MOMMY DEADLIEST

Fitzpatrick told ABC he found Stacey to be a bad trip, a personality that rubbed irritatingly at his ability to sleep at night. Sometimes, Fitzpatrick said, the most frightening thing is the coldness with which people operate. Most women with a failing marriage might contemplate divorce. They might hire a lawyer. Or maybe they would try to glue the pieces back together again and seek counseling. But none of that seemed practical to Stacey.

"She just poured a drink," Fitzpatrick said.

Killing two husbands was one thing. But Stacey went immediately to the head of the coldness class, the coldness hall of fame, when she tried to kill Ashley.

"You could seek out someone with more degrees than a thermometer and they could tell you that, in their experience as a psychiatric practitioner that this woman suffers from this or that. It is just bald-faced *evil*."

Assistant D.A. Christine Garvey had another word to describe the defendant. "I think she is *diabolical*. What she has done over the course of seven years is unimaginable."

MOMMY DEADLIEST

MICHAEL BENSON

PINNACLE BOOKS
Kensington Publishing Corp.
http://www.kensingtonbooks.com

PINNACLE BOOKS are published by

Kensington Publishing Corp.
119 West 40th Street
New York, NY 10018

All Kensington Titles, Imprints, and Distributed Lines are available at special quantity discounts for bulk purchases for sales promotions, premiums, fund-raising, and educational or institutional use. Special book excerpts or customized printings can also be created to fit specific needs. For details, write or phone the office of the Kensington special sales manager: Kensington Publishing Corp., 119 West 40th Street, New York, NY 10018, attn: Special Sales Department, Phone: 1-800-221-2647.

Pinnacle and the P logo Reg. U.S. Pat. & TM Off.

ISBN-13: 978-0-7860-2206-9
ISBN-10: 0-7860-2206-X

First printing: December 2010

10 9 8 7 6 5 4 3 2 1

Printed in the United States of America

Acknowledgments

The author wishes to thank the following persons and organizations, without whose assistance the writing of this book would have been impossible: Michael Birchmeyer; Frank Brackin, forensic computer expert; Lara Bricker; the Cayuga County Community College Library; Mary Ann Cerretani; Taylor Clark, Voices editor at the *Post-Standard*; Kelly Cullen, librarian, Port Byron High School; Margaret Devereaux, photographer; my agent, Jake Elwell; William F. Fitzpatrick, district attorney; Linda M. Foglia, assistant public information officer, New York State Department of Correctional Services; Dr. Francis Gengo, Dent Neurologic Institute in Amherst, New York; my editor extraordinaire, Gary Goldstein; Charles Kurtz, tax specialist; Rachel Lewis, Skaneateles High School librarian; Tim McCarthy, D.A.'s investigator; Patricia A. Milite and Lauren B. Levi at the Inmate Record Office, Bedford Hills Correctional Facility; Janice Mary Poissant; Maureen Southorn, K–12 school library media specialist, Weedsport Central School District; Dr. Christine Stork at the Upstate New York Poison Center; Nancy Stoneburg; Renee Tawczynski; Sergeant Robert Willoughby.

Foreword

Oh, *it did it,* all right. *It* did it once, twice, three times. Felt no guilt at all. Just the removal of obstacles, a snuffing out of irritants. In between the lethal liaisons bloomed the planning, plotting, scheming—and the anticipation. Shangri-la was just around the corner. All that was needed was an elimination or two in the cast of characters.

Oh sure, *she* loved them all. But that was *her.* She loved her heroes; she loved the angels with fresh mouths; she loved all of them.

She had dreams of building the perfect nest. While still a teenager, she found her dreamboat, her knight in shining armor. She clasped her hands in front of her bosom, gazed dreamily skyward and watched the cartoon red hearts drift toward heaven, swell and burst.

So how could she help but feel disappointed when, after the intoxication of new love wore off and passion turned torpid, dreamboat revealed himself as just a man-child—a guy whose first wife took a hike, telling tales of drug abuse and cruelty.

Oh, how he loved to party, *needed* to party. When he wasn't partying, he was wondering where the party was. With her eyes now focused and her mind clear, she saw him as a mean little boy who had been at the party too long. Now her former knight was on the other side, trapped on the dark side of inebriation.

Even as *she* popped out two kids, beautiful daughters, he diminished in her eyes until he was just a man, with man smells, a wandering eye (and penis), a man temper. He was an idiot—just like men were always idiots.

While she told friends of infidelities, *it*—the monster within—grew increasingly impatient.

It emerged. . . .

It shattered her suburban nest, leaving shards of death and betrayal. *It* took over. *It did it* for the first time. Simple, really. A savage concoction, antifreeze and rat poison in his drink, make it look like natural causes. *Till death do us part.* Freedom called. *It* would shuffle this knight right off the mortal coil.

It got away with it. No one even glanced. No one said boo. Doctor said death was probably caused by a heart attack. Want an autopsy? Nah, she said. She trusted the doctor. Won't be necessary. *Hell, they didn't even know that* it *existed.*

It, the thing that killed, now shriveled and shrank back inside. She searched and searched until she hooked another dreamboat and saw another impressive bouquet of exploding cartoon hearts. But, just as before, her euphoria was ephemeral, wispy, and windblown. Again, the heavenly butterflies in her impassioned loins morphed in reverse, and returned to their cocoons, where they devolved into caterpillars.

Trouble started quick. Her daughters didn't see the cartoon hearts. They saw just another man, rigid and combative, someone who thought he could order them around like the f'ing king of the f'ing castle.

War erupted, and she couldn't help but notice her daughters' unhappiness. Truth was, she wasn't happy, either. Her marital disappointment felt familiar.

So *it did it* again. This time, things didn't go nearly as smoothly. Dreamboat number two became violently ill. He died, but he died too slowly. The image was hideous. *It* had to use a turkey baster to squirt—inject!—the poison into him.

The first one lay down and expired—decent of him, really. This one convulsed and vomited and flop sweated for hour after hour. *It* had to get away from him.

That did the trick. Absence made his life grow dimmer, and flicker out. Trouble was, this time, all the fuss brought the heat. *It* felt crowded, in need of some space—in need of a scapegoat.

And so it was that *it did it* for the last time. *It* turned its deadly sights on her oldest daughter, who according to its plan would both die and claim blame for the deaths of the two men.

There came a time in the middle of the night when *it* was busy, pushing a lethal cocktail of prescription medicines down her daughter's gagging throat.

Die! it thought.

We submit for your approval, our nominee for *worst mom ever*: Stacey Ruth Daniels Wallace Castor.

Although this is a true story, some names will be changed to protect the privacy of the innocent. Pseudonyms will be noted upon their first usage.

When possible, the spoken word has been quoted

verbatim. However, when that is not possible, conversations have been reconstructed as closely as possible to reality based on the recollections of those who spoke and heard the words.

In places, there has been a slight editing of spoken words, but only to improve readability. The denotations and connotations of the words remain unaltered.

In some cases, witnesses are credited with verbal quotes that, in reality, only occurred in written form.

1

"Bring him back! Bring him back!"

"Police communications, Nicole, how may I help you?"

The dispatch recording system automatically registered the date and time: Monday, August 22, 2005, two o'clock in the afternoon.

"My husband has locked himself in our bedroom for the last day and he is not answering his phone," said the stressed Stacey Ruth Daniels Wallace Castor. "He didn't show up for work this morning."

As she gave her name, the name of the man she was worried about, and their address, her voice skirted the fringes of panic.

Stacey said she was especially concerned because of the way her husband had been acting.

"How had he been acting?" Nicole asked.

"Friday night, we were arguing, and he told me and my kids to get out, and then five minutes later, he said if I left, he would make me sorry, that I would be sorry if I ever left him."

"One moment, please," the operator said, and transferred the call to Sergeant Robert Willoughby, of the Onondaga County Sheriff's Office (OCSO).

An eighteen-year veteran of the force, Willoughby was the OCSO hazardous devices technician, which meant if there was a bomb, he had to defuse it. But that had nothing to do with Stacey's call being routed to him. It was just luck of the draw.

The caller told the sergeant she didn't understand anything. She didn't understand why her husband would do something like this.

She wasn't at home now, no; she'd checked the house and she'd called her home repeatedly, throughout the night, but no answer. "I pounded on the door, but I got no response," she explained.

His name: David Castor. The caller ID'd herself as his wife, Stacey.

She repeated the address in the town of Clay— which, with a population of sixty thousand, was Syracuse's largest suburb. It lay north of the city, bordered on the west by the Seneca River and on the east by Route 81.

Although the town had gone through the normal American construction of tract housing during the second half of the twentieth century, there were still rural sections of Clay, with crops and cows and barns, which—if you ignored the highways with their speeding automobiles—looked much as it had one hundred years before.

She gave her husband's date of birth correctly as June 12, 1957. He was the son of Joyce Castor, of Baldwinsville, and the late Philip A. Castor, who'd passed away on July 22, 2005, exactly one month before.

No, she wasn't there now. She was at work. She had a key. She agreed to meet Willoughby at the specified address.

Her husband, David, was feeling down in the dumps, and she knew for a fact that he had been damaging himself with drink. She hoped he hadn't done anything rash.

"Okay, go to the house right now, Mrs. Castor, and meet me."

"All right."

As Sergeant Willoughby arrived at the beige-colored ranch house and pulled his OCSO squad car into the driveway, he saw a tall redheaded woman sitting in a lawn chair under a tree in front of the house.

The first thing that struck the officer was that the woman's body language was all wrong. It didn't say "emergency." He wasn't sure what it said. She was casually smoking a cigarette, seemingly too relaxed to be panicky over a suicidal husband—even too relaxed to be *mildly* concerned with his safety.

Willoughby would have looked like a cop even if he hadn't been in uniform. As he got closer, she could see he had kind eyes and a vertical crease above the bridge of his nose, a man who held the public safety and justice very close to his heart.

Willoughby noted to himself that the house was a typical single-level suburban home, with the driveway and garage on the right, and two mailboxes out front next to the road, one for the mail and one for the daily newspaper. On the front lawn, which was neatly mowed, there was a fancy bird feeder built to resemble a lighthouse. A small tree offered privacy, preventing motorists from looking in the living-room window. Lawn surrounded the house on three sides. On the side lawn, the side closest to Glenwood Drive, was a tiny white wishing well.

Standing on the front stoop to the side of the front door was a statue of a pink flamingo. On the side of the house, someone had recently been painting the frame around the bedroom window and had stopped halfway so that half of that frame was fresh and white and the other half dingy and gray. He knew it was the bedroom window because he had a friend who lived nearby, and a lot of the houses were laid out the same.

She told him she had a key to the front door, but since she'd been instructed to meet him outside, she hadn't gone in.

"Open up the house, please," Willoughby said, and Stacey fished the house key out of her purse. Sergeant Willoughby entered the house and strode purposefully to the master bedroom. The woman stayed outside at first. She eventually did step inside, but she didn't make it past the kitchen. Again, Willoughby thought this was odd.

"I know if I was the one sick in that house and someone had to break down the bedroom door, my wife would be over that guy's shoulder," Sergeant Willoughby said. He pounded on the door and identified himself. Nothing. He jiggled the knob to verify that the bedroom door was locked.

Before causing any damage—after all, he didn't even know for sure if the guy was home—he walked outside and circled around the house in hopes of seeing through the master bedroom window.

All of the property was to the sides of the house and in front. Behind the house, only a few feet from the back of the house, was a tall wooden-slat fence along the property line. On the side of the house farthest from Glenwood was a large tent with mesh walls and lawn furniture inside, someplace to go at night where you didn't have to worry about mosquitos. Another wooden fence, much like the one in back, had been built outward from the corner of the house so that people in the tent could not be seen from the street. There was also a wooden shed painted yellow with crimson trim. On the back of the house, off the kitchen, was a glassed-in porch addition, which now served only as a storage space and was filled with mattresses, rugs, and what appeared to be large pieces of Astroturf-like indoor/outdoor carpeting.

At the bedroom window, Willoughby found the blinds shut. He even went to the garage, got a ladder, and tried to look into the master bedroom through the top of the window, but he still had no view. He returned to the front door, leaving the ladder against the side of the house. He took a quick glance behind the house, and the only thing perhaps out of place was a girl's bicycle lying on its side.

Now he was going to have to cause damage. He reentered the house. Again, he thought she would follow, but instead she went into the garage. With a splintering of wood, Willoughby kicked the bedroom door open. There was a cracking sound, then quiet, a super stillness. It was the nothingness and silence that accompanied death.

* * *

David Castor had been a nice-looking fellow, with hair even redder than that of his wife, and a square hairline that made him somewhat resemble football coach and TV commentator Mike Ditka. He had a moustache, even though moustaches had gone out of style years before. He'd shaved the moustache off a couple of times, but it always came back sooner rather than later. Though often smiling, he was a man who sometimes handled stress, and sometimes mishandled it.

But that was before, facets of a personality that Sergeant Willoughby would never know. For now, the furrow in David Castor's forehead was gone, and he was naked, lying across the bed, turned onto his side with his face toward the wall. Brown matter, apparently bloody vomit, pooled under his head. Vomit was also on his hands and caked under the fingernails of his left hand. That hand was resting on the pillow that was partially under David's upper torso, the fingers frozen in a clawlike configuration, as if they had become still while gripping a glass, a glass that had subsequently been removed. Only his feet stuck off the side of the bed, his toes pointing toward four o'clock.

Willoughby checked the man on the bed for vital signs. No pulse.

The sergeant scanned the room and soaked in the scene. The bedroom and adjacent bathroom were cluttered with piles of clothes and bedding, some of it visibly stained with vomit. At first, it looked like there'd been a party. But upon closer examination, it must have been a very weird party, indeed. Sure, there were two glasses and a bottle of Hiram Walker apricot-flavored brandy, but there was also a blue plastic bottle of PEAK antifreeze next to the bed. The container had a built-in plastic handle at its top, a white plastic cap, which was screwed on, and a label on the front that displayed the brand name, along with an image of a snowcapped mountain.

And one of the glasses contained a fluid that didn't look like any drink Willoughby had ever seen. The liquid in the glass was green, a bright, almost glow-in-the-dark green. *What the . . . ?*

Willoughby went outside and called to the woman. He said he needed for her to come inside, and she entered as if walking the last mile.

"Is he all right?" the woman asked, her voice quavering.

"No—no, he's not," Willoughby said. She looked into the bedroom she had shared with David, saw him naked on the bed, and began to scream. After a brief but frenzied display of exhausting hysterics, she went into a protective state of denial.

"Bring him back! Bring him back! He's not dead. He's not dead!"

As the widow broke down, Willoughby got on the horn and called for big-time backup—investigators, forensic scientists, the medical examiner all needed to be notified—and when everyone showed up, he followed orders and searched the house.

The woman's friend Lynn arrived on the scene and found her friend, the new widow, in a questionable mental state. Even after the emergency medical technicians (EMTs) left because David was dead, Stacey continued to sniffle and whine.

"Make them come back. Make them come back and save him."

The medics were gone and they hadn't taken

David. How could they save him if they didn't even put him in the ambulance?

"Stacey, honey, it's over. There's nothing they can do," Lynn said. She tried, as soothingly as possible, to get reality to sink in—but it wasn't easy. The widow was stubborn.

"Make them come back," she said in a diminished little-girl voice.

The reinforcements called in by Willoughby included Detective Sean Price, who would recover an empty bottle of prescription medication at the scene, and crime scene photographer Deputy Lawrence Knapp, who would confiscate the bedside green-fluid drinking glass. The body, they all agreed, appeared to have been dead for only a short time.

Deputy Knapp noticed that there was mucus coming out of the dead man's mouth and nose, which was frequently a sign that death had been caused by some sort of poison.

Outside, one deputy stood guard at the door, while others ran police tape around the perimeter of the property, preventing pedestrians or concerned friends from walking onto the lawn or up the front walk, where they could potentially contaminate the scene.

Before memorializing the suspicous glass's location with photos, Deputy Knapp gave it a sniff. It wasn't liquor. There was some other chemical involved. Maybe antifreeze. It looked at first glance like a case of self-administered poison. Knapp and the others came to the initial conclusion that the victim killed himself.

Price looked at the green fluid in the glass and then at the container of antifreeze that was found on the bedroom floor. The PEAK antifreeze container was made of blue plastic and couldn't have been more obvious. It was practically on display, on the floor next to the bed, directly underneath David Castor's overhanging feet.

That glass was next to the bed, the antifreeze container on the floor. It painted a clear enough picture. Too clear, maybe. Too pat. Too obvious by a half.

Detective Price couldn't help but think it was not a random picture, but rather a creation by design— an attempt to deceive. The container of antifreeze's position demanded attention.

There were indications that some sort of event had occurred in the adjacent bathroom as well. Part of a towel rack had been torn off the wall and was on the floor in front of the toilet. In the corner of the bathroom, positioned at the right foot of someone sitting on the john, and now a silent witness to the happenings that preceded David Castor's death, was another pink flamingo, identical to the one on the front stoop.

A search under the victim's bed produced a loaded shotgun.

As the investigators and crime lab personnel did their jobs, Willoughby was told to search the kitchen, and he set about his task methodically. Upon first glance, he felt that nothing seemed amiss. There was a teakettle and some pots and pans atop the stove. On the kitchen counter was a cutting board, with the word *SALSA* painted on it. On the far wall, under the window, was a rack holding two pairs of oven mitts and a green plastic watering can. To the left of the rack was a white plastic trash basket lined with a white plastic bag.

The widow was already being questioned. What had she been doing all weekend? Well, she was away all day Sunday. Doing what? She spent a lot of time in Wal-Mart, shopping. Could she prove it? There was a receipt. No, she didn't remember what she did with it, probably threw it out. Now Willoughby had a new instruction: be on the lookout for a Wal-Mart receipt. Just routine, to corroborate Mrs. Castor's story.

Willoughby searched the kitchen wastebasket. There were a few papers on top of the trash, so he picked them up, one by one, and examined them, checking efficiently to see if they were the receipt he'd been ordered to look for. He had only made his way through a few pieces of paper when he found the case's most unusual clue: a turkey baster.

Odd. The baster had been discarded, but there didn't seem to be anything wrong with it. No wear and tear whatsoever, not that the sergeant could see. He would have sworn that the baster was close to brand-new. It seemed to him that this baster wasn't so much discarded as hidden. Hidden—but not very well.

The baster hadn't even been buried in the kitchen trash. There were only a couple of pieces of paper on top of it. Was it purposefully hidden, yet not hidden well? Did someone *want* the baster found?

Willoughby took a closer look at the baster and could see that there were tiny droplets of green fluid inside it. He couldn't identify the liquid by sight, so he pulled the rubber bulb off the baster and gave it a sniff. He picked up a strong scent of alcohol, but he couldn't be more specific. Maybe it was brandy. Maybe antifreeze. Couldn't tell.

The sergeant looked around the kitchen and deeper in the trash basket for signs of food. Had the dead man been eating during the days and hours leading up to his death? Men who were drinking themselves to death didn't eat. He saw no evidence of food or food preparation. Brandy and antifreeze were alone on the menu.

Willoughby was surprised when he learned a loaded shotgun had been discovered underneath the victim's bed. The whole time he had spoken with Stacey Castor on the phone, and then in person at the house, she hadn't mentioned the weapon. If he had known the man was potentially armed, he would have handled the kicking in of the master bedroom door differently.

Every bottle and glass in the room was carefully bagged, labeled, and transported to the county forensics center for processing. Later, it would be processed in the crime lab as potential evidence in a suspicious death.

Back in the bedroom, Deputy Knapp first noticed something that would turn out to be important. On the side of the bed closest to the door, there was a stain indicating that vomit had run in a stream there, and directly beneath that stain was another, the same color, on the rug where vomit had pooled. The antifreeze container sat on the pooled vomit, yet there was no vomit on the container. This indicated to Knapp that the antifreeze container had been placed where it was *after* the man vomited at this location.

2

"David had been acting strangely. . . ."

The widow was thirty-eight-year-old Stacey Castor. At first, Stacey was questioned on the lawn in front of the house. "David was drinking copious amounts of alcohol, and he wasn't acting himself," she said.

Later, she and her two teenage daughters were taken to the police station. While there, she gave Detective Diane Leshinski an eight-page statement, detailing her activities with and without her husband that weekend.

Leshinski was a veteran when it came to taking statements from people who were in shock, including new widows. She knew that it could be like pulling teeth. People in that condition tended to babble, to weave in and out of reality, and to scramble chronology, as to make their statement unintelligible. But not Stacey. She was shaken, that was for sure, but her communication skills remained intact.

Stacey's was one of the most detail-oriented statements Leshinski had ever taken. Stacey didn't just mention that she'd gone to a fast-food restaurant, she also added that she'd gone to the drive-through window and listed every item she ordered and in what size. She didn't just say she ran into the convenience store, she said she bought cigarettes and she mentioned the brand. She gave a list of everyone with whom she spoke on the phone. She gave a list of every friend she saw in person.

Any marital difficulties? Well, Stacey had a boyfriend, if that was what she meant. Yes, that was what Detective Leshinski meant. Name? His name was Mike Overstreet (pseudonym).

Her husband, David, she said, had been acting strangely for about a month. He frequently said he didn't have long to live. His blood pressure, he claimed, was sky-high. Any day—*boom!*—he was going to keel over dead.

"He told me he didn't have to worry about retirement or Social Security or any of that, because he didn't think he would ever live to be sixty-five," Stacey said.

He was a "melancholy" person, she explained, a condition that was exacerbated by his dad's death, just a month before. She said he'd been saying things that upset her—for instance, "What if I die? What would you do? How would you survive?"

David wasn't afraid of death, she explained. If he dropped dead tomorrow, so be it. Lightning might strike. He could walk out into the street and get flattened by a car. You never knew when your number was up.

What he really worried about was having a heart

attack or a stroke that would incapacitate him but not kill him. He worried about the effect on the family of long-term medical care. He might become a cruel burden on the family, a drain on the family's finances. The repo men would come to visit. They might end up losing the house, just to pay his hospital bills. He mentioned something about "burial plots."

During the previous week, she said, they had been arguing frequently. They had had their second wedding anniversary on Tuesday, August 16, 2005, but their romance had not been sparked.

According to Stacey, David said he wanted to do something to put the romance back in their relationship, something that would heat things up a little bit—get it back to the steamy way things used to be when it was all fresh and new.

David wanted to go away on a second honeymoon, an extensive trip to an amusement park—two weeks, just the two of them. But Stacey had shut the idea down.

The plan was nice but not doable, she said. She told her husband that her youngest daughter was still too young to be left home alone. If they went away, they would have to take the girls with them. That triggered the fight—and it had been a doozy.

The aborted honeymoon plans opened an old wound. David had never cottoned to being a stepfather in the first place, and felt jealous whenever Stacey chose to give her daughters attention instead of him.

Most of the quarrel took place in the garage. There had been an initial flare-up, at which time David locked himself in the bedroom and Stacey fell asleep on the couch.

Then, late Friday night, he'd come out and she met him in the garage, where the marathon argument took place. A wide range of topics were addressed. Stacey wanted to be out there because her girls were home for at least part of the argument, and she didn't want them to hear.

Though they took breaks, the argument went on for something like seven hours.

It had crossed her mind that he might try to hurt himself. She said that during the fight, he was drinking Pepsi. At one point, she asked him for a sip.

"Get your own," he said.

At the time, she thought he was just being difficult. Now she was thinking, maybe he put something in the Pepsi, something to hurt himself with, and he didn't want her to have any.

They'd had numerous fights, almost always over the children. Not that fights were unusual, but lately they had gone from every once in a while to all the time.

No, not violent. Just nasty—nasty, and growing nastier. The potential for physical violence, she had to admit, was ever increasing. Lately, Stacey said, she was "afraid" to talk with David.

Finally, she concluded, he guzzled Southern Comfort and threw up for two days.

Still, she explained to police, early on during that final binge, the day after the argument, she tried to be a good wife. She tried to be nurturing.

David had told her that his feet hurt, so she rubbed them for him. Didn't that make her a good wife? What other wife would do that when her husband was being such a jerk?

Then came the vomit. Like Niagara F'ing Falls.

The first time that he threw up all over himself and the sheets, she said, she helped clean him up. She had him on his hands and knees in the bathroom, his head over the tub so she could wash his hair. She changed the sheets on the bed. She tried to keep him hydrated and brought him drinks of Ocean Spray Light Cranberry Juice Cocktail and water.

Stacey, right up until the end as it turned out, had always tried to be a good wife. She had been *such* a good wife. When he passed out, stark naked, she put underwear on him, and that wasn't easy when a man was out of it and not cooperating.

"I had repeatedly been asking David, throughout Saturday, if I could get him an ambulance or medical attention," she told a detective. "He refused to get any medical assistance."

Stacey's hysterics were through. She was speaking calmly. Yes, she thought it was odd that a man would choose to drink antifreeze, but maybe not so odd in David's case. After all, now that she was talking about it, she remembered that there was that TV show they'd watched—that must be what planted the seed in his head.

"What TV show is that?" Detective Leshinski asked.

"David and I watched the *48 Hours* about a year ago where a woman killed two husbands by putting antifreeze in green Jell-O," she said. "I think this show was on again about a month or two ago, because David and I watched it a second time," she added.

Detective Leshinski asked all of the questions, but the interview of Stacey was observed by Detective Dominick Spinelli, who was destined to become the case's lead investigator. Spinelli, born and raised in

New York City, was a well-conditioned man, his thickly muscled body the product of the modern gym workout; yet he had a surprisingly youthful face, a face that hadn't changed very much at all since he was a little boy.

Stacey's last comment, about the murder-by-antifreeze TV show, created an almost audible click in Detective Spinelli's mind. The comment pinged what Spinelli called his "sixth sense." It was the same sense that allowed Sergeant Willoughby to know the turkey baster was important. Spinelli couldn't quite put it into words. It was something akin to intuition, something you acquired from years and years of being a cop.

Spinelli was thinking: *Note to self—widow is the first to mention a wife killing her husbands (plural, husbands) with antifreeze. Switch the green Jell-O for cranberry juice and apricot-flavored brandy, and you have a workable scenario for what happened to David Castor.*

The previous poisoning-by-antifreeze case Stacey was referring to was that of Lynn Turner, a former emergency operator from Atlanta, Georgia, who in 1995 killed her husband, Cobb County police officer Maurice Glenn Turner, by putting antifreeze in his green Jell-O. In 2001, Turner killed her firefighter boyfriend, Randy Thompson, in the same way. Until the coincidence of both deaths was noted, it was thought the men had died of natural causes. Later tests indicated they had died from ethylene glycol poisoning, that being the lethal chemical that was produced when the body tried to digest antifreeze. In both cases, Turner's motive was said to be money, as she collected on the insurance policies of her victims. In separate trials, in 2004 and 2007,

Turner was convicted of both crimes. At the first trial, the prosecution was allowed to note the similarities between the deaths of the two men. Turner's second trial was one of the longest in Georgia history. Jury selection began just after the New Year, and the jury convicted her near the end of March.

Although the case did garner a lot of media attention, and Stacey would have had ample opportunity to learn about the case through TV, producers at *48 Hours Mystery* said they had never featured that case in an episode.

Answering Detective Leshinski's questions, Stacey continued her explanation of her husband's demise: On Saturday, David passed out on the bedroom floor and she had to call a friend of hers, Michael Colman, to come over and help get him back into bed. Detective Spinelli made a mental note to check out this part of the story.

Later, Spinelli would talk to Michael Colman, often called Mike, and verify that it had happened the way Stacey said it had.

"David was completely out of it," Colman said. "He didn't even recognize me, and I've known him for years."

After the binge started, Stacey was in and out of the house a couple of times. The first time she returned, he was on the floor, kneeling next to the bed, naked. That was when she put the underwear on him. She tried to get him to stand, but he didn't have the equilibrium for it. One time, she did get him to stand up briefly, but he immediately fell and hit his head on the nightstand. That was it for the standing.

At five o'clock in the morning on Sunday, she heard

him getting sick in the bedroom and opened the door. She saw his body convulsing as he dry heaved.

She claimed that when he saw her standing there in the doorway, he yelled at her: "Get out. Leave me alone. Get the fuck out of my house—and take your goddamn kids with you. This is my house. I bought it before you even knew me."

So Stacey shut the door, and that was the last time she saw him alive. Stacey gathered up her two daughters and left the house. She was concerned for their safety. Who knew what would happen with him out of control like this?

"There was no point in being in the same house with him if he was going to be like that," she said. She was afraid to be in the house. She feared there'd be a "blowout" with her husband.

It seemed like he wasn't going to stop until he had drunk himself to death, and she was sick of watching and hearing the process. She certainly didn't want her daughters to be around while that was going on.

Stacey repeated that her husband had been depressed, anxious, and stressed. His father had recently passed away and he took it hard. Besides his dad, there were problems on the work front as well. David had his own business, Liverpool Heating and Air Conditioning. He'd owned it since the autumn of 1994, when he purchased it from his first wife's dad. Stacey worked there also. She was the office manager, so she knew. Whatever you wanted to know about that business, she knew. David had business trouble, the financial blues.

Those were the external problems that David was having, but it went deeper than that. There were *internal* problems as well. She couldn't be specific—you can't read a man's mind—but she had a feeling that, deep down inside, David was unhappy with *himself* as well, his own physical person. Insecure, he worried about the *adequacy* of the man he had become. Bottom line, she said: a lack of self-esteem was compounding his depression.

On Monday morning—after a long, long weekend of dealing with, and worrying about, David's self-destructive behavior—she had gotten up and gone to work. She decided she would give him the morning to get his act together.

"Throughout the day, I started to have a bad feeling," Stacey said. "I was nervous and scared."

When Detective Leshinski's interrogation of Stacey was complete, the widow was informed that, whenever there was a strange death, and this one easily qualified, there had to be an investigation. She was told that her fingerprints, and the prints of her daughters, would need to be taken for comparison purposes.

Stacey said that was fine, so Lieutenant Craig Costanzo took her fingerprints.

While Stacey was interrogated, her daughters were also being asked questions by authorities. The girls corroborated their mother's story. Both had heard them arguing in the garage. Ashley said that at no time over the weekend had she seen David. Bree had, though. Bree looked into the master bedroom that weekend when Michael Colman came over, and she saw David on the floor in his underwear.

* * *

After listening in on Detective Leshinski's questioning of Stacey Castor, Detective Spinelli thought a number of red flags had been raised by her statement. The widow seemed to be alibi building. She emphasized how little she was with her husband during the time he was ill. She was specific about where she was and who could vouch for her whereabouts.

The investigator took a fresh look at the death scene. Every cop in the twenty-first century has watched modern crime shows—sometimes on a high-definition flat screen—they showed death all the time. But the television version wasn't like reality. Not even close. Death on TV was stylized, the creative manifestation of an art director's vision. Scenes were lit indirectly, sometimes with multihued fluorescents, so it looked like maybe the corpse died in a spaceship, and on the sound track, a techno band thumped its most hypnotic groove.

Real crime scenes were grubby, and without sound. A corpse's inanimation was overwhelming, even amidst chaos, and a lifeless human form radiated quiet and super stillness.

And this was a grubby scene. Spinelli studied it, first in person, and later via the crime scene photography. The reddish brown vomit, the sheetless bare mattress, and the PEAK antifreeze bottle on its side on the rug—so that it looked miles from its home in the garage—positioned on the set as if it were taking credit for the wasted life above.

There was an empty bottle of Ocean Spray Light Cranberry (Spinelli figured this bottle, because it was "diet," was purchased by one of the women of the house) and a bottle of brandy. Hiram Walker brandy. Fruity flavored. Again, to each his own, but what middle-aged man drinks himself to death with fruity brandy? Apricot. Where was the real booze? Then there were the two glasses, one half full of antifreeze and another, empty, just some brown crud at the bottom, like it once held cola.

As he looked at photos of the glass containing the green fluid he noticed how clean it was. Practically pristine. It didn't look like it had been handled by someone who was sick, sweating, and throwing up.

Simplest explanation, this was about the argument David Castor had with his wife over the aborted plans to go away together. The guy became depressed and committed suicide. That might have been the most simple scenario, but not the best fit. The woman mentioned seeing a TV show about a woman who murdered her husbands. What did that have to do with David Castor committing suicide?

As part of the Onondaga County Sheriff's Office investigation, Spinelli and others checked into the background of David Castor and his grieving widow, Stacey. It always helped to know the backstory.

Friends and relatives were interviewed. David knew a lot of people and he was extremely local. He'd never lived more than fifteen, twenty miles from Syracuse. Those friends agreed that at first, anyway, Stacey and David Castor had a marriage of domestic bliss. He treated her better than she had ever been treated before. No contest. In public, David treated Stacey as a princess.

He liked snowmobiles and motorcycles. A lot. He was a member of the Tug Hill Wheelers Four-Wheel

Club and the Snow Pals Snowmobile Club. Stacey
was always outwardly supportive of his interests. She
loved riding "bitch" on his motorcycle, although she
didn't care for that term. They were married about
two years ago. Just as Stacey had said, David Castor,
police learned, had been a successful businessman
with his own heating company, a business genera-
tions old, begun by his ex-wife's dad. Stacey was an
employee there—the ex-wife was gone by this time.
The company operated out of a large yellow building as big as two houses, with its own parking lot in
front and back. The front of the warehouse-type
building was about twenty feet high from the
ground to the peak of the roof, and featured only
two small windows and a white windowless door.
Stacey and David often commuted to work together
in the morning.

Stacey's friend, Lynn Pulaski—who was the practice
manager at the Beaver Lake Animal Hospital on
Genesee Road in Baldwinsville—said this looked like
a story that *had* to have a happy ending. Stacey had
already lost one husband, and then David came
along. Everything for Stacey was perfect. Lynn compared Stacey to Cinderella. Out of the gloom, the
black cinders of widowhood, a brilliantly shiny new
life had emerged. Happy, yes. Ever after, no.

Police learned that although the Castors' marriage
began on a blissful note, the real world caught up to
them. Problems arose, and the fairy tale cracked.

First and foremost among those problems were
Stacey's daughters—Ashley Kailyn Wallace and Bree
Lynn Wallace—who didn't get along with their new
stepfather. They were oil and water. Did not mix.
The girls had nothing nice to say about the new

living arrangements, living in the house of a man who they had no say in choosing.

Stacey thought about her daughters' complaints and could see only the positives of the new living arrangements. The house was only a half mile from the school. The girls could walk to and from school. How cool was that? And, in the other direction, one block from Oswego Road, where all the fast-food restaurants were.

Mom was just being Mom. David was the problem. The man who had not allowed his first wife money of her own had little patience for Stacey's daughters. According to the girls, David tried to be all large and in charge.

Ashley was the one with the mouth. She told him to bite it. The girls felt nostalgic for the good old days, before David was around, when it was just the three of them—Ashley, Bree, and Mom—and the daughters had their mother all to themselves.

Bree felt homesick for the days when she, her sister, and her mom would have dinner together. They would tell stupid jokes and laugh a lot and "just be girls." They did so many things together. Ashley recalled the happy trips that their mother used to take them on.

That all ended once there was David. Once there was David, and David was in charge, their mom had a whole lot less time for Ashley and Bree.

In addition to his mom in Baldwinsville, and his widow and her daughters, the victim had one son, David Jr., with his ex-wife, Janice. And big David had brothers and sisters, too. He had a brother Michael, the only sibling who'd left the area. Michael Castor lived with his wife, Jeanne, in El Paso, Texas. Brother Gary and his wife, Karyn, lived in East Syracuse. Brother Stephen and his wife, Sue, lived in nearby Cicero. His sister Sandra married Paul Santorelli, and they lived in Canastota, home of the International Boxing Hall of Fame. Sister Linda married Gary Horzempa, of Pennellville. David also left behind two granddaughters.

And all of those people seemed more upset over David's demise than Stacey and her daughters. And those three weren't the only ones thinking life was more pleasant without David. Stacey's mother, Judi Eaton, who was remarried herself, had a lot to say about the way her granddaughters despised Stacey's second husband. And, when it became apparent that police weren't wholly satisfied with the suicide scenario, she was also the most outspoken when it came to defending Stacey. And it was Eaton who was most vivid when describing the stress between David and her granddaughters.

Stacey spoke about it, too. She later recalled that David had made a begrudging-at-best transformation from being a bachelor to being a stepfather. David had a king-of-the-castle attitude when it came to his domain. "My way or the highway." He thought a simple dictator stance would be effective.

As it turned out, David grossly overestimated his ability to handle teenage girls. He figured he'd give the orders, and the girls would obey without question. Stacey knew that wasn't going to work and she told David so. But he didn't listen.

The girls' reaction to his orders was pretty near

opposite of what he'd envisioned. Instead of mind-lessly obeying his every order, Ashley and Bree were incorrigible—questioning *every*thing. Stacey remem-bered thinking that they were chips off the old block, that she, too, had questioned everything when she was young. The girls couldn't help it, Stacey thought. It was genetic.

Every word David spoke to his stepdaughters was contradicted. They were the monsters who were ru-ining his life, and vice versa. It drove him nuts. There were many arguments, the nastiest between David and Ashley.

Stacey's friends Mike and Dani Colman had known Stacey for fifteen years. Before David came along, Dani and Stacey worked together for years at the same ambulance company. Dani still worked there. She remembered how David treated Ashley. They recalled him calling his oldest stepdaughter "selfish and disrespectful."

"He made no bones about the fact that he didn't like the girls," Dani Colman said.

Asked about her relationship with her dead step-father, Ashley admitted that she and David "did not like each other at first." Ashley complained that David dished out mixed signals when it came to her and Bree. "He'd say he didn't want to be our father, and then he would try to be," Ashley recalled.

Dani Colman told police a story that jibed with Stacey's perfectly. Dani said that on the last weekend of David Castor's life, he had wanted to go away with Stacey, a fortnight getaway, just the two of them. Second honeymoon. Hotel room with champagne and a heart-shaped tub. But his plan had fallen through. As usual, the problem was the girls. Couldn't be left home alone. Ashley was only *sort of* an adult, and Bree no way. Bree was only fifteen.

And so David's plans disintegrated, just like everything else. Stacey described the ensuing fight to Dani after the fact. David had a temper, but this was the maddest she'd seen him. It was like he transformed into a monster. Stacey said David was so mad that his "head split open and an alien came out."

Stacey walked out on David. She didn't want to share space with a monster. With a lot of encouragement from Dani and another friend, Robert Ross, she spent much of the weekend with the Colmans.

Police asked Dani, "What was Stacey's demeanor that weekend as she stayed at [your] house?"

Dani said, "Stacey was pretty distraught almost all the time she was there. She said that David had stayed home and was just drinking and sleeping." A couple of times during the weekend, Stacey went to the house to check on David. "She told me that she put her ear up to the door and she could hear snoring."

Dani had asked, "Through the door?"

"Yeah, David snores like a Mack truck," Stacey had replied.

Stacey personally told her daughters that their stepfather was dead. Ashley was more confused by the news than anything else. Of course, it was a shock—but it also did not compute.

Sure, David could be an idiot sometimes, but why would he want to kill himself? She felt skeptical, like somebody wasn't telling her everything. All of a sudden, Ashley was supposed to believe that David was depressed to the point of being suicidal. Where did that come from?

Stacey talked about it like it was perfectly obvious, but if David had ever suffered the slightest bout of depression, Ashley had never picked up on it. "I had no idea he was hurting like that," she said. "I was crushed."

The victim's body had remained on the sheetless bed, purplish feet hanging off the edge, until he was officially pronounced dead, thoroughly photographed and examined. It was then wrapped in a sheet, lifted onto a stretcher, and carried outside to an ambulance for the slow, siren-free drive to the county morgue for autopsy.

Performing the postmortem surgery was Dr. Robert Stoppacher, who had been the Onondaga County deputy chief medical examiner (ME) since 2004. Before that, he was an assistant medical examiner in Milwaukee County, Wisconsin.

The doctor later summarized his findings: "We found crystals, and the presence of those crystals in the kidney indicated that he died of ethylene glycol toxicity. He died of renal failure from drinking antifreeze."

The medical examiner had seen thousands of dead bodies, and this wasn't the first case of suicide by antifreeze that he had seen, but it still shocked and amazed him that anyone would choose this method to end it all. It was simply *not* a pleasant way to go. The seductive nature of the liquid came from the ethylene glycol itself. That chemical comprised most of the fluid and had a naturally tasty flavor. The swallowed antifreeze would make it as far as the liver, where the metabolism would go to work on the ethylene glycol. The compound was chemically broken down into deadly acids, glycolic and oxolic, that struck first at the central nervous system. Already there would be intense discomfort. The room would be spinning, pain growing all over. During this phase of the poisoning, the victim might appear drunk. This was followed by an array of dehydrating symptoms; profuse sweating, frequent urination, intense thirst, vomiting. The internal organs shut down one at a time. It was agonizing.

Every once in a while someone commited suicide by drinking antifreeze, but it was always a safe bet they regretted it before the agony ended their life. Aware of no evidence that might suggest foul play, Dr. Stoppacher concluded that David Castor had committed suicide.

3

Case Not Closed

The medical examiner might have concluded that David Castor committed suicide, but Detective Spinelli had not. It wasn't uncommon for crime scenes to send mixed signals, but this was over-the-top.

He ran it through in his mind. It couldn't have happened the way Stacey said. *No one* would commit suicide in that fashion, so slowly and so painfully. Suicide by poisoning was so feminine, and the chosen poison—sleeping pills were common—offered a pain-free finale. Men preferred to blow their brains out. *Boom.* Over.

In addition to the feminine choice of chaser—apricot brandy and diet cranberry juice—there was that shotgun under the bed the whole time. The misery could have been ended swiftly.

Even if the victim was too dizzy and disoriented to actually shoot himself with a shotgun, he would have tried. But the shotgun remained untouched.

There was something *sadistic* about the way the

victim died. David Castor had been tortured to death, probably by someone using a turkey baster. (A turkey baster as a murder weapon? The case seemed preposterous. Key elements were straight out of a Hollywood movie.)

How did they know David Castor was depressed, anyway? The wife said so. That was it.

She said he was feeling inadequate. What man ever used that word?

And what about the two glasses? Why would a man committing suicide have two glasses? Poison with a chaser, maybe. Or a party for two.

And what of the 911 call? Almost all phone calls to an emergency operator are made from the scene of the emergency. But Stacey's call was remote, made from down the road at Liverpool Heating, and on the work phone rather than her cell.

Suicide? No, Spinelli thought. This was murder.

The rules in Onondaga County stated that the crime lab was not allowed to process evidence in cases of suicide. The assumption being that there were more important things for the lab to be working on. So, before the case could be further developed, Dr. Stoppacher would have to change his conclusion.

Detective Spinelli took his case to the medical examiner. He pointed out that there were solid indications that this was no suicide. There was vomit above and below the container of antifreeze, but none on it. Though the wife said the decedent was depressed, other friends and relatives said there was no way he would commit suicide. There was a turkey baster that reeked of antifreeze.

Dr. Stoppacher said this wasn't enough for him to

change his conclusion from suicide to homicide, but it was enough for him to change it to *inconclusive,* which would allow the crime lab to process the evidence.

The physical evidence confiscated from the death scene was transported to the crime lab in the Wallie Howard Jr. Center for Forensic Sciences. The center was named after a Syracuse police officer who was shot and killed by a fifteen-year-old during an undercover drug operation the day before Halloween in 1990.

The center was comprised of three main sections: criminalistics, forensic biology/DNA, and forensic toxicology.

In the criminalistics section, latent fingerprints—as well as palm prints and footprints—were analyzed. That section also handled questioned documents, forensic chemistry, firearms, trace evidence, and digital evidence. There the prints found at the scene of David Castor's death would be compared to prints supplied by family members. If there was no match, they would be run through the Statewide Automated Fingerprint Identification System (SAFIS).

The questioned documents section analyzed paper items for indentations, type of ink, obliterations, and handwriting comparisons. They would come into play later in the case when the victim's will was contested.

Forensic chemistry analyzed powders, tablets, and plant material, usually looking for the presence of controlled substances. This section of the lab was often involved in arson investigations, as it analyzed fire debris for the presence of possible accelerants.

If a gun was involved in an investigation, it was sent to firearms, where it was determined if the gun was operable. Bullets or bullet fragments were also analyzed here, using a microscope, and if possible spent ammunition was matched to the gun from which it was fired. This portion of the lab used a computerized database called the Integrated Ballistic Identification System (IBIS) to aid in connecting shootings from different crime scenes.

Trace was responsible for analyzing hairs, fibers, or other tiny pieces of evidence found at a potential crime scene. If a fiber found on a suspect's clothing matched one found at a crime scene, that might constitute evidence that the suspect was at the crime scene.

The digital evidence section examined electronic media, such as hard drives, optical discs, flash memory, and digital cameras, in search of relevant data, which might be in the form of text, photos, video, or audio.

The forensic biology/DNA section of the lab worked mostly on homicide, sexual assault, and burglary cases, in which a criminal might have left part of him or herself at the scene of the crime. DNA analysis of bodily fluids found at a scene could be used to either identify or eliminate a suspect.

Any DNA submitted as evidence was checked against the national database known as the Combined DNA Index System, aka CODIS. This database has been known to link unsolved crimes with one another, link crime scene evidence with previously convicted offenders, and to match remains with missing persons.

Toxicology usually worked in conjunction with the medical examiner's office to help determine the manner and cause of death. Methods used included gas and liquid chromatography, mass spectrometry, and immunoassay. Results showed whether or not drugs, alcohol, or poison was present in the submitted remains. In addition to cause-of-death cases, toxicology also worked on DUI/DWI cases, and sexual assaults in which drugs or alcohol were suspected of being a contributing factor.

A blood sample from David Castor was sent to the toxicologist who checked it for quantity of alcohol and antifreeze. The results were surprising. The victim had very little of either in his bloodstream.

This flew in the face of the scenario, as Stacey painted it, of a man who had consumed liquor for most of the weekend, and saved the antifreeze for last. The toxicologist concluded that the ingestion of booze and antifreeze had taken place but had stopped many hours before death. That jibed with the fact that the poison had been in the victim's system long enough to cause renal failure.

Liquids confiscated from the death scene by sheriff's detectives were taken to the crime lab for analysis. They were received by the supervisor of the drug section, Raymond Van Orden, a chemist/deputy sheriff assigned to the forensic science building. Back then, both sworn members of the OCSO and civilians worked in the crime lab. Only in recent years had the lab become 100 percent civilian.

Van Orden was born in Brooklyn, but he moved away when he was two. He grew up north of Syracuse in Phoenix, New York, and as an adult lived in the Syracuse suburb of Liverpool. He'd prepared well for his role in the lab, first earning an associate's degree in math and science at Alfred State College. Then to the State University of New York (SUNY) College of Environmental Science and Forestry at Syracuse, where in 1985 he earned his bachelor's degree. The educational process never really stopped and he earned his master's in biochemistry in 2008.

By his own recollection, Van Orden tested a "whole bunch of stuff," including the green liquid found in a glass on David Castor's night table, and brown residue from the bottom of the other glass.

He scraped some of the brown stuff into a container and squirted it with distilled water to dissolve it. He put the solution in a headspace vial and heated it in a special oven/analyzer called a headspace gas chromatograph/mass spectrometer, or GC/MS for short. It was the same process that he used to determine blood-alcohol levels. The residue turned out to be caramel and ethynol (drinking alcohol). This result was consistent with the glass holding a mixed drink, some sort of liquor or liqueur mixed with diet cola.

By the time Van Orden saw it, the green fluid had been removed from the container it was found in and placed in a sealed vial, which had been bagged and labeled at the scene. It was tested next, in the same manner as the brown residue, and was found to contain ethylene glycol—antifreeze.

The stuff appeared to be pure, not mixed with anything. It had a strong chemical smell, so Van Orden diluted it before running the test. "I didn't want anything blowing up on me," he later said.

He tested the liquid from inside the turkey baster,

the Southern Comfort bottle found on the counter, and other booze bottles found in the house. The liquor bottles contained ethynol, but no ethylene glycol. Vice versa for the baster.

"I tested a bunch of sheets that had been stripped off the bed that the victim had vomited on," Van Orden recalled. By the number of sheets he received, he could tell that the sheets had been stripped and changed, only to have the victim vomit on the second set as well. There was blood but no evidence of ethylene glycol in the vomit, which was one of the reasons he died. His body had already processed the stuff into crystals, which lodged in his organs. In other words, by the time he started to throw up, it was too late.

The testing of the sheets was done differently than that of the fluids. Ethylene glycol fluoresced, so the sheets were examined under a laser light source. Some small areas were fluorescing, so those areas were cut out and tested for ethylene glycol. All of those tests came back negative.

David Castor was laid out at the Jewell Funeral Home on South Seneca Street in Weedsport, the same funeral parlor where Stacey's first husband, Michael Wallace, was waked. Friends were invited to come visit from five to eight o'clock on the evening of July 22, 2005. Those who wished could make contributions in David's name to the Hospice of Central New York in Syracuse.

David's first wife, Janice, came to the funeral parlor early so that she could say good-bye without the risk of running into Stacey or her friends. David

Jr. would attend the funeral and meet Stacey, but
Janice knew she wasn't wanted.

David's sister Linda Horzempa looked at her
brother in the casket and felt it must be a bad dream.
Why are you lying there? What happened? she pondered.

Then the similarities between Michael Wallace's
and David Castor's funerals became downright
creepy. Castor was buried in a plot at Owasco Rural
Cemetery, adjacent to the plot for Michael Wallace,
Stacey's first husband. Some found it pretty odd—
raise-the-eyebrows odd—that Stacey had buried her
two dead husbands next to one another.

Then again, some figured maybe it wasn't so odd.
Just efficient. This way, she could visit both graves
at the same time.

While the little hairs on the back of Detective
Spinelli's neck were standing on end each time he
processed the facts of the case in his brain, life at
the Castor household proceeded happily, with little
mourning. It was more like a weight lifted than a
burden added.

Stacey had gotten over her hysterics quickly. She
had to be strong for the girls' sakes. She still had her
boyfriend, so she wasn't lonesome.

Topics that would one day become important to
the point of being all-consuming were ignored by
Stacey and her daughters during those ignorance-
is-bliss days. There was no mention of causes and
methods of death. David Castor was gone, out of
their lives forever, and the case could not have
been more closed as far as the three were concerned.
They weren't missing David that much. Ashley found

that things were getting peaceful and silly again, just as they had been when it was just the three of them after Daddy died, but before David was in the picture. Those were good times and now they were happening again. Ignorance *was* bliss.

There were immediate changes in the interior and exterior decoration of the house and property. Signs of David disappeared, *poof!*

In the meantime, authorities never stopped going over the evidence in the suspicious death of David Castor.

Sometimes Ashley would think about how weird it was. Her own father had died of a heart attack years before, and now her stepfather was dead, too. She thought her mother had the worst luck, that she had been "dealt a bad hand when it came to relationships."

Detective Spinelli wasn't alone with his goose bumps. They were felt also by David's sister Linda. She'd go over it in her head. He was in the heating industry. He worked with cars and motorcycles.

"He knew what antifreeze could do," Linda said. "He knew what antifreeze would do to him and how painful it would be, and he would never do that to himself." She remembered walking up to her brother's casket and wondering, *Why is he lying there?*

Janice was also confused by the suicide. She knew in her heart of hearts that David was too full of life, *in love* with life, in love with all of his toys, to kill himself. *Ever.* David Jr. recalled his mother never once thought his dad killed himself. She "knew something was up" right away, never changed her mind. *It didn't happen that way,* Janice thought, and she wasn't quiet about it, either. She pestered the detectives in charge of the case early and often—in particular, Detective Spinelli.

Back at the crime lab, the criminalistics section was methodically ID'ing prints found near David Castor's body. Three readable prints were lifted from the drinking glass that contained the antifreeze. The early assumption was that they belonged to the victim, to the man who'd killed himself. Those fingerprints were placed on a card labeled, *Latent Print L2 (Item 1-5 drinking glass)*.

Comparison revealed that the prints on the glass were Stacey's. Of course, there would have been plenty of reasons for her prints to be there. She lived there and could have touched the glass at any time. She was probably the last one to wash that glass, so her prints might have been on the glass already by the time antifreeze was poured into it. Her fingerprints were probably on a lot of glasses in the house. Her fingerprints were bound to be on anything, and there was no way of telling how old a fingerprint was. Still, it was odd. Odd in the sense that a pattern was forming.

A palm print was found on the antifreeze container, but it was *never* identified.

As it turned out, the better piece of evidence was something that wasn't there. Why weren't David Castor's fingerprints on the glass that contained the poison? Still, it wasn't enough without a confession. Why weren't his fingerprints on the antifreeze can? Why weren't they anywhere? Did he wear gloves during his own suicide, gloves that magically disappeared after his death?

Or, was his participation in his own death extremely limited? Was there a lethal bartender serving David Castor his final drinks? Was that last shot—one more for the road—administered via turkey baster?

Or—and come to think of it, Spinelli liked this idea better—maybe it was all pure theater: art direction. Was the drinking glass with the small amount of antifreeze in it just a prop? Perhaps David Castor never drank out of that glass. Maybe every single drop of antifreeze to enter David Castor's body came through the baster?

Phone records were acquired—more damnation for the widow. Stacey claimed in her initial interview with police that she had called the house regularly during the weekend that David was sick. But the records showed that she had only called once. They checked her cell, her work phone, any line she might have used. One call.

Cops knew she'd only called once, but she didn't know they knew—a factor Spinelli hoped to exploit somewhere farther up the road.

There turned out to be other problems with Stacey's scenario. The time element struck Spinelli as peculiar as well. Why would a woman show up for work at seven-thirty in the morning and wait until two o'clock in the afternoon to call 911? On its surface, it resembled the behavior of someone who was waiting for a victim to die.

If she had called from the house, that would have seemed normal. If she'd called from her cell phone, that would have been cool. But she called from her work phone. And that didn't add up.

After being thoroughly dusted for fingerprints, and its contents identified as antifreeze, the turkey baster was sent to forensic scientist and DNA expert Kathleen Hum. She began her examination of the baster at the tip and then worked her way slowly back toward the bulb.

The only visible material on the outside of the baster was toward the tip. She carefully moved that material and created a series of swabs. She then created a DNA profile of the material on the swabs, which turned out to be a match with a DNA sample that had been taken from David Castor's remains.

"The interesting thing about the turkey baster," Hum explained, "was that the amount of DNA that was recovered was significantly more than one would expect if someone had just casually come in contact with it."

The DNA was from saliva and it was plentiful. The conclusion was clear. At some point, the tip of the turkey baster had been inserted into David Castor's mouth. The chances that this insertion was voluntary were minuscule.

Now a clear picture was formed in Spinelli's mind: an image of the victim deathly ill and naked on the bed, and the murderer administering the slow and painful poison, one drop at a time, by squeezing the rubber bulb of a turkey baster.

4

The DA

The district attorney (DA) in charge of the case was William J. Fitzpatrick, a Brooklyn boy born and raised. Born in Brooklyn Hospital, he lived till he was five on Willoughby Avenue in Fort Greene; then his family moved to Bay Ridge. That was where he stayed, until he went away to college, and even then he returned during the summer.

William, often called Bill, graduated from Xaverian High, a school that sat upon the bay ridge for which the neighborhood was named, overlooking Shore Road Park, New York's upper harbor, and the Verrazano-Narrows Bridge.

He attended Syracuse University, at first intending to be a journalism major. But, as his freshman year came to an end, young Fitzpatrick had a heart-to-heart talk with a trusted teacher, the late Mike Sawyer.

Sawyer had studied Bill's proclivities and said, "Look, it's obvious you want to be a lawyer, a prosecutor." They talked for a long time, and by the end of the conversation, Fitzpatrick shifted his major from journalism to pre-law.

At Syracuse, he earned his bachelor's degree in 1974 and his law degree in 1976. The future top dog began working for the Onondaga County District Attorney's Office in 1975 as a law clerk. He was admitted to the bar in 1977. He was promoted steadily within the DA's office until, in 1983, he made it to chief assistant district attorney. He was the youngest person ever to be appointed to that position in the county.

Fitzpatrick first helped prosecute homicides during the 1980s for the Felony Trial Unit, where he also handled other violent felony cases and was responsible for overseeing the prosecution of all homicide cases in Onondaga County. He eventually took charge of the Homicide Bureau in 1983.

Over a three-year period, he tried twenty defendants for murder with a perfect conviction rate. In 1985 alone, he successfully prosecuted seven consecutive murder cases, and all seven individuals were sentenced to life sentences for their crimes.

His other noteworthy convictions included that of Cynthia Pugh, who was convicted of murdering her boss/lover James Pipines, an executive of a Manlius roofing company. Pugh served twenty-four years in prison before being paroled in 2008.

And he put away Jeff Cahill, who—during the spring of 1998—hit his wife over the head at least four times with a baseball bat. The wife didn't die, but lingered in the hospital, so Cahill used forged documents to acquire potassium cyanide, and obtained a fake hospital ID card so he would be able to enter the hospital where his wife was recovering. He also acquired a wig, glasses, and a uniform similar to that worn by the hospital's custodial staff. During the fall of 1998, Cahill donned his disguise, and carrying a mop and the poison, he entered his wife's room. He forced the cyanide down her throat, killing her. During the penalty phase of the trial, he was sentenced to death, a punishment that was reduced to life in prison in 2003.

As chief assistant district attorney, Fitzpatrick specialized in reopening inactive cases and, with the cooperation of various police agencies in Onondaga County and the state of New York, won cases that were thought to be unwinnable.

From 1987 to 1991, Fitzpatrick worked in general practice of the law, handling a variety of criminal, civil, personal injury, and medical malpractice cases in Onondaga County and throughout New York State. In addition to his legal work, he served as an adjunct professor at Syracuse University College of Law from 1987 to 1988, where he taught a course on trial practice.

By January 1992, when he was sworn in as the Onondaga County district attorney, he had been working in the DA's office for twenty-eight years, and had served as a defense attorney for five years as well. He ran an office that included forty-six assistant district attorneys (ADAs), thirteen investigators, and a forty-person support staff. His jurisdiction, which included the entire city of Syracuse, had a total population of just under a half-million people.

During the 1990s, Fitzpatrick served a term as president of the New York State District Attorneys' Association. That organization awarded Fitzpatrick their Prosecutor of the Year award in 2003, and the New

York State Bar Association's "Outstanding Prosecutor" in 2005.

He was married to the Honorable Diane Fitzpatrick, a judge on the New York State Court of Claims. They had three grown children and lived in Lafayette, New York.

Fitzpatrick learned from Spinelli and others that the case was looking less and less like a suicide. The most profound evidence against suicide was the turkey baster. Would a suicide administer the fatal dose by squeezing a bulb? He quietly opened his own investigation into the death of David Castor. The DA put his team of investigators to work right away. He needed to know everyone's whereabouts during the seventy-two hours during which David Castor was dying.

"I couldn't limit my investigation to friends and relatives, either," Fitzpatrick recalled. He also had to check Castor's business associates. Did the guy have enemies? Did he owe anyone money? Did he have some sort of secret life that his family and friends didn't know about? Was he a gambler? Did he do drugs?

The answer to all of these questions came back definitively no.

Although Stacey was the best suspect, she wasn't the only one. There was a close family member, Stacey's mom, who did not think David Castor committed suicide and did not think Stacey Castor poisoned him. This was the "Ashley did it" contingent, and Grandma would always be the head spokesperson. Other members of this group included Stacey's boyfriend and the

Colmans, Stacey's friends. Ashley, not Stacey, they said, should be the number one suspect.

The war in that house was between David and Ashley, and that was the war that was resolved by his death. Ashley won, her grandmother thought. Judi Eaton loved Ashley just as much as anyone else in the family, of course—but the girl was a snot. And a brat. The old lady had no trouble imagining Ashley as being capable of murder.

With Stacey as its focus, the investigation forged ahead. The evidence gathered so far was promising, yet frustrating. Without a confession, Fitzpatrick believed, they still came up short of a conviction.

The reading of David Castor's will only encouraged the investigation into his death. David, as it turned out, left just about everything to Stacey. His only son was stiffed. The will didn't ignore David Jr. completely. He was given a bracelet, a gold chain, his dad's restored Dodge, and a handprint in plaster that David Jr. had made for his father when he was five. But Junior, who now had children of his own, got no money. Except for the car, everything of value went to Stacey. Junior was hurt. He couldn't understand why his father would stiff him—his only kid!—like that. What had he done? He'd thought things between him and his dad were okay. It was *that woman.* She had something to do with this.

Janice concurred. There was something "very wrong" with the will. "Dave didn't do that," Janice said.

Everything around Stacey smelled fishy, and now her dead husband's will smelled fishy, too. Janice pledged that she would help the detectives in any way possible to find the truth.

Janice remembered her part in the investigation

well. She called Detective Dominick Spinelli so many times, she said, "I couldn't begin to count them." The first time she introduced herself, she told him how well she knew Dave—they were married almost a quarter century!—and how sure she was that he didn't commit suicide.

Detective Spinelli went to her apartment and interviewed her. After he left, she did research on the Internet and called him every time she found something. She faxed him stuff. She looked up "murder" and "antifreeze" on the computer and found items regarding the Turner woman who killed two men in Georgia by putting antifreeze in their food. At first, it was thought they had heart attacks. Janice knew that Stacey had worked as something medical, and another job in a law office, so maybe she thought she knew things.

"I took time off from work to do research," Janice remembered. The will had to be fake. The will stated up front that David wanted his estate to go to Stacey in the case of his death, and that if Stacey died before him, it would go to Ashley and Bree. The estate would be theirs, the will stated clearly, "absolutely and forever, share and share alike." If the girls predeceased him, his estate would go to the girls' offspring. If Stacey passed away, the girls were to be taken care of by her sister, Darcey. The will was witnessed by Lynn J. Pulaski and Paul W. Pulaski, who, Janice correctly assumed, were friends of Stacey's.

The will read as if David Castor's family didn't exist. It was all about Stacey, her girls, her sister. David would never stiff his son. Janice had his original will from March 1989, the only real will he'd ever made, she believed. It left everything to her and David Jr. The notary public who stamped it was

Vivian D. Brown. Janice knew David would never make a will without doing it through an attorney and having it notarized.

Besides, there was the signature on the will. Not only didn't it look like David's real signature, it was tremulous and uncertain—which were not facets of his personality.

Janice took a day off from work and collected genuine David Castor Sr. signatures, which could be used in court to compare against the forged signature on the will Stacey produced.

The street-smart lead investigator, originally from New York City, didn't mind the regular phone calls from the victim's first wife. She was sincere, levelheaded, and prepared to do legwork.

Spinelli thought about the contrast between Janice, who couldn't have been more concerned about the lack of justice her ex was receiving, and the manner of Stacey, who projected a certain solemn serenity with her widowhood.

From outward appearances, and through the long talks they'd had on the subject, Spinelli knew Stacey had efficiently and effectively put the David Castor page in her life behind her and moved on—as had her daughters, for that matter. They moved on and didn't look back.

The investigator pondered the contrast. One woman saw Castor's death as a new problem in her life; the other maybe felt a problem resolved. It was a compelling way to look at the case, Spinelli thought.

5

Flashback

Stacey R. Daniels was born on July 24, 1967, the daughter of Gerald W. and Judith Daniels. Her dad, a car salesman, had been born in Syracuse, but he lived most of his life in Weedsport, a small town about twenty miles west of Syracuse.

Stacey grew up in a house on Bell Street in Weedsport. She had an older sister, Darcey A. Daniels, who later married a man named Geddings and lived in Baldwinsville. In January 1986, Darcey completed the nursing program at Cayuga-Onondaga BOCES and received her cap. She had been a nurse ever since, practicing in "several different areas of nursing."

Stacey also had a brother, Jamie, who lived in Weedsport. As a young man, Jamie worked for T.C. Timber—Habermass Corporation, a large toy manufacturer in Skaneateles.

All of the Daniels children, including Stacey, attended Weedsport Junior/Senior High School. The school district was so small that grades seven through twelve all attended classes in the same building.

Stacey's photo first appeared in that school's yearbook in 1979 when she was eleven. In a large group of thin, smiling preadolescents, Stacey appears sullen and pudgy. By the time she was thirteen, she was not just slightly overweight, but she towered over her classmates.

She came from a large family. Older brother Jamie, class of 1982, was on the Weedsport wrestling team, wrestling as a heavyweight.

It was during her senior year at Weedsport High that Stacey met a man. Introduced by friends in 1985, according to Stacey, it was love at first sight for the tall redhead and the gregarious twenty-four-year-old.

He was Michael "Mike" Wallace, son of Walter K. Wallace and his wife, Joyce. She was Stacey Daniels back then, a six-foot-tall (without shoes) teenager who looked like she might be able to slam-dunk a basketball if she got up a good head of steam.

Her 1985 senior portrait revealed a serious young woman, with a boyish haircut and the beginnings of a double chin. According to her high-school yearbook, she liked *purple, soaps, going to the movies, spending money, and looking for M.I. with Dipsey.* Her favorite saying was *We're talking wicked!* She was on the yearbook staff during her senior year, and on the prom committee as a junior. Her plans: *To be a lawyer and to make a million in my first year of practice.*

Stacey's height put some men off. But not Mike. He liked this woman's size.

"What's your sign?" Stacey asked Mike.

"Virgo, born September 16, 1961," he replied.

Stacey sized up Mike as well. Other than looking good, the first thing Stacey noticed about Mike was that he was always the life of the party. Standing next to this convivial man, she figured, would be a pretty fun place to be.

Talk about a small world. Mike had previously been married to Stacey's third cousin, Nancy. The two women had not known each other well, but they saw each other at family picnics.

"She lived in Weedsport and I lived in Port Byron, which are neighboring towns," Nancy said. "I didn't hang out with her or anything."

It was 1979 and Nancy was seventeen when she met Mike—seventeen and pregnant with another man's baby. Nancy and Mike met in high school, and Nancy remembered those early days fondly. God, it felt good riding in Mike's fast car. She could still hear the roar of his Mopar engine.

Nancy gave birth to a daughter, Renee, and later Mike and Nancy had a son, James. Nancy found that the fast car/Mopar phase of their relationship was ephemeral, and it turned into a tearful vapor. The rest was pain. Her memories of their marriage were not happy ones.

"He was a bad boy," Nancy said in 2009. "He got himself into some trouble . . . quite a bit." Mike was in and out of jail for "different things," including DWI, but drinking and driving wasn't the biggest problem, as far as his first wife was concerned.

"He was very abusive to me," Nancy recalled. "Physically abusive. Eventually it got so bad that I ended up leaving the relationship."

Nancy didn't want people to think Mike was a monster, however. "He was basically a bighearted guy," she said. "He would do anything for anybody. He was a good father."

Same old story, he was just a product of his family situation when he was growing up. Nancy and Mike were together for six years and broke up just in time for Mike to meet another high-school senior and start over.

When they first became boyfriend/girlfriend, Stacey was counting the days before graduation with a perfectly normal combination of anticipation and dread, and Mike Wallace worked as a setup operator at McQuay International, a manufacturer of heating, ventilating, air-conditioning, refrigeration, and building management equipment in Auburn.

In Mike, Stacey could see a viable future. He was "the love of her life." Wallace, likewise, was immediately smitten with the tall, redheaded teenager.

By all indications, Wallace was merely starry-eyed. Stacey was formulating a plan. Within five minutes of meeting him, she knew what she wanted. She could envision it: the wedding, honeymoon, babies . . . spending the rest of her life with him.

She knew, she knew, she knew.

Not that Mike Wallace didn't come with some emotional baggage, but nothing Stacey couldn't work through. He had an ex-wife and a couple of kids, but she'd known Nancy for years and things were civil.

Stacey's well-planned future almost lost out to that bugaboo known as unforeseen circumstances. When

Stacey was nineteen and still living at home, she was in the passenger seat of her mom's car, her mother behind the wheel, riding along Route 31-B, near Pump Road in the town of Brutus. They were struck by a car driven by John E. Terpening, a Weedsport seventeen-year-old, who, when the police arrived, was ticketed for failure to yield.

Stacey's mom was uninjured, but Stacey, who had been wearing her seat belt, complained of abdominal pains. She was taken to Auburn Memorial Hospital, the emergency room (ER), where tests for internal injuries came up negative.

Not long after, Stacey learned she was pregnant with Mike Wallace's baby. Mike did not do the right thing—at least not right away. Not only didn't Mike and Stacey get married just then, but they broke up. Stacey had a baby girl, whom she named Ashley.

During the weeks and months after Ashley was born, Stacey was "in love all over again." Ashley became Stacey's raison d'etre. She existed only to take care of that baby girl. As Ashley grew, she and her mother became best friends who did everything together.

"I knew from that minute on, my whole reason for being here was to take care of her," Stacey said.

Stacey's life course had again veered away from her vision, but she was tenacious and she never stopped working to get things back on track. The very aspects of Mike that were so appealing when she was seventeen—his "party hardy" personality—were prime drawbacks when it came to settling down and starting a family. She didn't quit, and she eventually got Mike back, got the ring on her finger, and set the date. While Ashley was still a baby, Stacey got to proclaim, "Mission accomplished."

In the wedding photos, Mike's dirty blond hair, thick and swept across his forehead, was otherwise cropped into a rocking mullet. Mike and Stacey, again an inseparable couple, were married in the Daniels home on Bell Street.

Stacey's mother later recalled Stacey's joy. This had been the best part of her life. "She was so happy with Michael, certainly happier than she'd ever been before," Judi Eaton said.

Mike maintained a relationship with his former family. There was even one Christmas when his ex, Nancy, and her two kids came over and joined the party with Mike's new family. There were other times, too, when Nancy would drop the kids off so they could see their dad and Stacey would invite her in.

Nancy's mind was boggled by the dynamics of Mike's new household. Here was a guy who had beaten her up until she'd had to flee, and yet his new wife not only didn't seem beaten, she seemed in charge.

"I don't understand it, but Stacey seemed to be wearing the pants in the family," Nancy remembered. "I thought she was a very smart woman who stood up for herself and got things done." Obviously, Mike and Stacey's relationship was very different from the one she'd had with him, and Nancy thought that was to Stacey's credit. Stacey tamed Mike, and by any standards, that was quite an accomplishment.

Years later, after all the bad things happened,

Stacey still talked about Michael Wallace as she would an idol. When discussing Michael, she still felt like a teenager with the world's biggest crush. She recalled that he was larger-than-life, like a Hollywood star.

He didn't change that. Just because he'd taken vows to love and cherish didn't mean he'd vowed not to party. Stacey remembered thinking there was an old cliché that applied to him. "You know, when he was good, he was very, very good," she said—but sometimes he was bad. He liked to drink and do drugs, and sometimes there were demons that burst forth from the mixed substances. "He had a problem with both drinking and drugs for a long time in his life," Stacey recalled.

Wallace's sister, Rosemary, put it differently. She said he was a rebel without a cause, to borrow the title of a James Dean movie. "He went way over the limits on just about everything he did. He was a good soul, though. He was a good man."

But everyone who ever saw Michael and Stacey together agreed on one thing. He loved her. He loved her like life itself. Michael *adored* Stacey.

Three years after Ashley, Bree was born, and she became her daddy's favorite. By this time, Mike still had the thick hair swept across his forehead, but now his hair covered his ears and the mullet was long gone.

Michael called Bree his "little princess." Friend Dani Colman remembered thinking it was odd that a man would so obviously prefer one of his daughters over the other.

By the time Bree was two, the Wallaces' hair styles were different again. Mike's golden brown hair was shortly cropped all over and he had a moustache. It was Stacey who sported the mullet.

Unlike their hair, the relationships within the family remained staid. There was never a single mention, as far as Dani Colman could recall, of any kind of relationship whatsoever between Mike and Ashley. It was always Mike and Bree, Mike and Bree. That was all Dani heard. The younger girl was "Daddy's little angel" who could do no wrong in his eyes. How to explain it? Was there a question of paternity in Mike's mind blocking his affection for Ashley? His first marriage featured one who wasn't his and one who was.

It's hard to say how much anyone thought about it at the time, but later Stacey said that Mike's obvious favoritism toward Bree was hurtful and harmful for Ashley.

Stacey said there were no shades of gray. Just black and white. Bree was Mike's favorite. Ashley was not. The favoritism was even supported by family photos in which Bree and Michael turned toward one another, while Ashley was turned away. There were photos of Mike and Ashley alone together, but none in which the pair looked happy. Dull-eyed and uncomfortable was more like it.

Stacey said that she was deeply aware of the emotional gap between her husband and her oldest daughter, and she stepped up to compensate. Stacey spent as much time with Ashley as she could. They hung out. Their relationship expanded beyond that of just mother and daughter.

"We were best friends," Stacey remembered.

Ashley, years later, said she didn't remember it being like that. She had no intense feelings of rejection. She would say that those were happy years, when she and her sister were little. Ashley remembered them as spontaneous days.

"We'd just go for a ride in the car, you know? For no reason, just take a ride. That was fun," she remembered.

During her first marriage, Stacey worked during the day as an ambulance dispatcher for the Rural/Metro Medical Services, an organization of drivers and paramedics whose slogan was "Fifty Years of Serving Others." Mike worked as a mechanic.

And while it was true that Mike and Stacey did quarrel sometimes—more often than not because he was drinking or doping too much—outsiders were unanimous in their opinion that during the first years of their marriage, the couple was happy, their relationship was working.

When asked what the arguments were about, Stacey preferred to say what they were not about—and what they were not about was money. "That's because we didn't have any," Stacey recalled.

The Wallaces lived in a serene-looking two-story semiattached house on East Brutus Street, the small town of Weedsport's premier east-west thoroughfare, where the lawns were manicured and the mature trees provided plenty of shade. The home was practically across the street from Weedsport Junior/Senior High School, which would have been extremely convenient for the girls, had they remained living there after their father's death.

Weedsport was in the northern part of the town of Brutus in Cayuga County, twenty-five miles west of

Syracuse. With a population just greater than two thousand, it was due north of Owasco Lake and the town of Auburn. It was tiny compared to Clay, only one square mile in size, a diminutive village—with five churches, one Catholic and four Protestant— originally built where it was because of its proximity to the Erie Canal and its basin, which allowed barges to turn around. The town was named after Elihu and Edward Weed, merchants who helped found the village.

In 1994 or 1995, Mike's stepdaughter Renee came to live with them. Renee was in her "wild, rebellious teenage years" and was having trouble finding people—including her parents—who were willing to live with her. She had been living with her biological father in Auburn, and both Mike and Renee's mom, Nancy, felt that wasn't a good place for her to be.

"She was having a lot of trouble there. It wasn't a good atmosphere for her at all," said Mike's first wife, Nancy.

According to Renee, her mom didn't want to take her back. According to Nancy, Renee didn't want to come back. So Mike, ignoring matters of paternity, volunteered to give Renee shelter. Renee brought her "wild child" act to Weedsport, causing instant alienation between her and Stacey.

The living arrangement only lasted for a couple of months. Stacey said Renee had to go. She feared Renee was a bad influence on her girls.

Today, Renee admits that her memories of that time are hazy, but Mike, Stacey, and the girls seemed, to her, to be a normal, functional family. The initial plans were for her to stay with the Wallaces long-term. She enrolled in school in Weedsport and moved in the spring, at the end of the school year, a tough time to start a new school.

"I remember the weather was nice," Renee said years later with a small laugh. Ashley was in Girl Scouts when her stepsister came to live with them, and the house was taken over for a time by the cookie sale. Bree was still little and enjoyed eating ketchup sandwiches.

"Just ketchup and bread," Renee recalled. "It was her favorite food."

Looking back, Renee theorized that Mike's role in her life was one of the reasons that she'd been wild in the first place. Up until the time she was fourteen, she'd believed that Mike was her real dad. She was an adolescent when her mother told her that this wasn't so. Mike was the guy her mom married after being impregnated by someone else. This came as quite a shock. She'd always called Mike "Dad."

She remembered the time when she and her brother had lived with her mom and Mike. They were never well-off. They lived in trailers. They had animals, a dog and a rabbit. She remembered how tactful Mike was when telling her the rabbit had passed away.

Renee had memories of being very little and being taken to visit Mike in jail. Why he was in jail, she doesn't remember. But she visited more than once and Stacey was already with him.

"My mother says that he was not a nice man to her. He was abusive to her, but as far as I could tell, not to Stacey—so maybe jail did him good. As far as I could tell, Mike and Stacey's relationship was great," Renee opined. The Weedsport house that Mike and Stacey and the girls rented was "not bad, but not wonderful." Mike, she recalled, had a farm job then and Stacey worked on an ambulance crew.

Looking back, Renee finds it strange that Stacey, the person everyone today finds so interesting, never much registered with her. She was her dad's wife, who didn't like her. So screw her. That's all.

"I remember her size. She was tall and not small. She was built pretty solid. Not fat, just big," Renee said.

After leaving Weedsport, Renee never saw the man she called her dad again. She only saw Stacey, Ashley, and Bree once more, and that was a few years later—at Mike's funeral.

About a decade into the marriage between Mike and Stacey, there was talk of trouble, with infidelity on both sides. Things got bad. Stacey's friend Kim remembered that Stacey had once told her that she'd contemplated divorce, but had decided against it because she didn't want to "upset the apple cart." There were always reasons. Not with summer vacation coming up. Not with the holidays coming up. There was no divorce.

It was around that time, late 1999, that Michael's health began to fail. He was riding a roller coaster of sickness, and no one could figure out what was wrong with him.

To a physician, he said, "I don't know what the problem is, Doc. I always feel drunk, even though I haven't been drinking. I'm dizzy. My equilibrium is off. One time, I got up off the toilet bowl and I could barely stand." It wasn't low blood pressure. It wasn't an inner-ear infection. It wasn't diabetes. There were plenty of things it wasn't.

* * *

Mike Wallace's sister-in-law, Melanne Keim (pronounced mel-ANN), since 1988, had been married to Stacey's brother, Jamie. Aunt Melanne, who graduated from Weedsport High School and the Bryant & Stratton Business Institute, saw Mike during the time he was sick. He was so dizzy that he was staggering like a drunkard.

The poor guy's nerves were worn raw by his own poor health. She asked him what was the matter and he said he didn't know, but it had been going on for a long time and he was getting sick and tired of it.

His mother-in-law looked at Mike and saw heart disease. She remembered the symptoms as well. Judi Eaton said Mike didn't look good. He had a cough. And he complained that his shoulder was hurting him. She remembered thinking, some people complain of pain in the arm or shoulder before they have a heart attack.

Mike had no energy. After the slightest exertion, he needed to rest. Judi told him that he should go see a doctor as soon as possible, but he never made it.

Judi Eaton wasn't the only one telling Wallace to seek out medical care. Rosemary Corbett, his sister, had also. Corbett remembered the Christmas of 1999. Her brother was a mess. He couldn't stop coughing. He looked fatigued and bloated.

The day after her grandmother came to visit and saw her dad all sick, Ashley—who was twelve years old at the time—recalled seeing her father lying on the couch and behaving peculiarly.

That couch was white with a red flower pattern on it. Like many couches, it was positioned so that you could lie on it and watch TV at the same time. But her dad's head was at the wrong end for TV viewing, and the TV was off.

"It looked to me like he was making funny faces," Ashley remembered. He stuck his arm up in the air and then he held it out at his side and then it just fell down, she recalled.

Ashley did not further observe her father's odd behavior because it was time for her to pick up Bree at school. That was the last time Ashley saw her father alive.

When she got home, holding her little sister's hand, there was an ambulance parked in the driveway. Her mother came outside and told the girls to go next door and wait there.

That was what they did, and later their grandmother came over to tell the girls that their father had passed away. It was surreal, like being beamed into a parallel universe with no way of returning.

Ashley couldn't remember ever being so frightened. She became obsessed with her last memories of her father alive. She told the story again and again. The faces he made. The arm. When she stopped saying it aloud, she continued to go over it in her mind. Thousands of times.

She couldn't help but wonder if she was somehow in part responsible for her father's death. If only she had said something, done something when she saw him behaving oddly on the couch. *If only, if only, if only* . . . but she was twelve, too young to even register that there was a crisis—and she did nothing.

Stacey, who was practically clairvoyant when it came to Ashley because they were so close, could tell that her oldest daughter was feeling guilty.

Ashley, in fact, blamed herself for her father's death for a long time.

Sometimes, Stacey remembered, Ashley would come right out and say it. "It was my fault," Ashley said. Stacey didn't know what to think when Ashley said that. Probably, Stacey figured, Ashley was referring to her belief that she could have saved Daddy and had not. "I've relived this day over and over again in my head, because what if there was something that I could've done?" Ashley said. "Like, I should've known, but I didn't. I was twelve!"

It was assumed that Mike Wallace had a heart attack. He had lifestyle issues. He'd had pain in his shoulder. His heart—that must have been it.

But there were those who were suspicious. One person raising a skeptical eyebrow was Mike's sister, Rosemary.

"The color of his skin from head to chest was deep, dark purple. And it was really weird," she said. Not that she was thinking about foul play. She just had an inkling that something, well, strange had killed her brother—something that wasn't *just* a heart attack.

Corbett remembered suggesting to Stacey that an autopsy might be in order. Stacey said no, and Rosemary's mom was freaked out at the thought of an autopsy on her son, so Rosemary didn't push.

Stacey said, "When the doctors told me that they believed he'd died of a heart attack, I believed that. There was no reason for me to question that." It wasn't like he was a fellow who took care of himself. He smoked Marlboro menthols.

She would later explain that she was in shock and not really making decisions for herself at all. If the doctors had recommended an autopsy, she would have said sure, go for it. However, they said it was a heart attack, that there was no urgent need for an autopsy, so she didn't request one.

As would become the norm, Stacey's mother agreed with her daughter on this and every other point. Judi Eaton said that she worked for one of the emergency room doctors who was working when Michael Wallace was brought in, and he assured her that it was probably a heart attack and no autopsy would be needed. Besides, he had that pain in his shoulder. That was a clear sign.

On January 13, 2000, the *Post-Standard* newspaper in Syracuse ran Mike's obituary. He was born and had been pronounced dead in the town of Auburn. He grew up in Owasco, New York, a town about five miles south of Auburn and Skaneateles, about halfway between Owasco and Skaneateles Lakes. It said he was a factory worker. Mentioned were his widow and two daughters, his son and stepdaughter by a previous marriage, and his surviving mom, Joyce, his brother, Walter, of Montezuma, a one-tavern town thirty miles east of Syracuse along the thruway, and his sister, Rosemary E. Corbett, of Cato, which was just a crossroads really, twenty miles northwest of Syracuse. The burial, which wouldn't take place until the spring because of the frozen ground, was to be at the Owasco Rural Cemetery.

Mike's body was laid out at the Jewell Funeral Home, and the friends and family who came to view the body and pay their respects all noticed how stoically Stacey was taking her husband's death. They never saw her cry. Not at the hospital. Not at the funeral.

"I would not classify her as the typical grieving widow," one friend said.

Ashley, too, noticed her mother's lack of emotion following Michael's demise.

"Not one tear," Ashley commented. She hadn't thought that much of it at the time. She chose to believe that her mother was just trying to "stay strong" for her and her sister's sakes. "I thought she didn't want us to see her sad."

And that was what Stacey said, too. She said that staying calm in the face of tragedy had been a conscious decision on her part. She didn't want to be one of those widows who just stayed in bed all day in a funk, whom people didn't want around because they were so weepy. She decided not to act like a widow, but rather to act like a mother. It was her job, in the final analysis, to set an example for her girls.

Folks accepted it, even admired it, when Stacey's demeanor did not quite match her circumstances. Consensus was that Stacey was an exceptional woman, a strong woman capable of holding herself together when anyone else would have fallen apart.

Stacey cashed in Michael's $50,000 life insurance policy and used the money to pay for his funeral. She paid off some debts, and she took the girls to Disney World. The three of them did their best to look ahead rather than look back, and they quickly adapted to Michael's absence.

The mood shifted from mourning to upbeat almost overnight. "We were happy that way," Ashley said, and then added the vague qualifier: "Or so we seemed."

That good mood was sullied only by the death of Stacey's dad, Gerald W. Daniels, at the age of sixty on

February 27, 2002. "Jerry" had been recovering when he took a sudden turn for the worse and died. Stacey was among his last visitors, seen entering his room with an open can of soda. At the time of his death, he was living in an apartment on Columbus Street in Auburn. He'd lived in Auburn since 1988 when he moved from Weedsport. Stacey's dad was employed for the last twenty-two years of his life by the Fox Auto dealership in Auburn. He was immediately cremated and Stacey became executrix of his will.

All of that happiness shared by Stacey and her girls flew right out the window as soon as Stacey started seeing David Wayne Castor Sr. He was her type, large and rubicund. And older. David, born June 12, 1957, was already in his forties when he met Stacey, who was a full decade younger.

Stacey and David were married on August 16, 2003. One photo taken in a park after their wedding showed the bride and groom grinning widely. At six feet, she was a little bit taller than he. She was wearing a white wedding dress, and David wore a black tux with a white tie. Standing on either side of them were Chauncey and Judi Eaton, the bride's stepdad and mom. Chauncey was also in a tux and wore a red tie. Judi's dress matched both her husband's tie but also the dresses worn by Ashley and Bree, who sat in front of the adults, both wearing glasses. Bree was smiling her prettiest smile and looking at the camera, while Ashley was sullen, looking downward. So Stacey and her daughters moved into the house on Wetzel Road with David Castor. Their new village was Liverpool in the town of Clay, northernmost of Onondaga County's fifteen towns, sprawling over more than fifty square miles between the confluence of the Oneida and Oswego Rivers. The town was named after Henry Clay, the nineteenth-century statesman and orator, who, despite the nickname "the Great Compromiser," had been listed among those responsible for the War of 1812. He unsuccessfully ran for president and was, during the mid-twentieth century, named one of the five greatest U.S. senators of all time.

The town of Clay was not just sprawling but heavily populated as well, with close to sixty thousand people, more than a third of the population of the city of Syracuse to the south. In 2008, it finished fifty-ninth on *Money* magazine's "Best Places to Live." It was also the home of one of the country's largest shopping centers, the Great North Mall, which opened in 1988.

6

Janice

Throughout the investigation into David Castor's death, Janice Mary Poissant, a pretty blonde who'd spent a quarter century with the man, remained the law's biggest ally. Janice thought Stacey did it, she loved David dearly, and she pledged she would do whatever she could to put *that woman*—*it*, the alien from outer space, she called her—behind bars for the rest of her life.

Years later, speaking with a writer, Janice would say she wasn't sure she had the strength to say some of her memories out loud. They were too powerful. She wanted to state up front that David Castor was not all bad. He was always a loving father, but she'd never before told the whole story of what it was like to be with him.

She wanted to be sure she told a balanced story, including the many, many highlights of her marriage, as well as the lowlights. But she wished everyone to know that the story of why she broke up with

David was not the whole tale. It was only the sad and just finale.

And they were so young when it started. Teenagers. Adolescents, really. Janice and David grew up less than a mile apart in the town of Baldwinsville. He lived on Dewitt Drive, she on Dennis Drive. Both streets were off Route 370, which was known as Cold Springs Road when it passed through town. She had an identical twin, Janet, and two younger siblings.

She knew David because they rode the same school bus to and from Durgee Junior High five times a week. To herself, she called him Rudolph, because his nose was always red—in the summer because of the sun, winter because of the cold.

Janice took notice of David, and not just his nose. He wasn't like the other guys. The other guys were mean and tortured the girls. He was *gentle*.

Besides, she was friends with one of his sisters, Linda. Janice and Linda had some of the same classes at school and they had been partners for a Halloween painting contest, for which they won first place. Following the contest, Janice spent her first night at the Castor home celebrating, but she didn't remember seeing David, just Linda's two youngest brothers, Gary and Steve.

David was the third of six Castor kids. They were, in order of birth: Sandra Lynn, Philip Michael "Mike," David, Linda Susan, Gary Lee, and Stephen Gregory.

David was also the neighborhood paperboy, riding his bike from house to house. Sometime after the Halloween painting contest, Janice remembered, David rode his bike over to her house for a visit, and this is when she had her first feelings of "true like" for a boy.

When she was thirteen going on fourteen, a horrific, traumatic thing happened to Janice. It changed her. In her own words, she went from being a "good girl to being a bad girl." She skipped classes, she caused trouble in school, anything to get detention and avoid riding the school bus home and facing the mean boys. She had no choice but to ride that bus in the morning, but twice a day was too much. She fought every day to quit school, but she was too young.

The more serious aftereffects of the traumatic event were a severe loss of self-esteem, and a worrisome self-destruction kick. She almost took her own life twice. The second time, she didn't make it home from school, and her father found her under a bridge at Baldwinsville's "Four Corners."

But somehow David was the magic man, and somehow he pulled her out of it and put a halt to her self-destructive nature.

"He asked me out two or three times before, and I finally said yes. We were outside a school dance." She hadn't gone into the dance. She was just hanging around outside the school talking. Janice and David were each with a group of friends outside, beyond the realm of chaperones. David had a friend of his go over and talk to her.

"David would like you to go out with him," the friend said.

Her immediate response was "No way." But then she began to think about how nice he was on the bus, how he'd visited her on his bike, and she started to feel that she could *trust him*. And so she eventually said yes.

David and Janice had their first date on October 3, 1973, when Janice was fifteen and David was sixteen.

From that point on, Janice and David were practically inseparable. Two months after their first date, David gave Janice a necklace, which she still owned. At first, her self-destructive behavior continued. She never told her parents about the bad thing that had happened, and they were confused and hurt by the change that had taken place in their daughter.

Because David and Janice were together so much, and Janice was still chronically getting into trouble at school, there were times that David got detention just because he was with her, a situation that caused him problems with his parents, Joyce and Philip.

Not long after they began dating, David moved in with Janice and her family. There was what Janice called a "misunderstanding" at the Castor home, and David felt he had to leave. When David told his parents that he was moving in with Janice's family, his dad cried.

The new living arrangements worked out well, because Janice's parents, Louis and Marion Poissant, adored David. They sensed the change in Janice and David's positive influence. They felt like they had their girl back.

Besides, as Janice's dad put it, they "couldn't have the boy living on the streets."

As her relationship with David grew, Janice shed her self-destructive persona, but she remained as eager as ever to quit school. She dropped out on her sixteenth birthday. David dropped out as well.

"If David had been with anyone but me, he probably would have graduated," Janice admitted many years later.

David and Janice wanted to go places and do things. They wanted to go to the movies and go bowling, the usual dating activities. So Janice's dad helped them buy a 1973 Dodge Challenger.

"David was so proud of that car," Janice recalled. It could "burn rubber."

Janice was almost completely dependent on David from the start. He always had a job, and when he'd leave for work in the Challenger, Janice would look sadly out the window, remaining until she could no longer see his taillights.

David and Janice's relationship was "progressing," she said, but Janice had reservations, and she knew she would one day have to tell David about the bad thing. David "made the transition bearable, though there were many tormenting stages that came and went. We survived!"

In September of 1976, David and Janice set out to look for a place of their own. David was nineteen, Janice eighteen. That abode turned out to be a mobile home on a two-hundred by eight-hundred lot, out in the country, in Pulaski, a good hour from Baldwinsville, which David purchased at the recommendation of his friend Leo for $6,000.

They were truly roughing it at first. The mobile home had no running water and no electricity. It pretty much had no everything. They carried buckets from a two-hundred-year-old well and lit kerosene lamps. They wore heavy clothes and "put about a ton of blankets on the bed."

Pulaski was right at the easternmost end of Lake

Ontario, in the direct path of the snow belt, an area frequently dumped on by "lake effect" snow. One time, it snowed so hard, it took David eight hours to dig them out.

They were making do. Eventually the water and electricity were hooked up and life became a tad closer to normal. The bigger problem was their parents, both sets, who were not pleased with their unmarried and cohabitating status.

One day, all four parents came to the mobile home and forced a discussion of marriage. When the young couple expressed a willingness on the subject, arrangements were quickly made before David and Janice had an opportunity to change their minds.

They were married on November 6, 1976, at St. Mary's Church in Baldwinsville, with a reception following at the local VFW. David's sister Linda made a JUST MARRIED sign and attached it to the back of David's Challenger. The newlyweds then took his parents' motor home to Niagara Falls for their honeymoon.

The Challenger, the very symbol of their freedom, eventually had to be taken off the road because they couldn't afford the insurance. For six years it sat.

It was a lonely time for Janice, who stayed home while David went to work. He would leave before daylight and return home after dark, and she was alone, not knowing the neighbors. The only person she knew was David's friend Leo, who first led them to the mobile home. She didn't even know him well, and he was born in 1909.

Janice focused her attention on being the best homemaker she could be, both inside and outside the home. On the outside, Leo taught her how to garden. She built a huge vegetable garden under his guidance. Together, they tilled and planted. Alone, she maintained and canned. Year after year.

On the inside, she was an immaculate house-keeper. Both of her parents worked and she'd learned to cook and clean from the time she was nine. She enjoyed thinking of her role in the marriage as "old-fashioned," taking care of the domestic end while David brought home the bacon. She would have dinner ready when he got home, even if she had to cook ahead of time and heat his plate up when he arrived.

Yet, there were times when Janice's loneliness was unbearable, and she struck out from her home, just to see new scenery and maybe meet a neighbor or two.

When David learned about Janice's midday wanderings, he became angry. "I have enough to worry about at work, without having to worry about you, too." Janice was to stay home.

And she did. But it was hard. It wasn't like David was great company when he *was* around. It wasn't his fault, but he often came home from work exhausted, and plopped on the couch—too tired for conversation.

Next came a period when he wasn't satisfied with her on any level. He was blind to the things she did and scolded her for the things she didn't do.

Janice knew the perfect cure for her loneliness. She should have a baby! She lobbied her case to David, saying, "Imagine how nice it would be to have a little David running around with his father's red hair and full of smiles!"

On February 27, 1978, Janice confirmed that she

was with child. On October 3, 1978, she had David
Jr. She'd been prophetic. Red hair. Full of smiles.

Liverpool Heating belonged to Stan Korzinewski,
back in the 1950s. Janice's dad worked there for
years and bought the business when Stan retired in
the fall of 1978. When her dad filled out the legal
forms, he listed the new owners as Louis Poissant
and his son-in-law, David Castor. Janice was *huge*
when David Sr. went to work at her dad's business. It
was exactly a month before David Jr. was born.

"My father taught David about the business,
taught him everything," she remembered.

It was a family business, and David Jr., when he
got old enough, always helped, too. Young David
said that he helped his dad with his work from the
time he could remember. He went on service calls
with him. Every summer, he would accompany his
father for furnace installations. And at home, too.
"I remember all the work we did together. I'd be
right there helping him, being his gofer, getting
tools for him."

Cousin John Howard was also part of the business.
He made service calls and performed installations.

The business was successful—and with a *zero* ad-
vertising budget. Their customers were loyal, and
word of mouth always worked to their advantage.
They provided quality equipment and service at a
reasonable price.

To keep an eye on her all the time, David gave
Janice a job. So she was a working mom with a baby.
A little busy, but it was better than being alone in the
mobile home without much to do.

For Janice, the most complicated part of her busy schedule was having both her dad and her husband as her boss. There were days when her dad would say one thing, and David would say another. She wouldn't know what to do.

Both Janice and her mother, Marion, worked in the office as secretaries/bookkeepers/office keepers. When Janice's mom quit and returned to her previous job with General Electric, Janice took over the office. She had a cordless phone so she could work throughout the facility. Taking over was a big confidence booster. Her lack of education worried her, but when the time came, she knew enough math to do the job.

After six years of being covered with a tarp, the Challenger was back on the road. The old muscle car needed a new engine. David ordered one and he and Janice did the labor themselves.

David's in-laws, the Poissants, built a new house in Pennellville, and everyone pitched in. David and Janice helped dig out the basement and shingle the roof.

Janice and David lived together, slept together, worked together. The *only* time they were apart was when he had to go out on service calls.

Luckily, David Jr. was a breeze to take care of. Such a good baby, and as a toddler content to play quietly with his toys. If he had fussed like other babies, life would have been much harder.

Janice's office was a sitting room furnished with a desk, couch, chair, and television.

One day, at her mother's urging, Janice went to the mall. The young woman had never done anything like that before. She spent the day window-shopping, reveling in this unprecedented freedom.

When she told David about the day she'd spent at the mall, he became angry. "If you do that again, we're going to end up just like our friends—divorced!" he said.

He explained that there was no need for her to have her own car or money. He would protect her. He would take care of her needs. He was all she needed.

When David Jr. was old enough to start school, September 1983, big David and Janice had a tough decision to make. They loved it, but they lived in the middle of nowhere. He could go to the centralized school closest to home, or go live with Janice's parents where the school was nearby. David and Janice signed papers making Louis and Marion the guardians of David Jr. during the school year. Janice and David still saw David Jr. every day, since they commuted back and forth anyway for work.

"As a family, we each had our snowmobiles. We each had our four-wheelers. David never took any of his big toys and went out with friends. It was always with us, as a family," she said.

Snowmobiling had always been big. David purchased a 1976 Olympic 440 Ski-Doo just before they got married. David Jr. started driving it when he was seven, in the field across the road. Later they would go on six-hour trail rides together from their home to the easternmost edge of Lake Ontario and back.

They were campers, staying in a series of ever-improving travel trailers pulled by a series of ever-improving Ford trucks. They'd go to Darien Lake Fun Country or River Forest Park, depending on the season. For fun on the water, they'd go out on the lake in David's twenty-foot Citation Cuddy Cabin, or buzz around in his Jet Ski. There were motorcycles, too—a series of Kawasaki bikes.

Janice recalled when David Jr. got his first four-wheeler, a brand-new 1986 Honda for his eighth birthday. Eventually big David bought a Suzuki for himself and a 1997 Polaris 400 Scrambler Automatic for Janice. They used to ride through the mud and come home laughing and covered in mud.

In 1985, her father found a perfect place to move the growing business. There was an existing house on Wetzel Road from which he could run the business and a lot in back, where they could build the warehouse/factory. Plus, it was only five minutes from his house.

The warehouse was built immediately, and it was enlarged in 1996 to its current size.

Janice felt her marriage was relatively strong until that Easter of 1987 when Dave had his accident. He'd tried to get Janice to learn how to ride a motorcycle. She liked riding behind him on his bike, but thought it might be fun to have her own and ride alongside him.

He bought her a Husqvarna dirt bike to learn on, but it didn't go well. She liked automatics and was never comfortable with anything she had to shift.

The dirt bike was too big, or her legs were too short. Either way, she had to stand on tiptoes when she straddled it, and it was difficult to keep her balance.

She finally gave up that spring after a praying

mantis landed on her shirt as she rode, sending her into a panic that caused her to lay down the bike.

After that, David just wanted to get rid of the thing. His brother agreed to buy it. So on Easter Sunday, David put on his helmet and took the dirt bike out for a test ride.

Janice and David Jr. stood at the front door, watching the field across the road where David was riding. First they saw engine parts shooting across the sky, and then a human body flying through the air.

Janice ran barefoot across the road. She could still remember the feel of the chilled blacktop on the soles of her feet. On the other side, she found David unconscious. The dirt bike looked as if it had exploded. There was something oozing from her husband's mouth.

"Go get the nurse who lives down the road and call 911!" she screamed. David was rushed to the hospital, where he was put in the intensive care unit (ICU) with a bad concussion and a deep cerebral contusion. The helmet he was wearing had saved his life.

When Janice first saw him in the hospital, David's arms and legs were tied to the bed. She was told that he'd been "extremely agitated" when he first regained consciousness.

Delirious, he'd said odd things. For instance, "Janice, untie me. Can't you do *anything* right?" Janice was hurt by this, until she learned from a nurse that he'd lost his memory.

The brain injury left him at first with amnesia so bad that he didn't recognize his son or his wife. "He knows the name 'Janice,' but doesn't recall who the name belongs to," the nurse said.

Doctors confirmed what the nurse had said. There was a possibility that he'd need to be taught everything all over again—right from the beginning, from infancy. They wouldn't know for sure until the swelling in his brain went down.

Janice stayed with him in the hospital and watched with hope as he improved daily. After a few weeks, he returned home, where he slowly and sometimes painfully recovered his memory. Eventually all of his memory came back, but he was never the same.

Perhaps the accident had caused a permanent brain injury and he no longer had mature impulse control. He grew rapacious for material things. He blurted out statements that popped in his head. He acted out without weighing consequences. Aspects of his personality, such as his preference for grown-up toys over people, became intolerable.

During the fall of 1987, "Grandpa" Leo, who had helped Janice plant her first garden, passed away.

Janice was an abused woman, but she couldn't see it. It wasn't as easy for her to see as it was for those on the outside looking in. She lived under these conditions day to day. She told herself that there was nothing wrong. The way she saw it, she was just old-fashioned. She hung the clothes outside on the line to dry. She cooked meals from scratch, and not from boxes. Dinner was always on the table waiting for David when he came home. She mended, she sewed. David was her hero. David saved her.

He had so many toys, it was difficult for Janice to find anything to give him for Christmas. One year, instead of buying him something, she gave him a "personal certificate," for a "daily head-to-toe fingertip-to-fingertip massage" for a whole year.

It took a long time to sink in. She had started with him when she was so young. Her body was now mature, but he treated her like the little girl on the school bus, the damaged one who'd been broken by cruelty.

And the nostalgic delusion was rich in her psyche, too. She saw him as she'd seen him on that school bus, with his nose red and not like the other boys. He would always be her knight in shining armor, the one who had gotten her out of her self-destructive mode.

He always said he did things because he loved her, because she needed protection. Wasn't it obvious? "You need a keeper for a husband," he maintained.

Janice remembered that her sister tried to talk her into going to Vera House, a local shelter for abused women. But Janice said no. She didn't know what Vera House was, and she didn't want to go there.

It sank in slowly, but it sank in. Janice felt smothered by David. She'd met him as a young girl, and now middle age was upon her and she developed an identity crisis. She needed independence. She tried to make him see, but he wouldn't. She talked to him. It didn't take.

"I felt like I was losing me," she said. He'd been verbally abusive ever since she knew him. "He would fight me and I would always back down, but I got to a point where I felt there was no more Janice."

Janice's sister echoed her feelings: "Where's my sister? I want my sister back," she would say.

The lightbulb went on the day in 1994 when sixteen-year-old David Jr. left home, complaining about the same controlling nature in his father that Janice felt. Her only child took off. He'd wanted her to come with him. He was gone for a while; then he returned long enough to finish school and enlist in the army for four years.

The Castors threw a graduation party on June 20, 1997, and things didn't go well. Big David tried to control the situation, oblivious to the fact that a certain amount of chaos was necessary for a successful party. He ordered that gates be put up in the house to restrict guests' movements. Guests were forbidden to use all of the bathrooms except for the one in the basement. During the party, as his father tried to suck the joy out of it with rules and restrictions, David Jr. turned to his mother and said, "How do you do it?" David's family had planned to have Thanksgiving at David and Janice's that year—they had never hosted the festivities before—but those plans were scrubbed when family members observed David's behavior at the graduation party.

She left him for the first time in 1997, but she went back after just a couple of days. After that, "things got good" for a little while. But he couldn't fix what was wrong, because he couldn't see that anything was wrong.

"My dad retired while David and I were still married, and after that, David was in charge," Janice said. Louis J. Poissant retired in October 1994 and sold the business to his son-in-law for $50,000, one-half contracted and one-half verbal promise.

In February of 1997, the Castors moved from their mobile home in Pulaski to the house on Wetzel Road in Liverpool. By that time, the marriage was in trouble. One night, while in bed, Janice and David argued. He wanted to, she didn't. "He got a gun out," Janice recalled. "He wanted me to shoot him." Luckily, he couldn't find the bullets, and the next day, he acted as if nothing had happened.

David told Janice that she had a good life. He provided well for her. They went on vacations—Hawaii, Colorado, Disney in Florida, Key West, Busch Gardens, Williamsburg. The vacations provided David and Janice with opportunities to relax, and good things happened.

The marriage's highlights were a checklist of joy: riding with the motorcycle club; cross-country skiing, which looked like it was going to be boring but was incredible; coating each other with mud from the rooster tails off their four-wheelers; racing on frozen Kasoag Lake on snowmobiles at one hundred miles per hour; the cross-country trek to Barnes Corners, when they stopped at a swimming hole with the beautiful waterfalls and stone walls; the outing on the boat and skinny-dipping in the lake, in awe of the complete freedom they felt.

There was Jacksonville to visit old-time friends; Houston to visit her twin, who was pregnant with her first child; in campers to Myrtle Beach; several trips to Niagara Falls—even after their honeymoon and always that same hotel with the mirror on the ceiling over the bed and the heart-shaped Jacuzzi.

David put her in the Jacuzzi with bubble bath, bubbles overflowing everywhere, and gave her a glass of wine. At the bottom of the glass was the first diamond ring she ever received.

Then back to Houston to meet the new niece, Mindy. Then to Hawaii, Janice on an airplane for the first time. They rented a condo in Avon, North

Carolina, and on one very dark night, she and David went for a walk, just the two of them, carrying only a blanket. They passed a group of people sitting around a campfire. One of them was playing guitar. David and Janice walked, hand in hand, into the pitch blackness. They came to the water, laid out the blanket, and made the best-ever love.

And Key West, 1999, which turned out to be the last vacation. Back home, back at work, the relaxed and fun David always disappeared.

After searching and searching, Janice finally located a book that explained her marriage. It was called *The Verbally Abusive Relationship* by Patricia Evans. She took the book's advice and wrote David a letter, a list of demands that she be treated more like a grown woman, with at least some of the freedoms that other women enjoyed, her own money, a car to go places.

Even if you were perfect, which you are not, she wrote, *I need more than just you in my life. Even if you made me feel one-hundred percent good, which you don't, I need more than just you in my life.*

David read the letter. "I don't deserve to go on after what I've done," he said.

"Yes, you do," Janice reassured him.

He said he would change, but the control he exerted was still there.

"He merely changed his tactics," she noted.

If she wanted to go somewhere, he made her feel *so* guilty. He told her she hated him and was making him suffer for all he had done to her.

And when she went someplace, wherever it might

be, she was only half there: there but not there. She would give up. Reliant on routine, she'd return home.

Sensing that he was losing the control he needed, David took the verbal abuse to a new extreme. She was f'ing stupid, he said, an f'ing idiot. No f'ing brains.

He was very mean, telling her that if she got her way, the horrific thing that happened to her before they started going out was going to happen again.

Was that what she wanted?

The abuse became physical. He grabbed her, his grip painfully tight, like her arm was being crushed in a vise grip. When she did manage a trip outside without him, there were hours-long interrogations when she returned. He told her they needed to be together all the time.

"When we die, you'll be buried next to me, right?" David would say. "I don't want to be alone."

Janice refused to make that promise. Nobody knew when their time was going to be up, and under what circumstances it would come.

"When we go, we go together," David said.

One of their rare good days came on July 24, 1999, when David Jr. married his longtime girlfriend, June. Janice and her husband danced to his favorite song, "Lady in Red," and when the band's time was up, David Sr. agreed to go in halves with June's dad to keep the band playing.

David and Janice were together for a long time, a lifetime. They split up after twenty-six years together and twenty-three years of marriage. She left him in January 2000 for the fourth and final time. The final straw came on a Saturday night when David "did an extreme" to her that nearly "did her in."

She loved Dave when she left him—but she couldn't do it anymore. She left with the clothes on her back and her purse. If you included the house and the business and everything, she left behind $300,000 in assets.

She went to a grocery store and felt her grip on reality slipping. When her senses snapped back, after she imagined hearing her son's voice, she called a friend and asked her to take her to "the shelter." She called David Sr. and told him she was going. He screamed for her not to leave, but she couldn't be dissuaded. She told him the van was in the grocery store parking lot and the keys were under the seat.

Janice's friend picked her up at the grocery store and took her to Vera House, named after Sister Mary Vera. For the first few days, she didn't eat or sleep. She was on her own among strangers for the first time.

While she was there, David drank and drove, heading who knows where, until he was busted for DWI.

"Leaving him was the hardest thing I ever had to do in my entire life," she said. "I had never been on my own before. It was traumatic. I went from one extreme to the other, from being completely controlled, to being completely free."

She lost her home, her job, and her husband all at once. When she left, she didn't leave a forwarding address and there was no way for Dave to contact her.

With Janice out of David Sr.'s life, David Jr. became the brunt of his father's frustrations. David Sr. was putting "every emotion you could possibly have" on his son.

"I could see that this burden was weighing heavily on David Jr.," Janice said. "He would tell me that nothing was wrong, but I knew better. I could tell."

Janice said she'd held no grudge against her husband when she left him. While it was true that their relationship was one of dominance and submissiveness, it was not a sadomasochistic relationship.

David wasn't controlling because he wanted to be mean and she didn't stay because she enjoyed being mistreated. It was just the way things had developed.

She just wanted big David to learn from his mistakes and be happy. The business remained his. She didn't want to take it away from him. She just did what she had to do.

"I didn't want to beat him up or destroy him, and the business was his livelihood," she recalled. "Although in the state he was in, he was going to lose the business."

Janice's father-in-law stepped in and helped David, and saved the business for him. Her mother-in-law said she was hurt terribly by the separation, but she wanted Janice to know she still loved her and she would always be welcome in the Castor home.

Janice left Vera House after receiving a phone call from Texas from her twin sister, Janet. Their mother was gravely ill, her heart, so Janice flew there to be with her.

Miraculously, her mom recovered, doctors shocked her heart back into working order, but while in Texas, Janice learned from her twin that David had told her family, including her mom and dad, all about the horrible thing that had happened when she was thirteen.

"He said that it had been haunting you and that's why you left him," Janet explained.

Janice was stunned. For one thing, she had never wanted her father to know her horrible secret. For another, David was refusing to take any responsibility for their breakup, and was blaming her past.

On April 10, 2000, Janice returned to the shelter. Two days later, she retained a divorce lawyer from Hiscock Legal Aid. At first, she attended counseling classes, "Onward and Upward," designed to teach her to be more independent.

After a few weeks in class, she moved on to the "Displaced Homemaker's Program," where she learned work skills, such as how to use a computer. When she "graduated" from the shelter, she went to live with friends for a time, and then shared an apartment with a couple she hardly knew.

She bought a beat-up old car to get around and got a job at a hotel just down the road—which was a good thing because she'd been denied unemployment.

Life went smoothly until August when, against Janice's instructions, the Department of Labor gave her address to David. That meant she had to move.

She stayed briefly with old friends in Onondaga Hill before finding a nice apartment in Syracuse. For nine months, she'd lived out of a suitcase, and now, for the first time in her life, she got to set up house for herself and only for herself.

There was an enveloping feeling of independence that most people feel as teenagers, many others as young adults. Janice, on the other hand, was forty-two.

It wasn't long before David again learned her address. She couldn't move again, because she had a yearlong lease, but she did put an extra dead bolt on the door.

In April of 2001, a friend of Janice's was murdered by her husband in Weedsport. The former couple shared custody of their son. He shot her and then turned the gun on himself in front of the kid. That incident amplified Janice's domestic terrors.

That summer, Janice earned her GED.

David got a new girlfriend named Jenny. He brought her in to work at the office and forced his father to leave. His dad had brought a TV with him to work to watch an hour-long show he enjoyed. David had a fit. He cut his dad's pay and gave himself a raise. Predictably, his father split. David asked Jenny to marry him, she said no, and they broke up. He quickly recruited another girlfriend, this one named Valerie, and repeated the pattern. He proposed; Val said no; Val was gone.

David and Janice's divorce became final on August 31, 2001. Janice was not impressed with the job her lawyer did. In retrospect, Janice thought she would have been better off paying the lawyer not to represent her.

Janice gave away what little money she got from the divorce, but she did keep the trailer in Pulaski, and that was where David Jr. went to live after he got out of the service.

By that time David Castor's divorce was final, Janice Poissant was promoted to supervisor at the hotel, and Stacey Daniels Wallace was a widow wondering how she was going to raise two girls on her own. She spotted David and, like fishing in a barrel, easily hooked him.

Predictably, Stacey was hired on as girlfriend/

office manager at Liverpool Heating, just like Jenny and Val and Janice before her. But when David asked this one to be his wife, she answered with an enthusiastic yes.

David and Stacey were married on August 16, 2003. David didn't tell his parents until after the fact, and his parents notified his ex-wife. Using the same grapevine, Janice received occasional updates on David's new family. All Janice knew about Ashley and Bree was that they didn't clean up after themselves and this drove David nuts.

When Janice heard David had remarried, she instinctively knew that there was no love there. "He was a perfect target with a lot of assets," Janice recalled. He owned a good home and had a very prosperous business. Plus, he had all of those toys. The new wife wanted what he had more than she wanted him, and he was so desperate not to be alone that he couldn't see it.

The year 2005 was one of death. On January 17, Janice's dad died in Texas after a long asbestos-related illness. David wanted to attend the funeral. Janice said no, but she felt bad about it.

On July 22, David's dad passed away from mesothelioma—also from asbestos exposure. Janice went to the funeral home. She didn't remember if she saw Stacey, but she did say hi to her ex-husband. She'd thought he was his brother Steve and didn't realize her mistake until it was too late.

Janice's first distinctive memory of Stacey was at the Pine Plains Cemetery in Clay, standing around the burial plot. She briefly saw her standing next to David and looked away.

At the grave site, Janice did a surprisingly bold thing. She asked if she could say a few words, and, of course, David's family said sure. So Janice said, "Dad, I love you so very dearly!" That said, she shifted the subject: "I would like to thank David Sr. for our time together." One would imagine that got Stacey's attention. "Thank you for what we had," Janice continued. Without their *long* and *loving* relationship, she noted, there would be no David Jr. She also thanked David's family for always being so kind to her.

Unknowingly, David Castor Sr. had one month to live.

After his dad's funeral, there was a family gathering at Mom Castor's, and Janice and Stacey found themselves in the same house. They did not acknowledge one another, but Janice admitted to looking at her as much as she could.

Mostly, Janice remembered Stacey standing at the picnic table in the garage helping herself to some food. Janice could see the lack of love there. Stacey was emitting some troubling vibes. Maybe it was what Janice had said at the grave site, or maybe because she sensed that Janice didn't trust her, but Stacey gave off very strong keep-your-distance vibes. One time Janice glanced over at Stacey and felt shivers run up and down her spine.

David Jr. asked for Janice's permission before speaking to his father. She gave it wholeheartedly, reminding him that their marital problems had nothing to do with him. This broke the ice and David Sr. got to meet his grandchildren before he died.

* * *

On August 22, 2005, Janice took her mom to a specialist. She had survived her major heart scare, but she still required regular medical attention. At the doctor's, her mom mentioned David. This caused Janice to burst into tears. She cried hard and long. It was a bizarre reaction to a casual mention.

Janice would come to blame clairvoyance. She must have known somewhere deep inside that the love of her life had died. After taking her mother to her sister's, she became restless and was taking a drive when her cell phone went off. It was her daughter-in-law, June, telling her to go to June's parents' house.

When she arrived, David Jr. was waiting for her. "Mom, Dad is dead," he said.

She refused to believe it. June's father said it was true. He'd driven past the house on Wetzel and saw all the cop cars and yellow tape. He stopped and asked and was told his daughter's father-in-law had committed suicide.

Janice lost feeling in her legs and crumbled to the ground at the edge of the driveway. She didn't remember much after that. She was taken inside and then home, all the time her brain swimming with *if only* this and *if only* that. She'd had a premonition in the doctor's office. If she'd gone straight to him, would she have been able to save him?

Janice knew right away that suicide was out of the question. Then, as she learned more about what Stacey was saying, she became suspicious. When Stacey told the story, she made David sound like an alcoholic, and Janice knew that wasn't true. He wasn't even a regular drinker. Just on special occasions.

David's siblings—well, mostly David's younger sister Linda—later gave Janice a full report on David's funeral. Stacey showed *no* emotion. Ashley and Bree *were* emotional. Maybe too emotional, and it occurred to some that the girls were enjoying the drama. They acted as if they liked David, when everyone knew they didn't.

"It was the weirdest funeral ever," Linda said. Something about it didn't feel right.

One old friend was overheard to say, "Stacey was a paramedic. She should have known what to do."

The murmurings of discomfort among David's friends and loved ones at the funeral boiled into a teeth-grinding fury as they proceeded to the grave site—which was, as more than one complained, in the "middle of freakin' nowhere." Stacey was putting David in a place he didn't belong. No one could believe how far away it was. The anger grew when they arrived at the grave site and saw that David was to be buried next to Stacey's first husband.

A few days after the funeral, Janice received a letter from Stacey.

It read: *Janice, Although I don't know if you'll ever read this letter I feel I need to share something with you.* Stacey wrote that she wanted to thank Janice for respecting and honoring the promise Stacey claimed to have made to David by not coming to the funeral.

I hope you know that it had little to do with my personal feelings, but I made a promise to him and I had to keep that, Stacey wrote. Stacey didn't know whether or not Janice chose to go to the funeral home on her own. *As long as I don't know, I didn't break my promise.*

She also wanted Janice to know how proud she should be of David Jr.: *I'm positive you already are,* Stacey wrote. *You raised an amazing young man.*

Stacey wrote that she felt *very cheated* that she hadn't had an opportunity to get to know David's only son better. Stacey wrote that young David was probably the *gentlest, kindest young man* she had ever met. And she knew it was due to Janice's influence in his life.

I hope this has not upset you in any way, the letter concluded. *That was not my intent at all. I hope both you and David Jr. find peace in your lives. You both deserve it. Sincerely, Stacey.*

As soon as Janice read that letter, she told her son that she was reading between the lines. She told him that his father, first of all, would never ask that Janice wouldn't be allowed at his funeral, and second of all, why would he ever say such a thing in the first place? He didn't know he was going to be murdered.

"I knew that it was Stacey who didn't want me there. She threw in that stuff about David Jr., even though it was true, just to keep me happy," Janice said.

That part about David Jr. and her finding peace in their lives—that was Stacey's way of telling them to move on with their lives and leave everything to her.

Around that time, David Jr. also received a letter from Stacey. It said she was in possession of his father's will. She was sorry to inform him that he was not mentioned.

Stacey requested an in-person meeting at David

Jr.'s home to discuss the things of his father's that he wanted. David showed the letter to his mother, who fumed.

Janice was worried that Stacey would take advantage of her son, so she gave young David a pep talk. *"Don't trust her,"* Janice said. "Your emotions are high. You're not thinking straight. That's normal. It's not a good time to negotiate. Even if you do take some items, don't finalize it. Tell her you need more time to think about it. Don't sign anything! Don't trust her!"

Janice promised to be in the car somewhere in the vicinity at the time of the meeting so she could swoop in and save her son, in case something happened. "I can be there in a few seconds if you need me," Janice emphasized.

The meeting was short. Afterward, Stacey left so Janice could pick up her son in private. Janice picked up David Jr. and asked him how it went. "She brought some stuff to the house for me," David Jr. replied. They were army savings bonds, a teddy bear, a toy truck and car, a handprint he had made in plaster when he was in grammar school, some jewelry of his dad's.

"Did she show you a copy of the will?" Janice asked.
"No."
"Did you sign anything?"
"No."
Yes, he named some items he wanted in addition to those he'd just received. No, he did not finalize negotiations in any way, and, yes, he asked for more time to think of items he wanted.

Time passed and eventually Janice advised her son

it was time to get back in touch with Stacey. They would run an experiment to gauge Stacey's sincerity.

"What were some of those items you said you wanted from your father?" Janice asked.

"Some tools and stuff," David Jr. replied.

"Call Stacey, tell her you want to come over and pick up the tools. Tell her you're working on one of your vehicles and you need the tools."

David Jr. called Stacey, and she said, sorry, he couldn't have the tools because "everything needed to be liquidated."

"She has no intention of giving you anything else," Janice said. "She wants it all."

Janice first learned that the authorities were investigating David's death through his youngest brother, Steve. It was also from Steve that Janice learned David died of antifreeze poisoning. It was a tough time. She was working two jobs—at a welding company and at the hotel—and was having trouble keeping anything organized in her personal life. Steve also said that Janice probably knew some things that would be of interest to the sheriff's deputies who were investigating David's death. Steve gave Janice the name and number of Detective Dominick Spinelli, the investigator in charge. She called and introduced herself to the detective as a woman who had been with the victim for twenty-six years, 24/7, and she knew he didn't commit suicide. Spinelli said he'd come to her and they chatted. She gave Spinelli the letter Stacey wrote to her a few days after David's funeral. She told him about the will her son still hadn't seen, that it was impossible for that will to be real if it didn't mention David's son.

Janice got in touch with Frank Josef, the attorney who prepared David's real will. She requested a copy of that document so she could show Spinelli what a *real* David Castor will looked like. She next called David Horan, her ex-husband's Prudential Life Insurance agent, who verified that Stacey had received the money. She checked on David's three retirement funds and discovered Stacey had cashed in all three.

She didn't really want to know, but she couldn't help herself, and she looked up death by antifreeze. She was horrified by what she read. During her research, she encountered stories about the Turner murders in Georgia. There were so many similarities.

Janice knew that Stacey's first husband also died prematurely. Police needed to look into that. She called Spinelli, who said they were on top of it. "These things take time," he told her, and swore her to secrecy.

She continued to help with the investigation in every way she could, supplying Spinelli with contact information for employees of the business, including the names of the two women David had proposed to before meeting Stacey.

Sometimes Spinelli would call Janice with specific questions: "Who's Bob Ross?" It was a name he'd seen in the contested will. Janice explained that Robert and Cindy Ross were friends from way back, but they had sided with David after the divorce. Janice spoke with Cindy on the phone once after David's death and expressed her disbelief regarding

David's "suicide." It didn't take long for Janice to realize the Rosses were on Stacey's side, and the conversation was not a long one.

Janice made sure the grapevine remained open between her and the Castor family. Everyone who drove past the Wetzel Road home kept an eye out for Stacey or other activity. It was through word of mouth that Janice learned Stacey had a boyfriend. She'd been seen out with him, kissing in public. He'd been spotted pulling a Christmas tree into the house.

After Janice's father died in January 2005, David owed Janice's mother money from when David bought out the business. Now that debt belonged to Stacey, so Janice contacted an attorney to help her mother collect. The attorney recommended just calling Stacey and asking for her to pay up, thus saving legal fees, so that was what Janice did.

"Hello."

"Stacey?"

"Yes, who's this?"

"Janice."

"Janice who?"

"Janice Poissant! I'm wondering if we could meet someplace and talk."

"I wish never to speak to you. Don't call me again," Stacey said, and hung up.

7

Bad Mojo

Following David Castor's messy demise, just as she had after Michael's death, Stacey put on her strong face and kept her focus on the future.

Ashley and Bree remembered when their mother acted that way after their dad's funeral, so this time it didn't seem as odd. Everyone dealt with mourning in his or her own way. That was the common wisdom.

She buried David right next to Michael. One day, she would lie between them. David's gravestone read:

CASTOR

DAVID W. SR.

HUSBAND OF STACEY R.

JUNE 12, 1957   AUG. 22, 2005

Between the date of David's birth and that of his death, chiseled into the stone, was an engraving of a man straddling a snowmobile.

There was something creepy about the proximity between the grave sites of Mike and David. Part of the reason was that when Stacey designed Mike's gravestone, she didn't consider the possibility that she might one day remarry and bury a second husband.

Mike's gravestone had been designed to cover a double plot for Mike and Stacey. Underneath the word "Wallace," there were two hearts, with a pair of interlocking wedding bands between them. Inside the left heart it said: *Stacey R. July 24, 1967*. On the right, it said: *Michael E. Sept. 16, 1961–Jan. 11, 2000*. Chiseled into the stone beneath the interlocking rings were the words: *Together Forever.*

And Stacey, as always, dealt with things with a stiff upper lip, viewing her new domestic status—single mother (again)—as an opportunity of sorts, a chance to start her life anew.

She decided to think big. She would become a lawyer! Just like it said in her senior yearbook. *No, no, no.* She hadn't been to college, so it would take *too* long.

Ah, but she could do the next best thing. She could become a legal assistant. So she took a job at legal aid, where they supplied legal services to those who otherwise would not be able to afford them.

While Stacey thought about the new life that was opening up for her, like a rose blossom, she perhaps failed to consider properly the downside of her circumstance.

The police were, after all, steadily closing in on her.

* * *

From a romantic point of view, any middle-aged woman who has been twice widowed is apt to be considered bad mojo by prospective future suitors. Twice-widowed women carry baggage—weighty suitcase after suitcase filled with ominous dark clouds. Yet, for those of a certain mind, the risk can be intriguing.

Stacey's friends thought Stacey had to be one of the unluckiest women ever, positively snakebit.

From an investigatory point of view—and even before his conversation with Janice Poissant on the subject—Spinelli found the similarity between the two deaths intriguing. Upon closer examination, Mike Wallace's death wasn't so open-and-shut, not nearly as obvious as Stacey and her mother had made it sound. The ambulance attendant said it didn't look like a heart attack. During the days before his death, Mike Wallace had complained of feeling like a drunk man. That sounded like David Castor, a realization that gave Spinelli goose bumps.

Because of the similarities in the deaths of Stacey's husbands, Spinelli amped up his investigation during the summer of 2007. He could now obtain a warrant to tap Stacey's phone, and to set up surveillance cameras in locations that Stacey frequented. The warrant gave authorities permission to set up a surveillance camera outside Stacey's home so they could keep track of when she left and came home, and who her visitors were.

Another camera was set up at the cemetery where Stacey's two dead husbands were buried, side by side. A plot for Stacey was reserved, right between them. As it turned out, the cemetery surveillance camera wasn't important for images that it recorded, but for images that it did not record. The camera proved beyond argument that at no time had Stacey visited her husbands' grave site, not even on the second anniversary of David Castor's death.

That bothered Spinelli. She never put flowers on either grave site. This made her cool demeanor seem more like chilliness than a mask donned out of maternal considerations. Spinelli felt this was a sign that Stacey was so cool following her husbands' deaths *not* to set an example for her girls, but because she didn't really care about her dead husbands.

Spinelli understood that there was only one way to find out once and for all if Michael Wallace died of a heart attack, and that was to exhume the body and autopsy it now. Better late than never.

It seemed like a great idea at first. But after some thought, the idea ate at him. What if they exhumed the body only to verify that he'd died of a heart attack, after all? The last thing Spinelli wanted was to be responsible for the needless disruption of a body at peace.

Since David Castor died in Onondaga County, and Michael Wallace died in Cayuga County, cooperation between jurisdictions was required—no problem, the two neighboring sheriff's offices worked together regularly.

Spinelli, of Onondaga, called the Cayuga County Sheriff's Office (CCSO) to tell them Stacey's second husband had also dropped dead. The Cayuga deputies were all ears and agreed to take a second look at the Michael Wallace case.

Cayuga County DA James B. Vargason contacted Judge Thomas M. Van Strydonck, who had been the administrative justice for the Seventh Judicial District since the summer of 2000. He was extremely active in victim advocacy and other charitable causes. The judge had a nose for crime, and Vargason was fairly certain that he'd agree that one doozy of a crime had been committed here.

After reading over Vargason's report, he found significant cause to autopsy the remains of Stacey's first husband and signed the order to have Mike Wallace's body exhumed.

8

Exhumation

On September 5, 2007, a heavy-digging machine rolled into the Owasco Rural Cemetery and used its clawed bucket to gouge out the earth covering Michael Wallace's casket.

Perhaps the most nervous cop during this procedure was Onondaga County sheriff Kevin E. Walsh. He had a long history in law enforcement. He was military police (MP) in the army, and earned a Purple Heart. Back home, he earned a bachelor's and then a master's degree at SUNY Oswego. After that, from start to present, he was with the OCSO for going on forty years, hired as a deputy in 1966.

Well, not the full forty. He retired as a captain in 1986 after putting in his twenty, and took a job as the director of Public Safety with the SUNY College of Environmental Science and Forestry. He was elected sheriff in 1984, and served double duty from 1990 through 1995 as an Onondaga County legislator and was head of the legislature's Public Safety Committee.

As the Castor case broke, Sheriff Walsh was still wearing a variety of hats. He was adjunct faculty at Keuka College, and he taught at the National Sheriff's Institute in Colorado. He was on the executive committee of several councils, boards, and associations.

Sheriff Walsh was nervous because the buck stopped with him. If this turned out to be a false alarm, and Wallace's body had been exhumed for nothing, he would have to face the cameras.

Spinelli stood nearby and watched as the hole was dug and the casket lifted from the grave. He wondered if Wallace was looking down on this and saying that it was about time they took some action on this, about time they realized that he didn't just die on his own.

Wallace's casket was transported to the Onondaga County morgue, where the belated autopsy was performed by Dr. Stoppacher, the Onondaga County ME, the same man who had performed David Castor's postmortem surgery.

Wallace's organs—what was left of them—were removed and prepared for examination. There was no indication of heart disease. There was no cause of death that could be determined with the naked eye.

The day after the autopsy, Dr. Stoppacher looked at a piece of Michael Wallace's kidney through a microscope, and he noticed something unusual: crystals.

New high-tech toxicology tests were performed on those crystals and showed that Wallace died from an overdose of ethylene glycol, the primary chemical in antifreeze, the same chemical found in David Castor's body. The ingestion of antifreeze caused the crystals to form inside the body, and seven years after death, an autopsy surgeon could discover them. After examining the crystals in Michael Wallace's kidney tissue, the doctor reexamined the crystals found in David Castor's kidney. They were identical.

One thing found during Mike's autopsy was different from David's, however. In Mike, they found evidence of rat poison, in addition to the antifreeze. Law enforcement kept the rat poison part secret. Anyone who knew Wallace had rat poison in him had to be the killer.

The whole disruption of Wallace's remains was kept low-profile. Wallace's son Jimmy and Mike's first wife, Nancy, were among those most shocked when they heard about the better-late-than-never autopsy. The ex-wife and her son by Mike were not officially informed of the exhumation. Nancy heard about it because one of her cousins married one of Mike's cousins, and that was how the grapevine went.

Matching crystals meant it was only a matter of time before Stacey was arrested. The medical examiner's conclusion that David Castor had committed suicide now seemed ludicrous. Murder could be the only conclusion.

Fitzpatrick ran a computer check on antifreeze ingestion as a cause of death. It happened more often than he would have thought. Accidents, suicides, and murders. He learned that murder by antifreeze was not that uncommon.

"There were literally dozens of cases across the country," the DA said. Why? The substance was so prevalent, he explained. There were huge chunks of the country where winters were *real* and you could find a large can of antifreeze in just about every garage. Another factor was that it was relatively simple to get a potential victim to drink antifreeze because it was easily disguised when mixed with another liquid. Plus, you didn't need the victim to drink very much antifreeze for the results to be fatal. Two or three fluid ounces of the stuff would do the trick. That was, two or three shot glasses full of antifreeze could kill a grown man.

Cayuga County sheriff David S. Gould had been a cop for a long time. Gould's law enforcement career began in 1970 when he joined the New York State Police (NYSP). He stayed with that organization for thirty-four years, and retired in 2004. He spent the next two years as a special investigator for the Seneca County DA's Office. He was elected sheriff in 2007, and under his initiative, every one of his deputies had been issued a new weapon. Sheriff Gould had seen a lot of cases, and this Stacey Castor case was an odd duck. It had a different feel, an otherworldly feel. It was so strange that it didn't seem quite like real life. "It's unique, more like a movie plot than real life," he concluded.

Gould told reporters to spread the word, detectives wanted to interview anyone who might have ever known Michael Wallace or Stacey Wallace-Castor. If he received any tips involving other possible victims, he would be sure to follow up on them, the sheriff added.

Sheriff Walsh in Onondaga County was off the hook and wouldn't have to "face the cameras." But Sheriff Gould in neighboring Cayuga County wasn't as lucky. Gould took on the task of explaining to newspaper reporters why a murder had been originally ruled a death by natural causes.

"Unless you know or have suspicion about what may have caused a death, you would not look at that unless there is an autopsy done. In a lot of cases in this country, there is not an autopsy done if it's not a suspicious death or if a family member doesn't request it," he said. Gould said that the lesson learned here was that police officers and medical examiners needed to be "more aware of what was happening."

He guessed that the number of people being murdered by poison was higher than were being investigated. It was a type of murder that currently could fool law enforcement, he imagined, and that had to stop.

He said, "Wallace had been sick for some time and he'd been going to see his physician, so there was nothing out of the ordinary to be determined by an autopsy." Nobody back then had any inkling that Wallace's death was a crime. No police report had ever been filed on the death. Police didn't write an incident report on everybody that died, unless there was something out of the ordinary. Wallace was just a "sick person that died." Maybe they hadn't shown adequate interest in Wallace's death in 2000, but they were now eager to make up for lost time.

"We are definitely looking for people who might know anything, back in 2000, about the relationship between Stacey and Mr. Wallace, and anything people might know that would be useful for our investigation," Sheriff Walsh said.

* * *

The day after Dr. Stoppacher found crystals in Michael Wallace's kidney, Detective Spinelli, along with Detective Valerie Brogan, paid Stacey an unexpected visit.

Stacey expressed shock and annoyance when she answered the door and saw the detectives. "I thought that was over and done with," she said impatiently.

"No," Spinelli replied. "The case remains open. Just a few more questions to close it out."

"Well, okay," she said, and let the detectives in.

They informed Stacey of the medical examiner's conclusion regarding Michael Wallace's death. He mentioned the antifreeze, but not the rat poison.

Detective Brogan was often called in when cases involved women. She was a onetime winner of the Sister Mary Vera Award, presented by Vera House, Inc., the shelter and organization dedicated to helping those affected by domestic and sexual abuse.

During the subsequent interview, Stacey made a strange comment. "I'm sick of being controlled by someone from the grave," she said.

Brogan remembered shooting Spinelli a glance at that moment, a look that said, "That was a really weird thing for her to say."

The detectives told Stacey that they would like to continue their conversation at headquarters and Stacey said okay. They took her to the county sheriff's office on South State Street in Syracuse, where she was questioned for the next three hours.

Stacey was placed in a small room with a table, two chairs, and a two-way mirror. This time, Spinelli asked the questions. Brogan was on the other side of the mirror, observing the interrogation.

Spinelli knew that she had lied to Diane Leshinski only minutes after the discovery of David Castor's body. He pulled out a copy of the eight-page statement Stacey had given to Leshinski. He got right to the point.

"How many times did you call your home over the weekend?" Spinelli asked.

"Several times."

"How often?"

"Every half hour, forty-five minutes."

"We looked up your AT&T phone records, Stacey. Says you only called once."

"Well, I called from my cell," she said.

"We have those records, too. You only called once. You called the house from your work phone, just before you called 911."

Detective Spinelli asked Stacey to tell him again about the incident when David was ill and she needed help getting him back into bed.

Stacey explained that she was in the living room when she heard a thump. She went to investigate and found her husband lying on the floor, unable to get up.

Spinelli said that was an interesting answer, because back at the time it happened, Stacey said she was helping her husband back to bed from the bathroom, and that was when he fell and couldn't get up.

Spinelli showed Stacey a photograph of the night table next to David Castor's body.

"Stacey, I want you to show me which glass you gave David his cranberry juice in."

"Well, I poured the antifree—I mean, I poured the

cranberry juice into this glass," she said, pointing at the empty glass, the one that wasn't fluorescent green.

Spinelli asked why Stacey's prints were on the green glass, and nobody else's.

"That's it. I'm done," Stacey said, and she literally pressed her lips together.

That ended Stacey's voluntary cooperation with the investigation. As Brogan later remembered it, "She just shut down." Stacey got up to leave and Spinelli straightened his papers. As Stacey turned to leave, she caught something in the corner of her eye. It was a close-up photo of a turkey baster.

"What's that? What's that for?" she asked, gesturing at the photo.

"That's a turkey baster," Spinelli replied.

"Why? What is it?"

"Sorry, you discontinued the interview. I can't talk to you anymore."

When Stacey got home following that grilling by Spinelli, she had an urgent message for her oldest daughter.

"The police are closing in on me," Stacey said, according to Ashley's recollection. "The cops think I killed both Daddy and David."

"That can't be right. You couldn't have murdered them," Ashley recalled saying. "They issued death certificates saying he committed suicide, and Daddy died of a heart attack."

"I know," Stacey said. "I didn't do this."

Stacey, feeling crowded by law enforcement, hired a lawyer. She did something she hadn't done before.

She visited Michael's grave. Police had the site under electronic surveillance.

The visit was short and without sentimentality. She needed to know if Mike's exhumation was a bluff, and she left as soon as she verified that his grave was freshly disturbed.

While Stacey reeled from the news of the exhumation, and the forensic results, police were still listening to Stacey's phone conversations. She repeatedly talked to her friends about how anxious she felt regarding the investigation.

"It scares the shit out of me, because I didn't do this," Stacey told one friend. "And I don't believe for one second that they found antifreeze in Michael's body. I don't believe it."

Stacey realized her situation was dire. She could no longer rely on others *not* suspecting her. She was actively going to have to prove that she was innocent.

How to do that?

It had a plan.

9

"They came to my freakin' school."

Ashley's luck kept turning from bad to worse. The exhumation and its aftermath coincided with her first week of college. She was just starting classes at Bryant & Stratton Business Institute, where she planned to study to become an accountant. The school had been around for 150 years and had eight campuses across Upstate New York, in the Buffalo, Rochester, Syracuse, and Albany areas. The campus Ashley attended wasn't far from home—"Syracuse North" on Carling Road in the town of Liverpool.

On Wednesday morning, Ashley was in line to put her signature on a sign-in sheet before the first day of one class when a woman from the school's administration came and got her.

"I need you to come with me," the woman said to Ashley. She was led to waiting policemen who told her, all in one devastating fell swoop, that her father's body had been exhumed, that crystals from antifreeze were found in his kidneys, and that he had been murdered.

Ashley told them they were wrong. A mistake had been made. "My dad had a heart attack," she protested.

Ashley called her mother. She had no idea the police tape recorder was rolling.

"Hello."

"Mommy, they came to my freakin' school."

"They came to your school?" Stacey said with moral outrage. Then maternal: "Are you okay?"

Ashley thought about that for a moment before answering, "Umm, I'm going to be okay—but I'm really freaking out right now."

Ashley started crying and she couldn't stop. It was too upsetting. She wondered, *Why would they dig up Daddy?* It was inhumane. He was resting peacefully.

"Do you want me to come and get you?"

"No, I have to be here," Ashley replied.

"All right, calm down and go to class." They each said "I love you" and "Bye," and that ended the conversation.

Stacey did drive to school to pick up her daughter, but not until Ashley's classes for the day were completed. It was in the car on the way home that Stacey did an unusual thing.

She told Ashley that the two of them had sure had a tough day. Ashley agreed. It had been a tough week, in fact. "Let's get drunk," Stacey suggested.

That made Ashley practically swallow her gum. She'd known this woman her entire life and she'd never before heard her say anything remotely like that. Who was this woman?

Oh sure, Stacey had allowed Ashley to try alcohol in the past. Like one beer or something, and she always hovered over her the whole time to make sure she didn't chugalug or whatever.

It was unexpected, sure, but it didn't seem insane on Stacey's part. It made sense, kind of. They *were* upset after all this business with Daddy, and being embarrassed at her new school.

Alcohol might prove to be therapeutic.

Maybe it was just what the doctor ordered. It was just a little out of character, that's all. "Let's just drink, drink until we're drunk." *This is new. Cool,* Ashley remembered thinking.

Stacey bought a six-pack of Smirnoff Ice, watermelon flavored. It never occurred to Ashley to say no. She felt elevated by Stacey's suggestion. This was a graduating moment. Getting drunk was such a grown-up thing to do.

"What kind of teenager wouldn't think that was awesome?" Ashley later asked. "A parent just gave you permission to drink. Sweet. So I drank with her."

Stacey poured Ashley's first drink from the twelve-ounce bottle into a glass for her, but after that, Ashley drank directly out of the bottle. After a while, Ashley began to feel sick to her stomach. Stacey said nausea was normal.

"I'll give you a pill that will help you sleep it off," Stacey suggested, and Ashley took the pill.

The next day, Thursday, Ashley felt a little hungover but not incapacitated. She managed to get up and get to school. She only had one class that day, in the morning. After attending it, she returned home. Stacey was waiting for her.

"Let's drink again," Stacey said.

"Mom, it's not even noon," Ashley complained.

"By the time we get our stuff done, it'll be noon," Stacey said, according to Ashley.

There might have been a small voice in the back of Ashley's head that sent out a warning signal at that moment, but she did not listen to it. She said okay.

"I went ahead, and I did it," Ashley recalled. "I did it because, you know, I still trust her. She's my mom."

A surveillance camera at the neighborhood liquor store captured images of Stacey that morning, buying booze just when Ashley said she did.

Just as she had the day before, her mom served her the first drink in a container. Stacey sent Ashley into the basement to move some laundry from the washing machine into the dryer, and when she returned, her mother had her cocktail ready.

This time it was the hard stuff, real vodka, mixed with orange juice. Stacey said it was called a screwdriver. Ashley remembered it being a large cup.

"My drink looks funny," Ashley complained.

"Stir it up," Stacey urged. Ashley thought this was kind of weird.

"There's stuff swirling around in my drink," Ashley said.

"That's the spice I put in. That's why you have to keep stirring it," Stacey said.

Ashley stirred and stirred and took a sip. *Yuck!*

"It tasted really gross," Ashley recalled. "I don't even know how to describe the way it tasted. It made me gag, it tasted so bad."

"Oh, go ahead and take another sip," Stacey urged.

"Mom, I still can't drink this," Ashley said.

"Let me show you a trick that I learned when I was a kid," Stacey said. "Put the straw in the back of your throat and count to ten while you're drinking."

Ashley did as she was told and drank to a ten count with the straw pushed deep into her mouth, allowing her drink to get to her throat without touching any taste buds first. After that, the next thing Ashley remembered was that she didn't feel good and had to go to her room and lie down. Ashley lay down, but she didn't get up.

Stacey admitted that she had gone into Ashley's room a few times to check on her daughter but found nothing amiss. A wiretap on Stacey's phone picked up her comment to boyfriend Michael Overstreet that her daughter was asleep, "drooling normally."

At one point that night, Matthew Gandino, Ashley's boyfriend, stood outside her house on Wetzel Road. Some of the lights in the house were on, but Ashley's bedroom was dark. He called her cell phone again and again. Eventually Ashley's mother answered the phone. That had never happened before. Stacey said to call back on the landline. She made the request to save a few pennies, not realizing that she was also switching from a secure line to one that was tapped. Matthew called the new number and Stacey picked up right away. Matthew hesitantly asked for Ashley, and Stacey said Ashley was sleeping and couldn't be disturbed. Stacey asked the young man what he had done to her daughter to tucker her out so severely. Matthew said he hadn't done a thing. Then he asked for a favor. Without telling her that he was right outside the house, Matthew said he'd lost his ATM card and he suspected he might have left it in Ashley's room. Could she go and look for it for him? Stacey said sure. A short time later, Stacey returned to the phone and told Matthew that she had looked for it thoroughly and it wasn't in Ashley's room. Matthew knew she was lying. The light in Ashley's room never went on.

In the Wetzel Road side yard, a screened-in tent had been built so adults could enjoy the evening breezes as they smoked cigarettes and had cocktails without worrying about mosquitos. There were plastic chairs and a couple of tables in there. As Ashley lay in her room, Stacey entertained in the backyard.

10

"My daughter took some pills."

Nine days after the exhumation, at 6:30 A.M. on September 14, 2007, Stacey's twenty-year-old daughter, Ashley Wallace, was discovered in a sorry state.

That discovery was made by Ashley's younger sister, Bree Wallace. It had been eighteen hours since Ashley had learned the straw trick, and she was a sick woman.

Bree later recalled the scene and her big sister's condition. It was horrible to think about, but she could see it all in detail: Ashley's mouth was open. Her eyes were open. But there was a frightening glassiness to those eyes. Bree knew Ashley wasn't seeing anything, even though her eyes were open.

There was a funny expression on Ashley's face, too. It was a sort of composite, one she had never seen before on her sister's face. It was half scared and half blank.

Thinking that Ashley was dying, Bree called out her sister's name. Ashley didn't answer. Bree called out her name again, now screaming. It was then, according to Bree, Stacey came flying out of her bedroom to see what was the matter.

It was immediately apparent that Ashley was in distress, so Stacey called 911.

"911. What is your emergency?"

"I think my daughter took some pills. My youngest daughter came into her room and screamed and I just woke up. She's having trouble. She sounds like there's something in her throat." At that moment, vomit erupted from between Ashley's quivering lips. "Oh, she's throwing up, she's throwing up," Stacey said.

"Okay, take her on her side," the operator instructed, and Stacey rolled Ashley over so she wouldn't choke. Stacey gave her address. "Ashley. Oh, my God. Oh, my God. Oh, my God!"

"Are you talking to me?" the operator inquired, then tried to calm Stacey by telling her to breathe normally. At the operator's request, Stacey pronounced and spelled her daughter's name.

Stacey later recalled that she was in a state of complete shock and panic at that point. Ashley was her baby. All she could think was *Is Ashley okay?*

"Can you try to determine what she took?" the 911 operator asked.

"Ambien," Stacey said, referring to the brand name of zolpidem, a specific prescription sleeping pill.

"Do you know how many?"

"No, I don't," Stacey said. "The prescription was just refilled—and she drank an entire bottle of vodka."

* * *

Months later, Stacey answered questions regarding the words she'd used during that 911 call. Some of her facts were wrong. Stacey said she was surprised that she managed to make any sense at all. She might have babbled incoherently in her panic, and Ashley might have died. She'd stayed cool—at least cool enough to give the operator all essential info.

Indeed, there was no babbling. She managed to utter complete sentences and get the thrust of her message across accurately. She'd gotten an ambulance to come to her address, so, as far as she was concerned, mission accomplished.

But why did she say her daughter took pills, and why did she say this and why did she say that, she had no idea. Looking at her daughter in that sorry state was one of the hardest things she'd ever had to go through in her entire life.

The scene in Ashley's room was of such horror that Bree fled. Bree left Ashley's room when her mother entered, but she fought back her fear and—after a short time, she really had no idea how long—she reentered her sister's bedroom. Stacey was still on the phone with the operator.

As soon as Bree reentered, she noticed something that she hadn't seen before. It was a piece of paper resting near the head of the bed. She hadn't seen it before, yet it was perfectly obvious when she reentered the room. Bree picked it up and opened it.

The single piece of printer paper was folded once in the middle.

She began to read it, but Stacey snatched it away from her. Stacey now had the piece of paper in one hand and the phone in the other.

"What do I have to read? She left a letter," Stacey said clearly into the phone.

"She left a letter?" the operator asked.

"She left a note," Stacey said, trying a different and more descriptive noun. "Oh, my God! This is not happening." Stacey was emoting, clipping off her syllables for emphasis: "Hap. En. Ing."

As the ambulance rushed to the scene, the dispatcher kept Stacey on the line. At one point, apparently fearing a reputation as a slatternly housekeeper, she fretted and moaned that the room was a mess.

Ashley was rushed by ambulance to the SUNY Upstate Medical University Hospital. She'd OD'd on something. Doctors and other emergency personnel were pretty sure of that. First test: blood/alcohol level. Whoa. Spiking.

Ashley's gurney was wheeled into the emergency room and her case was given absolute first priority. The area became a flurry of activity. Ashley's life needed saving, stat.

Bree could hear a muddle of sharp orders and urgently reported quickie test results. Only a few words came through clearly. Bree understood that Ashley's heart was trying to beat right out of her chest, and that her big sister was "basically unresponsive."

Bree recalled that Ashley had been trembling

violently, convulsively, with a violent teeth-chattering shiver. And she was soaking wet from sweat.

At Ashley's side was her mother, repeating mantras of comfort and hope to her stricken daughter. In a flash, though, doctors separated the patient from her clinging mother. Better to treat the patient without a hysterical woman draped over her. Ashley was wheeled into a room, and the door closed on Stacey and Bree.

The first member of the sheriff's office to arrive at the Castor house on Wetzel Road was Sheriff's Deputy Michael Cox. Detectives Valerie Brogan and Bob Pitman were right behind and confiscated a number of pill bottles at the scene.

In the meantime, at the hospital, Bree told police that she had been worried about Ashley the day before her poisoning. Bree said that when she found Ashley, she was unconscious with pillows on top of her head. Bree said she found a note that she thought might be a suicide note—she'd only read the first few lines before giving the piece of paper to her mother.

"I told her I loved her, and that was the last thing I got to say to her," Stacey recalled.

An ER doctor who treated Ashley remembered that a monitor of Ashley's heartbeat revealed frightening results. Her heart rate was between 170 and 190 beats per minute. It was the heartbeat of a hummingbird, only erratic.

The key to saving Ashley's life lay in determining what she had consumed. Any continued mystery on that front and she would surely die.

* * *

Ashley had some memories of the emergency room. She could tell she was in a hospital, but things were blurry. She had tunnel vision, like she was looking at the world through a cardboard tube. She couldn't distinguish faces. There was a clutter of melded noises, some of it comprised of rat-a-tat-tat rapid-fire human voices echoing in her head.

According to Dr. Daniel Olsson, who was in the ER that day, Ashley was alive only because she was discovered when she was. If she had not been discovered, her heartbeat would have grown increasingly erratic until she expired. She wouldn't have lived past 10:30, 10:45. Bree had saved her sister's life.

Ashley's ability to perceive her surroundings slowly improved. She still couldn't see clearly, but understandable words emerged from the cacophony.

"How many pills did you take?" those words said. "What did you do? What did you drink? What did you take?"

A large man was leaning over her. She could see him silhouetted against the ceiling. He was looking down at her face.

That man firing the questions was Sergeant Michael Norton, of the OCSO. Sergeant Norton could see that Ashley was improving, but still not fully cognizant of reality.

He waited.

As Ashley slowly recovered from her near-death experience, word of the "illness" reached Onondaga

County's top cop, Sheriff Walsh. He assigned Detective Valerie Brogan as the lead investigator in the poisoning of Ashley Wallace. Because the Ashley case was so clearly associated with the David Castor murder, Dominick Spinelli was told to return to the Castor home. This time, the crime scene was in a different bedroom.

Police had the situation scoped out fairly quickly and planned to act just the second they felt they had all of their ducks in a row. According to Sheriff Walsh, his deputies were already thinking that this was no suicide attempt, even before the victim was awake and coherent enough to say so in person.

Firstly, loved ones in Stacey's vicinity tended to ingest poison. Secondly, it didn't *feel* like a suicide. There were none of the earmarks. She had only recently enrolled in a local business college. She had just started, and she was excited about that. She had a boyfriend with whom she was getting along well.

"Was I in a car accident?" Ashley asked, and it was then that Sergeant Norton knew she was coherent enough to answer his questions.

He gave Ashley the bad news: They had found a typed suicide note at the head of her bed. The note indicated that she had killed her father and stepfather and had then attempted suicide.

"She looked at me like I was out of my mind," Norton recalled.

As Norton questioned Ashley, she just shook her head from side to side. She wrote no note, killed no dads, took no pills.

They were in a room with the door closed. In the hallway just outside, Stacey and Bree were informed that it looked like Ashley was going to make it.

Bree remembered there were police everywhere. And it wasn't like that was normal. They were there because of Ashley. Bree also recalled her mother's behavior in the emergency room that evening. Stacey was obsessed with getting into that room so she could be with Ashley.

It was wrong to separate a mother from her child that way—just plain wrong, Stacey said. "I don't know why they won't let me in to see her," Stacey said, according to her younger daughter. "I'm her mother! I should be in there!"

In the meantime, inside the room, Ashley's mind was working again, and her thoughts were rushing in several different directions at once. What did she remember? What was the last thing she remembered? Then there was the police who had this whole scenario they believed in, and none of it jibed at all with her previous knowledge of the world and her own domestic situation. She thought of the foul-tasting alcoholic beverage that her mother had induced her to drink.

"When the detective was asking me what I did, I just knew that I didn't do anything, so somebody had to have done it," Ashley later said.

It didn't take Ashley long to figure out who, and it wouldn't take police long to figure it out, either. Her mother had just tried to kill her. Mom had been telling the truth when she said the cops were closing in on her. How could she be such a bad mom? She killed her daddy and David. She murdered them.

* * *

Back in the ER, Stacey was more stressed than ever, indignant that she was unable to see her stricken daughter.

Stacey was asked a lot of questions. No, she didn't read the note. How did she know it was a suicide note? Well, she'd glanced at the first couple of lines, but that was it.

What did Stacey think happened to her first husband? Well, she had no choice but to believe the note. Ashley confessed in black and white to poisoning Mike's Gatorade.

Stacey became indignant. She didn't like the tone the police were taking with her. That indignation would evaporate in a moment, however—replaced by a new and deeper anxiety. Detectives Spinelli and Brogan approached with purpose in their steps.

Spinelli was angry, partially at himself. He'd been on this case for years and never once considered the possibility that Stacey's daughters were in danger. He was a father himself, and what Stacey had apparently done was something he "just couldn't fathom." How could Stacey play God? How could she decide which of her children was going to die?

According to the sheriff's office, Stacey was destined to be arrested, anyway, but they had hoped to accumulate more evidence against her before making the bust. When people started getting hurt, that changed everything. Police had been keeping a "watchful eye" on Stacey ever since she arrived at the hospital, and made sure she didn't have alone time with her stricken daughter. They were worried Stacey might try to finish the job.

At 5:00 P.M. on Friday, September 14, 2007, Stacey was still at University Hospital, still trying to get in to see Ashley. Cops were approaching, and one of them was Spinelli.

"Stacey Castor, you are under arrest for murder. Please turn around and put your arms behind your back," Spinelli said. The woman was compliant.

For Stacey, this was one of those horrible, horrible days that refused to bottom out. She'd been wondering how this day could get any worse. Well, here it was. The day presented for her a diverse menu of problems, all unthinkable and devastating. Murder?

"Murder of whom?" she asked Spinelli, her arms behind her back.

"The murder of David Castor," the investigator replied, snapping the cuffs in place.

She couldn't believe what she was hearing. They thought she killed David.

"And for the attempted murder of Ashley Wallace," Spinelli added.

They thought she tried to kill Ashley! How absurd was that? Just the fact that anyone thought she broke any laws was just so bogus. "I had a speeding ticket when I was a teenager," she later said. "That's the closest I ever came to a brush with the law. To be arrested, handcuffed—I was terrified. I couldn't believe it was happening."

Stacey was taken to the sheriff's office headquarters— and there she was booked for murder and attempted murder. The transfer was not a difficult one.

The sheriff's office was right down the street from the hospital where Ashley was winning the battle with the fistfuls of poison that her body held. The commute went by in a blink of the eye. Stacey had been questioned and arrested and booked and caged, and none of it fazed her.

How could it?

How could she think about herself when her eldest lay so close to death? During the first few hours of her incarceration, she only had one thing on her mind—the state of her daughter Ashley's health.

The poor girl had one foot in the grave and now her own mother wasn't there to comfort her. Stacey said nobody had told her that Ashley was conscious and speaking, and that everything was going to be all right.

Stacey initially felt this was just a big mistake, a clerical error or something. It was that exhumation that started all of this. Maybe those scientists were drunk that day, or something, and the results were a joke. Maybe it was all an elaborate bluff. Maybe there really had been no exhumation and they just disturbed the dirt of Mike's grave to string her along. Maybe . . .

But after a while, she conceded to the fact that she was in deep trouble here. There were people, she sensed, willing to believe ridiculous nonsense, that she was a heartless black widow willing to harm her own child.

"Anybody who knows me, and knows how I feel about my kids, knows I could never do that," Stacey said. "I could never hurt them like that. My kids are my whole life."

She wanted to continue believing that Mike died of natural causes, that David committed suicide because of his acute self-doubts, and that Ashley had tried to pull the same stunt. But that mind-set, she felt, was growing increasingly naïve. She was going to have to face it. Murders really had occurred.

Stacey knew one thing for certain: she was not the murderer of Michael Wallace and David Castor. Mike's exhumation and Ashley's attempted suicide—and suicide note!—could lead to only one conclusion, as painful as that might be: in addition to trying to kill herself, Ashley had killed her father and her stepfather.

Stacey came to believe that. A surprisingly large team of Stacey's relatives and friends believed it, too. But Detectives Spinelli and Brogan didn't believe it. To believe that, you had to conclude that twelve-year-old Ashley—a good kid but disorganized, maybe even scatterbrained—had the capacity to commit a near-perfect murder.

Stacey knew it was a tough sell: My daughter did it. But it was the only possible solution, the only scenario that fit all of the facts as she understood them. Even though it crushed her soul, she had to believe Ashley was a homicidal monster.

The enemy was unthinkability. It was easier for people to get their mitts around a woman killing her husbands—it happened all the time—than to grasp that a little girl had murdered her own father and stepfather. People thought Stacey did it because she was forty years old. But a little girl killing her father? Very rare. Happened once in a blue moon and always caused a sensation.

A girl whacking her daddy was apt to be sensationalized by the press and become one of those 24/7 cable-news stories like O.J. or JonBenet or Natalee.

Little girls not only killed their daddies rarely, but only under the most horrible circumstances. They killed Daddy because Daddy was a monster. Ashley showed no outward signs of abuse.

But all of that unlikeliness didn't mean Ashley was innocent and Stacey was guilty. That was the point Stacey would have to make when talking to lawyers. That was public-relations point number one. Message: don't believe something just because it is easier to accept.

Another point: maybe it wasn't as rare as everyone thought. Maybe it happened more frequently but received no publicity out of respect for the families. Or maybe it happened in the ghetto, where it was hard to make the newspaper. But maybe it was common. Stacey was willing to believe that there were a lot more killers who were children than was commonly thought.

Talking to David Muir, of ABC, Stacey slowed down the cadence of her speech to emphasize the importance of this message, a message she was delivering straight to America: "Children are killing children, and children are killing other people. Every. Single. Day."

And, when asked, she delivered her best plea of "not even remotely guilty." Stacey said, "I did not kill either of my husbands. I loved them both very much."

Stacey loved to show off her tattoos, one on each shoulder, in memory of both of her deceased spouses. Each tatt was of a teddy bear with angel wings sitting on a cloud. Above each bear was the dead husband's birth date, below the bear his death date. Stacey haters believed those tatts had a completely different meaning—they were more like notches on a sniper's rifle.

Stacey came to think it for a long time before she could say it aloud. She found it difficult to say that Ashley wrote the suicide note. She'd just say that she, herself, didn't write it.

Others could conclude whatever they wanted. There was going to come a day, Stacey said, when she was going to prove that she did not write the suicide note, and that the wrong person was under arrest. She was "very confident" that with time the truth would come out and she would be vindicated.

"I know that the truth is going to come out of this," Stacey said. "It will come out that I am innocent— and I will go home."

Back at the house, detectives were again going over the house with a fine-tooth comb. On the kitchen counter, in front of the microwave, were three empty plastic bottles of Diet Pepsi, each with the cap screwed back on. The bottles were photographed in place, then bagged as evidence.

On the floor of Ashley's room were two partially filled Diet Pepsi bottles, a couple of water bottles, a partially drunk blue Gatorade, two soft-drink containers from a fast-food restaurant with plastic lids on, and a straw protruding from one of them. This evidence, too, was photographed and confiscated.

There were clean and dirty clothes strewn across the floor, as well as a Pez candy dispenser on its side, with the head of a cartoon princess on it.

Police were particularly interested in the computers, as the note found by Ashley was computer generated. It might turn out to be useful to figure out which computer produced the note. There were two desktop personal computers (PCs) and a small notebook. The notebook couldn't do word processing; so, unless the note was done outside the home, it must have been one of the two desktops. The two computers looked very different. One had apparently been David Castor's computer, a Komodo PC. The work area was completely empty.

Then there was Stacey's computer, a Dell PC, which was surrounded by clutter, a bottle of window cleaner on its side, coupons and receipts and brochures and magazines. There was a brochure or leaflet, or possibly a magazine, promoting the heavy metal band Buckcherry. There was an empty pack of Marlboro Lights, a plastic lid to a coffee container, a bottle of nail polish remover, a porcelain dove, empty Tupperware. There was a glass ashtray with one butt in it, and a brown purse, which was open. The notebook computer sat on a shelf above and to the right of the desktop. It was slightly open and a bottle cap rested on the keyboard. Next to it were a series of glass bottles holding clerical supplies, such as paper clips and rubber bands.

Next to this computer was a printer that also looked like it hadn't been used in a while. A pair of bottle caps sat bent on the paper feed protruding from the front. On top was another clutter of papers, and a blue tape measure. Sitting on top of these, like the cherry atop a sundae, was a pair of upside-down sunglasses. On the floor next to the printer was yet another pink flamingo.

* * *

Like her mother, Ashley struggled in her attempt to process reality. The events that landed her in this hospital bed were disorienting. She understood what must have happened, but she couldn't understand—not even a little bit—why it happened.

"How can you sit there and blame your own child for something you know you did? I just don't get it. I didn't kill anybody, and I would never try to kill anybody," Ashley explained.

Ashley was informed that her mother had complained from her jail cell that she felt bad because she and Ashley had been best friends, and now this.

"She was my best friend, too," Ashley said. "She was my best friend, and then she took all of that away. I would have done anything for her, and then she tried to kill me, instead."

That same day, with the daughter still in the hospital, Lieutenant Craig Costanzo—the same man who had fingerprinted the family two years earlier—found portions of the "suicide" letter on the family computer. The family computer's hard drive revealed that the note had been written in stages over time, and that two rough drafts of its text had been saved. These were compared to the printed note found on Ashley's bed. There were changes. The final version of the letter read, with typos and punctuation left as is:

Mommy. When you read the letter just remember I love you and everything I did is because I love you

I'm sorry all of this is happening to you but now everyone is going to know what really happened and they know it wasn't you it was me none was every supposed to know about daddy I told you when daddy died it was all my fault and it was daddy was doing things you never knew about he was drinking when he was at pick n pull house and at lisas house he was smoking pot again to I saw him he was mean to you and me and he only ever loved bree I couldn't let him do those things to you anymore you think I don't remember how things were but I do and I didn't want to every live like that anymore it wasn't fair to or me daddy wasn't going to be good to you or be ever only bree I couldn't stand it any more the cops said there was antifree in daddys body but did they tell anyone about the rat poson too when I got home from school that day I knew what was going on daddy was barely breathing I knew he was gonna die that's why I didn't call you for help or anyone else I wanted to make sure he couldn't be mean to you or me anymore he died before I went to pick bree up from school I watched him and I knew he couldn't hurt you anymore then we were happy for while just the three of us and then you married david and he was mean to you to he was mean to all of us meaner than daddy and I knew you loved him like you loved daddy and you were going to let him treet you like he did and you wouldn't leave it wasn't fair mommy he didn't love you or me or bree I never thought anyone would miss daved none but you loved him it was harder than with daddy because you were always home or with him but it did it I made sure he would never hurt you anymore to that Friday when david came home so you could go to the post office is when I first did it it was easy I asked him if he wanted something to drink and I put the antifree in his glass with some soda he drank 2 hole glasses that was it only it took longer for david then with daddy once I put the antifree in daddys Gatorade it only took a day or so and that's when he died when you were sleepin on the couch after david locke himself in his room I tried to get him to drink som of that booze with the dropper thing but he was gout of it and wouldn't I poured the antifree in the glass and on the floor and left the bottle in the room and then I put the gloves back in the kitchen and got ready for wok you never knew and know all of these cops are saying all of this stuff about you to everyone you know and love mommy it's just not fair when you told me they dug daddy up I knew what was going to happen none was ever supposed to know mommy and now they do and they think you did it but you didn't it was me when the cops came to my school today I thought they had figured it out and I was going to go to jail but they didn't take me mommy I can't live like this and watch what they are doing to you not anymore but I can't go to jail for the rest of my life I can't put you through that I did the only thing I could to help you mommy I know you hate me for doing hat I did but mommy remember I love you more than anything and I did it for you and for us please forgive me mommy someday when all of this is over please forgive me make sure you take care of bree she is all you have left now remember how happy we all were together and you will be ahppy again I promis you mommy tell matt I love him and I'm sorry tell bree to be a good girl for you and I love her now too please don't hate me remember I love you. Ashley.

* * *

Costanzo noticed that the letter referred to antifreeze as "antifree." Was it a Freudian slip? Could just be a typo, but it also, in a way, equated the poison with loss of liberty.

A key piece of evidence turned out to be the date and time that the electronic version of the note was last accessed. Someone had called up the note at 2:27 P.M. on September 12, two days before Ashley's hospitalization.

Ashley was not home at that time. She was at the Bryant & Stratton Business Institute campus in Liverpool. Stacey, however, was home, and she would pick up her daughter at school at about 3:30 that afternoon.

With the Castor family in disarray—everyone except one was dead, in the hospital, or under arrest—Stacey Castor's youngest daughter, sixteen-year-old Bree, was taken in by relatives.

Ashley told the same story repeatedly. The last thing she remembered was her mother giving her some kind of foul-tasting drink.

Reading the "suicide note," Detective Spinelli also got to the word "antifree" and stopped. He recalled an interview he'd had with Stacey, not long after Stacey was widowed for the second time. During that interview, he noted that Stacey referred to the poison that killed David as "antifree." Spinelli didn't care about the Freudian interpretation of that typo, if it was a typo. A more immediate bell was ringing inside his head. He got in touch with Detective

Valerie Brogan, who had monitored that interview from another room. They didn't remember the syntax quite the same, but agreed that Stacey had started to say "antifreeze" and had left off the last sound. She'd said "antifree."

Spinelli and Brogan both remembered Stacey mispronouncing the word as part of an almost-admission. She had started to say, "Well, I poured the antifree— I mean, I poured the cranberry juice." Brogan thought that Stacey had caught herself midword. Spinelli thought she'd merely mispronounced it. When probed regarding what she had almost said, Stacey claimed that she innocently misspoke, blaming the stress of the interrogation for her meaningless blunder. Still, Spinelli felt the verbal error created a strong lingual similarity between the writing of the note and Stacey's spoken word.

Police interviewed Ashley's boyfriend, Matthew Gandino. Was she depressed? No. Any talk of suicide? Well, there was one discussion. When? Maybe a month before. What was said?

"We both had agreed never to do it," Gandino said.

He seemed credible. Why would Ashley try to end it all during her first few days of college? She was looking forward, not back.

About the arrest, Onondaga County sheriff Kevin E. Walsh said, "We were suspicious of Stacey Castor from very early on. From the beginning [when David Castor's body was found], we treated the case as a crime scene. When her daughter fell ill, it became obvious to us this woman presents a danger to other people. The arrest was made at this time because we feel she poses a public-health threat."

Detective Spinelli recalled how he felt when he first heard of Ashley's OD. His head had begun to swim. Homicide investigators are a hard-boiled lot. They grow emotional calluses. They don't stop caring, although some wish they could, but they do develop a certain professional nonchalance around violent death and mankind's capacity for cruelty. Spinelli had difficulty getting his mind around this monster that was Stacey Castor. Her own daughter . . . how? Spinelli couldn't help but theorize. He had to make sense of it. No matter how unbelievable something might be, it was human instinct to try to understand it, at least to understand it at some level, right? He came to the conclusion that Stacey had felt things tightening around her. She panicked. One chance: make Ashley the scapegoat.

Despite the hours of pondering, Spinelli never did figure it out. He would always wonder how Stacey could play God like that. This was the type of case that a cop took home with him. He thought about it at work, at home, when he was driving, all the time.

Stacey continued to deny that she had anything to do with the death of either of her husbands. It was Ashley. She'd done it, and then she'd tried to kill herself, because . . . who knows? Maybe she couldn't handle the guilt.

Stacey's demeanor was blank.

"She wasn't talking, wasn't reacting," Spinelli said. "She was emotionless. She didn't shed one tear. Here, you're being charged with one murder, you may be charged with another, your daughter is in the hospital, and nothing fazed her."

11

Judging Books
by Their Covers

At 11:30 P.M. on September 14, 2007, Stacey was arraigned on murder and attempted murder charges in Clay Town Court before Justice John M. Hall.

Standing at Stacey's side was Charles "Chuck" Keller, Esq. Stacey had not had to look far for her lawyer. The guy she retained worked in the same place she worked, at the Hiscock Legal Aid office (which, coincidentally, was also the same place where David Castor's first wife retained her divorce lawyer). In fact, Keller was Hiscock's chief of the criminal division.

He'd passed the bar in 1996. He was a go-getter and a tub-thumper, taking up causes that sometimes earned him publicity.

For example, in 2004, Keller became an expert in the Zen-like dilemma of "If no one complains about the noise of a block party, are the noisemakers committing a crime?" That is, assuming they really are making a crimeworthy level of noise.

Keller's client was nailed with a noise violation, even though police had not received a complaint. It was a judgment call to be made by the responding peace officer.

And what constituted an illegal level of noise was vague, as written in the Onondaga County law book. It wasn't like they set a specific decibel level.

Keller maintained that a police officer shouldn't be able to arrest someone for having an annoying party when everyone within hearing distance was at the party and no one was annoyed.

Keller's gripe was that the law his client had supposedly broken was "unconstitutionally vague." You can't be accused of disturbing the public, damn it, when the public wasn't disturbed!

A few years later, Keller was back in the news, seeking to make the criteria more stringent for government to interfere with families. He represented clients who had lost custody of a child with troublingly little evidence against them.

True, Keller was a clever young lawyer with bulldog determination, and, true, he was the head of his firm's criminal division. But he was still a rookie. He'd never done a murder case before. A lot of this was going to be brand-new.

Assisting Keller in Stacey's defense would be Todd Smith, a former prosecutor in St. Lawrence and Chemung Counties. Smith earned his J.D. at the University of Buffalo and had been a lawyer since 2002.

Keller thought Stacey had a pretty good case for being not guilty. If she had been an actress, she'd have been a damned good one. He personally interviewed

just about everyone who'd been in contact with
Stacey during the final weekend of David Castor's life,
and it was unanimous: she sounded and appeared
genuinely distraught over the fight she'd had with her
husband and his subsequent drinking binge.

Keller thought the old phrase "You can't judge a
book by its cover" was a bit of an oversimplification.
Really what it was saying was that you can't *always*
judge a book by its cover. There were times when the
cover of a book told you all you needed to know—
and that was how he felt about the note.

The other side wanted to put the note over as an
elaborate deception. Sometimes the simplest explanations were the best, and that, Keller thought, was
the case here. The note was exactly what it appeared
to be. It *could* be judged by its cover. It was a suicide
note and confession written by Ashley Wallace.

Luckily, Keller was a quick study and could think
on his feet. Though he banged his head against the
legal wall a few times, he had the wisdom to be patient. He was like a hitter facing an ace pitcher. If he
went one for four, he considered it a good day. Most
of the tactics he would try would fail. He was going
to hurl a big pot of spaghetti at the wall in hopes
that some of it would stick.

The first thing Keller did for Stacey was ask for
bail to be set, based on the family support she had
behind her. In response, DA Bill Fitzpatrick noted
the irony of Keller's request, and said that any
woman who would attempt to murder her own
daughter was a risk to flee the area. Stacey was ordered held without bail.

* * *

That evening, when a reporter tried to get a quote over the phone from David Castor's mother, Joyce Castor, who lived in Baldwinsville, New York, she choked up and was unable to speak.

Ashley was young and healthy and recovering more quickly than anticipated. On September 15, the day after Stacey's arrest, University Hospital upgraded Ashley's condition to fair.

The news of Stacey's arrest hit the Castors' Clay neighborhood hard. Reporters went door-to-door in an attempt to get comments from the neighbors.

While most were tight-lipped, John Strongosky said, "It's bizarre. It's like something you would see on *CSI*." The house on the corner had been a quiet home, he said—that is, until David's death. After that, it became the site of "frequent parties," and he noted that a gentleman caller was frequently there to see the merry widow.

Another neighbor, Maggie Racculia, said that she had found Stacey's behavior odd after David Castor died. For years, there had been a row of cedar trees separating her home from the Castors', but Stacey had those trees cut down not long after David died. The widow also was enthusiastically starting landscaping and interior-decorating projects. "It seemed to me that she was trying to erase all of David," Racculia said. "I don't understand how, if you cared about somebody, you just rip everything out that was part of them."

On September 21, Keller told the press that not only was Stacey innocent, but that her daughter Ashley was guilty—guilty of both the murder of

Michael Wallace and David Castor. The proof, Keller explained, was in the suicide note, which also functioned in this case as a confession.

For reporters, Keller filled in previously unreleased details. He said that at the time Ashley was found seriously ill, a suicide note was also found. He admitted that he had only recently been supplied a copy of that note, and that he had not had an opportunity to go over it in detail. At first glance, it appeared to be a genuine suicide note written by Ashley Wallace in which she confessed to double murder. Keller said the note was proof that his client was innocent.

Reporters ate it up. That mother-versus-daughter angle was made in journalistic heaven.

On September 23, nine days after Stacey's arrest, a reporter from "News 10 Now" in Syracuse called Ashley Wallace, who had just been released from the hospital, and asked her how she was feeling since her suicide attempt.

Ashley said she did not try to commit suicide, that her mother had drugged her by giving her a mixed drink. She remembered having one drink that her mother had prepared for her, and then she passed out.

Why would her mother do something like that?

"My mother must have been looking for an easy way out," Ashley said.

She added that she did not write the suicide note, and she believed her mother wrote that letter in an attempt to frame her for the murders of her father and stepfather.

* * *

A week later, on Sunday, September 30, there was a row at the Castor home. It started when Michael Overstreet, Stacey's boyfriend, showed up at the house with a trailer and tried to remove items from the home. "As many items as he could carry," said one observer.

Ashley and Overstreet got into an argument. As was true of all human conflict, what happened is vague, agreed upon by no one. Here's the best guess: After Ashley and Overstreet quarreled, she screamed at one point that he had better "watch his back." That was when it got really nasty, and Ashley decided she needed backup.

Ashley summoned her boyfriend's father to the scene, and another fight ensued between Overstreet and Mark Gandino. Ashley's beef was that Stacey's boyfriend was not just taking stuff that belonged to Stacey, but stuff that belonged to Ashley as well.

According to Overstreet, Gandino said to him, "You are going to be fucking dead. I know where you live."

Later, Gandino reportedly asked Overstreet, "How does it feel to be driving a dead man's car?"

Overstreet felt threatened and got in his car and left. Gandino, Overstreet claimed, got in his car also and followed him around the neighborhood, prompting him to call the police.

The next day, Monday, October 1, 2007, Overstreet had Ashley and Gandino arrested, based on a warrant issued by Clay Town Court justice Christopher S. Gaiser. That afternoon, in Clay Town Court, Ashley Wallace was charged with aggravated harassment, a misdemeanor, and Gandino was charged with harassment, a violation. Having cooperated fully, both were released under their own recognizance.

Really pissed off now, Ashley fired back.

In the meantime, on September 27, the DA held a press conference in his office to announce that, in addition to the murder charge that was almost two weeks old, Stacey Castor had been arrested in jail for the attempted murder of her daughter.

As he spoke, Sheriff Walsh stood at his right shoulder.

Bill Fitzpatrick told the gathered reporters the story of how, on September 14, Ashley had been discovered in extreme distress by her sister. The distress was a result of a substance she'd "ingested with her mother."

The DA's office, he said, believed that substance was a mixture of narcotics, other drugs, and poisons. The final lab results were not yet prepared, but they knew there were foreign substances.

Ashley believed that she was ingesting alcohol, and alcohol only, with her mother in a "celebratory opportunity with her mom." That was not the case, however.

He described the note, which, he said, could be interpreted as a suicide note written by Ashley in which she confessed to killing her father and her stepfather. Members of the sheriff's office, however, had investigated that note, had done a forensic analysis of the computer found at the home, and had concluded that the actual author was Stacey, *not* Ashley, and they considered the note to be a significant piece of evidence for that reason.

"She was arrested in jail?" a reporter asked.

"She was arrested in jail and brought before Judge Gaiser this morning," the DA replied.

Bail was set at $50,000 cash, $100,000 bond, but those figures were irrelevant because Onondaga County Court judge Joseph E. Fahey had already held her without bail for the murder of David Castor.

"A lot of the evidence you got to support this new charge comes straight from the daughter?" the reporter asked.

The DA explained that, for days after the poisoning, Ashley had been unable to give a complete statement, and the primary concern for her at that time was for her safety and the return of her good health. Only after they got the medical okay did Sheriff Walsh direct that she be interviewed.

Despite being conflicted by her own statements, the DA explained, Ashley had been 100 percent cooperative. She didn't kill anybody and she wrote no note. This didn't surprise him. The substance of the note, the way the note was written, all pointed at Stacey as the note's author.

"Is it only a matter of time before she is charged with the murder of her first husband as well?"

"Sheriff Walsh has been in discussion with his colleague Sheriff Gould in Cayuga County, so I'll let him answer that."

"Sheriff Gould has assigned his detectives to work this case on a full-time basis," Sheriff Walsh said. "They are working with our people. I can't give you a timeline, but, hopefully, they will be able to put together sufficient evidence to bring charges [for the murder of Michael Wallace]."

* * *

On Tuesday, October 2, Onondaga County judge Anthony Aloi signed a court order stating that Stacey's boyfriend, Michael Overstreet, would no longer be allowed to go to her home and remove property. The court order also said that the removal, sale, or transfer of property from the house was forbidden. Ashley had informed police detectives of Overstreet's behavior and it was the sheriff's office that requested a court order forbidding the boyfriend from entering the property.

The reason given was that there was cause to believe Overstreet was tampering with evidence. According to Ashley Wallace, who witnessed the behavior, Overstreet had gone to the Castor home repeatedly since Ashley got out of the hospital, and each time, she believed, he had removed items from the house and left with them.

Judge Aloi ruled that that behavior on the boyfriend's part would have to come to a stop.

The family was keeping the court schedule busy that day. On that same date, the judge signed a court order requesting that Stacey "show cause" why she should continue as executrix of her late husband's estate. Since the legitimacy of the will was in question, so should be Stacey's assignment as the will's executrix.

Back in 2005, when David Castor died, his will was contested in surrogate's court by David Castor's only son, David Castor Jr. David Jr. filed a suit. Stacey filed a countersuit.

Just as Janice had guessed years before, the Pulaskis, Lynn and Paul, the people who had witnessed the so-called will, were Stacey's friends from Baldwinsville. In February 2006, the Pulaskis,

Stacey's friends who "witnessed" the ersatz will, were interviewed on David Jr.'s behalf by a representative of T.W., Private Investigations. The married couple reiterated their story, that they had gone to the Wetzel Road house the day after Stacey and David's wedding, and that the newlyweds were preparing to leave for a honeymoon in Las Vegas, and that it was David who suggested they witness the signing of the will.

Caught up in the "Sue-Me/Sue-You Blues," David Jr. had agreed on June 23, 2006, to withdraw his objection to his father's will in exchange for his father's car. But now, he was back. If the will was bullshit to begin with, then all bets were off. David Castor Jr. was represented in 2007 by lawyer James Meggesto. He formally reopened his client's case against Stacey as executrix of his father's will.

David Castor Jr. and Ashley Wallace, as it turned out, had a common enemy. David's counsel brought up the Michael Overstreet incident. Overstreet had been removing things from the Castor home, possible evidence, things that might be part of David Sr.'s estate. Meggesto admitted that he did not have an accounting of what those items were, but common sense dictated that it was probably evidence that might disqualify Stacey as executrix of David Castor's will.

Meggesto requested that Judge Aloi demand an accounting of the items that had been removed from the home and that those items be returned. Overstreet must have felt picked on. He was just trying to do what was best for Stacey, to make the woman he loved look good. When all this blew over, he was going to take Stacey away.

* * *

The case next hit the court docket one week later, this time with Judge Joseph Fahey on the bench. As it turned out, Judge Fahey would stick with the case until Stacey's murder trial was complete.

Judge Fahey was a rotund man with glasses. He was bald, with a ring of gray hair stretching around the back of his head from temple to temple, and a closely cropped gray beard.

On the agenda—again—was possible bail for Stacey. The thought of Stacey walking the streets was upsetting to friends and relatives of Michael Wallace and David Castor. They feared for Ashley's safety, too.

Speaking for this group that morning outside the courtroom was Janice Poissant, who said, "We want to make sure she doesn't get bail. She has to suffer for her wrongdoings."

During the hearing, Stacey's defense attorney Chuck Keller asked the judge to change Stacey's status from no bail to $100,000. Even though Keller knew that Stacey did not have the means to pay that sum of money herself, he stated that he was hopeful her friends in the community, the many who thought she was falsely accused in this case, could chip in and get her out of jail. The court hearing was not long, and when it was through, Stacey remained in custody without bail.

After this hearing, Keller emphasized to a reporter that Ashley was the real author of the suicide note, and that the note was written on the home computer. This made perfect sense because if Ashley were to write a suicide note, "she would use the computer at home," Keller reasoned.

* * *

Police did not release the names of the people who "witnessed" the fake will, but Jim O'Hara, of the *Post-Standard,* looked up the surrogate's court file and learned it was the Pulaskis. The records showed that on November 23, 2005, the Pulaskis each signed an affidavit stating that they had been present back in 2003 when David Castor signed his Last Will and Testament, and that they thereafter signed the will at the request of, and in the presence of, the dece-dent. None of this was true. David Castor was dead and in his grave the first time the Pulaskis ever saw that will.

Now Lynn insisted that she hadn't a clue that she was doing something bad when she signed that will. Stacey had been through so much. Lynn would have helped her in any way possible, and just a quick John Hancock didn't seem like such a big deal.

"I figured that if I could help things go smoother for her, then why not? I never in my wildest imagina-tion thought it would turn out to be what it was," Lynn Pulaski said.

Investigators scared the Pulaskis. It was explained to Lynn by her interrogators just how much trouble she was in for fraudulently signing that document. And maybe not quite so much trouble if they coop-erated fully with the investigation.

Lynn and Paul cooperated fully. The Pulaskis as-sured their questioners that they'd do whatever was asked of them. In exchange for that cooperation, the Pulaskis were not charged with a crime.

During one interview with police, Lynn was asked if Stacey had ever written her any letters. She said sure. At police request, Lynn turned those letters over to the investigation.

Meggesto said that the indictment supported what his client—David Castor Jr.—had been saying all along: the will from Stacey was bogus. The "witnesses" had admitted that they hadn't actually seen the deceased sign the document. The signature had no witnesses. The will was invalid.

The major asset in his father's estate was the home on Wetzel Road, in which he died, and in which his stepmother had been living at the time of his death. But if the will was declared invalid, or if Stacey was convicted of murdering him, the house would go to his son as next of kin.

The will purported to have been signed by David himself, along with the two witnesses, on August 17, 2003, which was the day after David and Stacey were married. Stacey submitted the will to surrogate's court on December 20, 2005. Meggesto first filed the challenge in February 2006.

On October 17, 2007, the subject of David Castor's will came up in Judge Fahey's courtroom, although that was hardly the main event of the day.

The headlines were grabbed by Glen W. Shoop Jr., who was arraigned on a sealed indictment charging him with first-degree murder, first-degree aggravated sexual abuse, and two counts of second-degree murder.

Already in prison on charges of domestic violence, Shoop was accused of sexually abusing and killing a grandmother as she walked to her granddaughter's house in July.

At the same court hearing, a Syracuse woman named Michelle K. Cormier pleaded guilty to fatally stabbing fifteen-year-old Kyle Bradbury outside a grocery store. Allegedly, she was intoxicated and he had made vulgar comments about her looks.

Two arsonists were sentenced, a man pleaded guilty to abusing a nine-year-old boy, and finally, to a tired courtroom, came the relatively dry matter of David Castor's bogus will.

On December 20, 2007, Stacey was indicted not just for second-degree murder in David's death, and attempted second-degree murder in Ashley's poisoning, but also first-degree "offering a false instrument for filing."

In response to Stacey's arrest for murder and attempted murder, and her indictment for forging a will, surrogate's court judge Peter Wells issued an order barring Stacey from disposing of any of David Castor's property until there was a "resolution of the matter."

Stacey sat in her jail cell over the Christmas holiday and she could practically feel the walls crumbling down on her. She was in the Patrick J. Corbett Onondaga County Justice Center, named after the man who had been county sheriff from 1963 through 1978, the first Democrat ever elected to that post.

Stacey's biggest ally remained her mother, Judi Eaton, an attractive white-haired woman. To understand what really happened, Eaton figured,

was to come to grips with a few agonizing con-
clusions.

Ashley.

It kept her awake at night. What happened to her
family?

Judi was Stacey's most frequent visitor in jail. After
one visit, Judi explained that it was difficult to visit
Stacey in jail because her daughter was sick with suffering in that cage. She did not deserve any of it.
Stacey was innocent. The suicide note was real. The
note contained information that only the killer
could know, so the killer had to be Ashley.

Judi closed her eyes sometimes when she talked
about it. She couldn't bear to say the words and look
at the world at the same time. Too painful.

"Ashley had ample time and ample opportunity,"
Judi said. "And I don't like to say that because I love
that granddaughter as much as anyone else in the
family."

Ashley's grandmother then presented her own
case against Ashley. For years, she explained, there
had been warning signs that there was trouble between Ashley and the men in the family. Ashley was
"literally jealous" because her father preferred Bree.
Bree was "Daddy's girl," and that was that. Ashley
had loud arguments with David. Both deaths made
Ashley's problems disappear.

"I've seen her temper," Eaton said. She believed
in her heart of hearts that Ashley was capable of
double murder.

Stacey was asked if she was surprised that her
mother had sided with her over Ashley. Stacey
replied that she was surprised, and she had asked
her mother about it.

"She said she still loved Ashley very much, but I was her daughter," Stacey said.

Detective Spinelli was thrilled with the new phony will charge against Stacey. This proved that Stacey was deceitful. Once her credibility was shaken, it would be easier to convince a jury she was a murderer.

Although it wasn't essential that a prosecutor prove motive in a murder case, it sure did help. Jurors were far more likely to vote guilty when they understood why the defendant committed the crime. Forgery charges supplied that motive.

Stacey, it could now be efficiently shown, had a financial motive for killing David.

On the defense side, Chuck Keller worked the phone, seeking expert witnesses who could give testimony damaging to the prosecution's case. One of the calls he made was to Dr. Francis Gengo (JEN-go), a University of Buffalo pharmacologist who worked at the Dent Neurologic Institute in Amherst, New York. Keller described the case and asked Dr. Gengo if he would, for a fee, be willing to review some of the pertinent medical and toxicology records, and to give him his interpretation as to what they meant. The doctor did subsequently analyze those documents, and the conclusion he would come to would fly in the face of the prosecution's—and Ashley's—version of what went down.

Keller also called Brooklyn College linguistics

professor Dr. John Roy. He asked Dr. Roy a similar question. Would he be willing to look over the written communications associated with this case—the so-called suicide note and letters known to be written by Stacey and Ashley? Dr. Roy agreed to do that, and after studying those documents, he, too, came to a conclusion supportive of Stacey's innocence.

Stacey sat in jail, aware that she'd become a bit of a celebrity, people from TV shows coming to visit her and all—but she couldn't have felt lonelier. Ever since she got arrested, she had had no contact whatsoever with either of her daughters. She couldn't help but wonder a little, in the back of her mind, anyway, that she might never talk to Bree or Ashley ever again, that they had abandoned her forever.

They hadn't even written her a letter in prison. She sensed that Ashley and Bree had come to a conclusion regarding their mother, and they no longer wanted to have anything to do with her.

No matter how they felt about her, she was going to love them always, love them more than anything, and she spent many hours in jail worrying about her daughters' well-being.

It was her maternal instinct. She couldn't help it. Her eyes filled with tears when she thought of them. Were they okay? Were they safe? Stacey called it "mom stuff."

12

Discovering *It*

District Attorney William J. Fitzpatrick had an unhappy feeling of déjà vu when he first heard about this case. This was the second time a case involving murder by antifreeze had come across his desk, and the first one, as far as he was concerned, hadn't gone well.

In March 1999, a man named Timothy Badger died from, according to the prosecution, drinking coffee laced with antifreeze. His ex-wife had invited him over for coffee and cake. He'd complained at the time that the coffee didn't taste right, that it was sweet in a way it shouldn't be sweet, and a couple of days later, he was dead. Charged with the murder was his estranged wife, Mitzi.

With Fitzpatrick as prosecutor, Mitzi's first murder trial resulted in a hung jury. The problem with the prosecution's case was that tests on Timothy's blood were negative for ethylene glycol.

In fact, those tests were conducted by Raymond

Van Orden, the same lab chemist who would later look at David Castor's vomitous sheets under a laser light.

Problem was, the investigation took a big hit right off the bat in the·Badger case. A lot of the Badger evidence was taken to the emergency room, where the victim's health was swiftly deteriorating. He was transported to the ICU, and the people cleaning up the ER accidentally threw away much of the evidence.

Van Orden tested a cup and the icing from the cake Mitzi had served, but he found no evidence that either was the source of the victim's poisoning.

Mitzi testified in her own defense that her ex-husband had a leak in his radiator and kept antifreeze in a Mountain Dew bottle in his car. Mitzi said he must have had a tragic accident and drank out of the wrong bottle.

A majority of the jurors thought a grown man should be able to tell the difference in taste between soda and antifreeze, and a majority of the jurors felt Mitzi was guilty. But a unanimous vote was necessary for conviction.

The second trial, which was held without a jury, resulted in a flat-out acquittal when visiting Lewis County judge Joseph McGuire ruled that the prosecution had not presented solid enough evidence to meet the burden of proof.

Interestingly, Judge Joseph Fahey would have been the decider of Mitzi's fate rather than Mc-Guire except he was out of town attending school in Buffalo.

Fitzpatrick had argued before Judge McGuire that Mitzi, and Mitzi alone, had the means, motive, and opportunity to poison Timothy. Mitzi's defense attorney, James McGraw, argued that there were discrepancies between the medical evidence and the prosecution's theory.

The judge agreed with the defense and Mitzi walked. The case still haunted Fitzpatrick.

This time around, Fitzpatrick would be aided during the preliminary hearings and the subsequent trial by the raven-haired ADA Christine Garvey. She was no stranger to notorious cases. In 2004, she successfully prosecuted a father who had raped his eleven-year-old daughter, who later hanged herself. The forty-six-year-old man was convicted of rape, sodomy, and endangering the welfare of a child. He was sent to the Clinton Correctional Facility for fifty years, where he, unfortunately, needed special treatment. As a daughter raper, he'd be eaten alive if allowed five minutes among the general prison population.

For the upcoming trial of Stacey Castor, Fitzpatrick and Garvey decided early on upon an interesting division of labor. Fitzpatrick would handle much of the questioning of witnesses, and was always the questioner during dramatic moments. Garvey—on the other hand, being easier on the eyes—would handle the long stretches of the trial during which the jury was most apt to be bored.

It was she who would introduce the seemingly endless list of prosecution exhibits; she who would introduce the forensic evidence, the fingerprints, and the telephone calls. And she would question the members of the OCSO who had been to the Castor home during the hours following David's murder and Ashley's poisoning.

This didn't mean Fitzpatrick was handling the important stuff while Garvey took care of more trivial matters. The strength of the prosecution's case was in the mountain of circumstantial evidence it had gathered, and it would largely depend on Garvey's presentation of that mountain to convince a jury of Stacey Castor's guilt.

Some of the evidence was admittedly too complicated and too plentiful for Fitzpatrick to master. "I can learn anything for a week," he explained. "But Christine was the one with rudimentary knowledge of computers, so she handled those witnesses."

Fitzpatrick later recalled, "Christine is an excellent lawyer, but there were some witnesses that I had to do because it's my case. I'm the lead prosecutor."

There were also some witnesses, Fitzpatrick recalled, who related better to Garvey during trial prep, and that was the reason she would question them when the time came.

Chuck Keller, prepping for his first murder trial, was youthful-looking, despite being a balding man with large ears. He had closely trimmed facial hair—really a glorified five o'clock shadow.

The defense attorney had the haunted, wide-open but sunken eyes of a thoroughly caffeinated insomniac. He was media savvy, knew how to feed the press bite-sized pieces of info. He knew how to best encapsulate his case for public consumption: "There are only two people in the world who know the absolute truth, and they are Stacey and Ashley," he told a reporter. This was a mantra to which Keller would stick. Keller noted that it was a terrible tragedy no matter how you looked at it, no matter what you believed and whom you felt was responsible. "There is no happy ending," he said, concluding his characterization of the case.

He deftly switched the subject to strategy. Preconceived notions, he said, were his enemy. He explained that during the course of his investigation, he had talked to many people associated with the case, and he was shocked to discover that the great majority of them believed Stacey was guilty. The reason why? That was what they had heard. People felt like Stacey should be "thrown away for good."

Keller said that this was America, and here we don't throw away people for good when there is a chance they are innocent. All it took was a chance. If there was just a single chance that Stacey was innocent, then she should walk. Those were the rules. Demonstrating that chance, that "reasonable doubt" for a jury, would become his passion, he promised. The task had been for him all-consuming, right from the instant he agreed to defend Stacey.

And he kept that promise. For almost two years, Keller prepared for trial. Piece by piece, he went over every follicle of evidence. He read and re-read every report, every transcript. The truth needed to be exposed. His client required liberation. His life became a tenacious search for that one piece of evidence that would prove Stacey Castor innocent.

Just as Perry Mason had Paul Drake to do his leg-work while preparing an aggressive murder defense,

Keller had Gabriel "Gabe" Ramos, a burly man with a graying beard and wire-rimmed glasses. Since the best defense is a good offense, Keller gave Ramos the task of searching for evidence that might prove Ashley to be the true killer.

In the course of his search, Ramos interviewed friends of Stacey's, Michael and Dani Colman. They'd known Stacey for twenty years, and like Stacey's mother, they were convinced she didn't do it. Ashley was responsible, they maintained. The Colmans told the private detective that Stacey's eldest daughter not only had the capacity to commit murder, they *knew* she did it!

Michael Colman explained his belief: "I've seen how jealous Ashley can be. I've seen how she can flip her temper very quickly."

"In my mind, in my gut, it makes more sense that Ashley could have done it as opposed to Stacey," added Dani Colman.

Michael said that he had "no problem" believing that Ashley killed her father, despite her tender age at the time. After that, Michael figured, killing David Castor was easy. She had gotten away with it once. Why not again?

But could Ashley, being just a kid, keep all of that a secret for all this time? The Colmans thought she could. "She was a very dark person," Dani said.

In March of 2008, Mike Overstreet had another altercation at the Wetzel Road home. This time, it was not Ashley Wallace who was trying to prevent Overstreet from taking items out of the house. Instead, it was David Castor Jr. and his mother,

Janice, armed with the court order forbidding the removal of any items from the house until the will issue was settled. Police came but refused to honor the court order, because, they said, the order was too general and didn't give specific names. The garage door was open, and Janice saw a fitness machine, the washer and dryer, and the disassembled pool table moved outside and ready to be loaded onto Overstreet's truck. Janice glared at Overstreet and he met her gaze with a self-satisfied expression she would never forget.

As the months passed and the investigation on both sides continued, the Castor home slowly emptied. David was dead, Stacey in jail, and the girls had gone to live with Ashley's boyfriend's family. During their search for evidence, Chuck Keller and Gabe Ramos made a thorough search of the Castor home. The place had been picked over by the police. The house was in disarray, and was in the process of being prepared for sale. The items that remained in the house were scheduled to be boxed up for storage or thrown out. Keller and Ramos did not have high hopes as they searched the house.

Keller and Ramos spent a lot of time in what had been Ashley's room, looking for writing samples that might be similar in some way to the style, spelling, and syntax used by the writer of the suicide note.

They also searched for evidence that might indicate motive, perhaps that Ashley was jealous because her father liked her baby sister better than her. Or that she felt David Castor, contrary to her mother's feelings, was an unwanted intruder in their home. Or that she was the type of girl who might attempt suicide.

It was toward that final objective that they struck pay dirt. While going over all of the papers that remained in Ashley's room, they found a letter that she had apparently started to write to her then-boyfriend.

In the letter she wrote that she would "die" if the boy ever left her. She explained that she wasn't threatening death just to freak him out, but that—from the time her father passed away until she met the boyfriend—she became stuck on the idea of death. She often contemplated what would happen in the world if she were to suddenly die.

She wrote that she had seriously thought about killing herself on two occasions, but both times she talked herself out of it. If she were gone, who would protect Bree? Her baby sister needed someone to watch out for her, a guardian angel, and who was going to step up and take the job if Ashley were gone?

Now, here was a document that Chuck Keller could work with.

"The letter to the boyfriend is crucial to the case," Keller said. "Because here is a person who has contemplated suicide." The letter was "absolutely consistent" with his theory.

In addition to the boyfriend letter, Keller also believed that he had discovered what he called "a pretty large hole in the daughter's story." When adequately scrutinized, Ashley's story "fell apart," Keller claimed.

"If the daughter is not to be believed, there is only

one reasonable explanation," Keller said, "and that is that Ashley is responsible, and the mother is not."

As preparations for the trial continued, it became apparent to both sides that this wasn't going to be a normal murder case. For one thing, it felt like ABC News was filming everything and had unprecedented access to the inner workings of both investigations. It was more like a reality show than reality. The reporter in charge of the ABC coverage was thirty-four-year-old David Muir, a veteran TV man. He had endured Hurricane Katrina, and had been in the Superdome when the roof blew off. He had survived war in the Middle East and was on the Lebanon border when Katyusha rockets struck inside Israel. Talking to a woman accused of murder didn't faze him.

The assignment, in fact, was a pleasant one for him. He'd grown up in Syracuse and happily took the assignment in his hometown. Muir graduated from Onondaga High School in 1991, and anchored the local evening news—WTVH, Channel 5—for five years.

Not only was Muir a handsome and charismatic feature of the Castor investigation and trial, but there was always a camera nearby for the players in this drama. If it wasn't in your face, it was across the room; and if it wasn't across the room, it was down the hall or around the corner ready to capture and reveal your image forever. No pressure.

Ashley, just as an example, felt like an Osbourne or a Kardashian—the subject of one of those so-called reality shows. ABC cameras followed her around for *months*. They filmed her when she was doing laundry. They filmed her when she put on her makeup. (Ashley, by the way, performed perfectly under the pressure of the limelight, and was described by ABC after the ordeal as a woman of "extraordinary strength.")

The fact remained, Big Brother really was watching. And, though some denied it, cameras change everything. Each day, the players were concerned with not just what they said aloud, but how they looked, about the facial expressions they were making as they spoke or listened. Self-consciousness was amped up across the board.

Not that there weren't still behind-the-scenes strategy meetings that even ABC couldn't infiltrate, but media was virtually pervasive—so much so, that even the normally theatrical set piece that is a courtroom and its environs was shellacked with a fresh coat of show business.

Some were affected more than others by the media coverage. One person who seemed unbothered by the prying eye of the media was the DA himself.

"You may not believe me, but it didn't affect me in the slightest," Fitzpatrick later recalled.

Part of that was his personality. Vanity had nothing to do with what he did. He didn't care how he looked, just as long as he got the job done. For another thing, he'd been in the limelight before and thus was more familiar with the added element of cameras.

Fitzpatrick's starring role on the ABC News

special would not be the DA's first brush with fame. Coincidentally enough, the first involved another case of a mother doing harm to her children.

Fitzpatrick's first high-profile case began in 1986 when he was prosecuting a father who was charged with killing two of his children. Three of his children had died, Onondaga authorities believed he killed all three, but one child had died in Saratoga County, outside their jurisdiction. The Saratoga prosecutor made a deal with the accused and charged him with manslaughter only. In Onondaga, however, no deal was made.

As Fitzpatrick was preparing for trial, he called in a forensic pediatric pathologist from Dallas, Texas, named Linda Norton. She and Fitzpatrick were talking one day about the case when Norton interrupted herself, and said, "Oh, my God! This is Syracuse. You have a serial killer here in Syracuse."

Fitzpatrick found this a "pretty provocative" thing to say.

She told him about a medical-journal article she had read that discussed the deaths of five siblings in the Syracuse area about fifteen years earlier. All of the children had apparently succumbed to sudden infant death syndrome (SIDS).

After the trial, at which the man was convicted, Fitzpatrick went to the Upstate Medical Center, and there read the article Norton had told him about.

"I said to myself, 'Oh, my God, there it is!' This guy was describing five homicides, only he didn't realize it," the DA recalled.

But the timing was off, Fitzpatrick was on the verge of leaving the DA's office temporarily, so he didn't do anything about it, and no one else did anything about it, either.

When Fitzpatrick became DA in 1992, he did look into it. He did research and sent out subpoenas. He found the mother, who was the prime suspect, living in Tioga County. Collaborating with the Tioga DA, Fitzpatrick put together a case. The result was the prosecution of Waneta Hoyt, who was accused and subsequently convicted of smothering her five children to death.

Following the Hoyt case, Fitzpatrick appeared on the *Eye to Eye* TV program with Connie Chung, and the case was the subject of the book *Goodbye, My Little Ones: The True Story of a Murderous Mother and Five Innocent Victims* by Charles Hickey, Todd Lighty, and John O'Brien. The DA also appeared on *20/20*, *Dateline*, *60 Minutes*, *Cold Case Files*, and *Women Behind Bars*, using his forum to increase national awareness regarding infant homicide and SIDS prevention.

Fitzpatrick says there was another factor in his ability to function during the Castor case without dwelling on the size of his TV audience, and that was the professional manner in which everyone from ABC handled themselves.

"Everything they said they would do, they did. They kept their word," the DA recalled.

The final factor was that the cameras themselves were designed and placed to be as surreptitious as possible. Before the first preliminary hearings were held, ABC had their tech people working on the courtroom. By the time proceedings commenced, the entire room was wired for sight and sound. In the modern courtroom where the preliminary hearings and trial would take place, for example, the cameras would be ultra–high-tech. Designed to be unobtrusive, they would be built into what appeared to be items of furniture. If you walked in unaware, you wouldn't know the cameras were there.

Fitzpatrick told ABC he found Stacey to be a bad trip, a personality that rubbed irritatingly at his ability to sleep at night. Sometimes, Fitzpatrick said, the most frightening thing is the coldness with which people operate. Most women with a failing marriage might contemplate divorce. They might hire a lawyer. Or maybe they would try to glue the pieces back together again and seek counseling. But none of that seemed practical to Stacey.

"She just poured a drink," Fitzpatrick said.

Killing two husbands was one thing, but Stacey went immediately to the head of the coldness class—the Coldness Hall of Fame—when she tried to kill Ashley.

"You could seek out someone with more degrees than a thermometer, and they could tell you that, in their experience as a psychiatric practitioner, this woman suffers from this or that. It is just bald-faced *evil.*"

ADA Christine Garvey had another word to describe the defendant. "I think she is *diabolical.* What she has done over the course of seven years is unimaginable."

Both sides saw the "suicide note" as essential, but for differing reasons. The defense took the note at face value. The prosecution felt the note differed from genuine suicide notes. It was much longer than the normal suicide note. People contemplating

suicide are in a state of emotional upheaval, not
known for their attention spans, and suicide notes
tend to be concise. Length wasn't the only problem
with the note. It also lacked the personal touches.
There was no handwritten component. It was purely
a computer printout. Suicide notes were rarely 100
percent typewritten. There were repeated mentions
of the mother throughout the text, yet only one
mention of the boyfriend, at the very end of the
note, almost as an afterthought. Didn't ring true.
Fitzpatrick had seen "many suicide notes," and never
before had he seen one remotely like this. The
Onondaga County crime lab processed the note
using its state-of-the-art equipment, and the only fingerprints found belonged to Stacy Castor. None
from Ashley. Including the investigation into David
Castor's death, Ashley's fingerprints had not been
found on a single piece of evidence.

Sure, the printed version of the note was important, but even more important were the practice
notes. The DA called those hard-drive versions "the
most damning evidence against Stacey." The prosecution merely had to show that Ashley did *not* write
the note and Stacey had to be guilty. QED. Case
closed. And with the evidence that the computer
expert had found regarding the multiple versions of
the note, Fitzpatrick felt certain that he and his team
could do just that.

Plus, there was the matter of personalities. Fitzpatrick prognosticated: "When the jury sees Ashley,
they are going to know that she had nothing to do
with it."

Still, proving a negative was hard. Fitzpatrick
didn't stand pat. He kept working. While tenaciously

preparing for the trial ahead, the DA read and re-read all of the written statements involved in the case: transcripts of police interviews, the so-called suicide note, letters Ashley and Stacey had written and that had later been confiscated. He was looking for minute details, pieces that fit, little Velcro hooks and loops that could make the case stick.

In the supposed suicide note, he read this passage: *I never thought anyone would miss daved none but you loved him it was harder than with daddy because you were always home or with him but it did it I made sure he would never hurt you anymore.*

Then Fitzpatrick read a letter written in jail by Stacey to her friend Lynn Pulaski. Stacey wrote, *Hopefully I won't be in here for to long. I hope I can get bailed out. It is only fair because it didn't do it.*

The DA stopped and read both documents one more time.

There it was. There *it* was.

13

Preliminary Hearings

On Thursday, April 17, 2008, a preliminary hearing was held before Judge Fahey to determine if there was sufficient evidence against Stacey Castor to hold her over for trial. The DA later counted the judge's even strain as one of the reasons that he, personally, was unfazed by ABC's coverage of the trial. Judge Fahey was simply not prone to histrionics, he explained.

At that hearing, William Fitzpatrick said he intended to prove Stacey killed both of her husbands, using more or less the same method five years apart. Although Stacey was not to be tried in Onondaga County for her first husband's murder, because that crime took place in Cayuga County, Fitzpatrick hoped to use evidence from Michael Wallace's murder, a previous "bad act," to demonstrate that Stacey had a preference for killing in the precise fashion in which David Castor was killed.

As it turned out, months would go by before Fitzpatrick would know for certain if evidence regarding Michael Wallace's death would be allowed into evidence at Stacey's murder trial. At this hearing, Judge Fahey admitted that he was leaning toward allowing it in, but he asked Fitzpatrick to submit in writing what proof he wanted to use relating to Michael Wallace.

Charles Keller called the DA's strategy "nothing more than circular thinking." Keller said Fitzpatrick planned to contend that one murder proved the other, and vice versa, when there was no evidence that she killed either of her husbands. Keller emphasized that it remained the defense's contention that Ashley had murdered her stepfather and subsequently attempted suicide.

The judge scheduled a hearing for May 16, at which time it would be determined which of Stacey's statements—including those made both before and after her arrest—would be admissible.

At the defense's request, the judge also agreed to review the court orders for searches and wiretaps that were used in the Stacey Castor investigation to determine if there was, as the defense contended, incidents of law enforcement misconduct.

At the May hearing, Detective Spinelli related the story Stacey had told him about opening the door while her ill husband was dry heaving, and how he had yelled at her until she left, closing the door behind her.

Spinelli said that Stacey told him she was frightened by the angry expression on David's face while he was sick in his room. Keller pointed out that

David's anger could have been the direct result of being poisoned.

Retired sheriff's Detective Diane Leshinski testified that she had been one of the first to see the crime scene and recounted how she had found what appeared to be brown vomit running down the side of David Castor's mattress.

As the summer began, players involved in the case made the news here and there—for both happy and sad reasons. At the end of June, Christine Garvey was given a promotion from senior assistant district attorney to chief assistant district attorney, as she was named to head the DA's Homicide Bureau.

On Sunday, July 6, 2008, Michael Wallace's mother, Joyce, passed away at the age of seventy-eight. She lived long enough to see Stacey arrested and strongly suspected of being her son's murderer, but not long enough to see Stacey's trial.

The next preliminary hearing was held on Tuesday, July 15, 2008. The defense asked Judge Fahey to suppress evidence gathered by police on September 14, 2005.

Testifying in support of the motion to suppress was Chuck Keller's co-counsel Todd Smith, who said that he witnessed sheriff's deputies searching the Castor home before a search warrant had been issued. "They were moving around inside the home," Smith said. "They were placing objects, which appeared to be bottles, on the kitchen table, and they were carrying cardboard boxes into the house." He admitted that he was with Chuck Keller at the time he witnessed these events.

Garvey argued that authorities acted properly when they conducted this search, because Stacey had invited them inside when they arrived, summoned because of her husband's medical emergency.

Keller argued that the fact that Stacey let the personnel into the house to help her husband did not mean that she had given them permission to search the house and confiscate evidence.

In particular, Keller wanted the turkey baster thrown out. Stacey at no time gave authorities permission to search her kitchen trash, where the baster was located.

Garvey noted that two years later, when Ashley Wallace was taken ill, police didn't wait until they had a formal search warrant signed before they again searched the Castor home for evidence. She admitted that there was a search of the house before the warrant was issued, but this was only in connection with the emergency, and police were only looking for evidence that might help them figure out on which substances and in what quantities Ashley had overdosed.

They weren't improperly gathering evidence, they were trying to save a life.

Keller argued that even on the occasion of Ashley's illness, there was no evidence that authorities drew the line where Garvey said they had. They used the medical emergency as an excuse to again commit an illegal search of his client's home, Keller explained.

Keller also asked Judge Fahey to hold a hearing about the legality of the tap police put on Stacey's phone during the days before Ashley's overdose. He said that a detective misrepresented the facts in order to acquire a court order for the tap.

Fitzpatrick explained that info on the court order request came from Mike Wallace's doctor. Judge Fahey said he would need a couple of weeks to make up his mind about the suppression motion.

On December 10, 2008, there were big doings. DA Bill Fitzpatrick and Sheriff Kevin Walsh were among those on the dais as it was announced by the U.S. Attorney's Office that twenty-nine individuals had been arrested in a marijuana-smuggling operation. The bust, the culmination of an eleven-month multijurisdictional investigation—involving Onondaga County, New York State, and Federal law enforcement—ended a flow of millions of dollars' worth of pot and cash from Canada into the Syracuse area through the St. Regis Mohawk Indian Reservation.

With Stacey's murder trial rapidly approaching, the grand jury continued listening to evidence. On December 22, 2008, a preliminary hearing in the *State* v. *Stacey Castor* discussed the relationship— appropriate and otherwise—between the ongoing grand jury investigation and Stacey's upcoming murder trial.

The legal sticking point involved the grand jury calling as a witness the private investigator Gabriel Ramos. Keller argued that the testimony of the private investigator would amount to a "deposition of defense witnesses" regarding the upcoming murder trial.

According to the *Post-Standard,* "At issue was a pill

bottle that was recovered from the Castor home after police, using a search warrant, investigated the house on Wetzel Road."

The pill bottle, discovered and confiscated jointly by Ramos and Stacey's boyfriend, Michael Overstreet, was turned over to the defense and should have been turned over as evidence, argued senior assistant DA Victoria Anthony White, who routinely handled points of law and appeal for the DA's office.

"It was not a secure crime scene," Keller argued. "This is an attempt to disparage the defense for secreting evidence. They make it sound like we sneak into the house under cover of night."

Keller pointed out that police had acquired a search warrant for that house and they had executed it. Thoroughly. There had been maybe a dozen officers, maybe more, searching with magnifying glasses and fine-tooth combs. "They searched every nook and cranny," Keller said, but they missed the pill bottle. "My obligation to my client does not preclude our raising a red flag and saying, 'Here's something you missed.'"

If the defense team had not acquired the pill bottle, it would surely have been lost to history, buried or destroyed. "When police detectives were through searching the house, the contents were either put in storage, thrown out, or destroyed in preparation for the new owners moving in," Keller said.

On the other side of the aisle, White rebutted that among the things the grand jury would examine was whether *any* of the evidence in the case was tampered with.

Judge Fahey ruled that the private investigator

would be allowed to testify before the grand jury. In his ruling he noted that Ramos had already provided prosecutors with an affidavit, and allowed Ramos to have his lawyer, Ed Klein, with him during the testimony. The judge ruled that the grand jury could only help the pursuit of justice by "further investigating the case."

At no time during the hearing did anyone refer to the contents of the pill bottle or allude to how it was involved in the case.

At this hearing, Fahey decided that the tapes of phone conversations police made during the days before Ashley's overdose would be allowed in as evidence. The judge ruled that there was legitimate reason to suspect Stacey of wrongdoing at the time the warrant to tap her phone was signed, and the possibility was strong that she might telephonically incriminate herself at that time.

The judge said he would reserve ruling regarding whether authorities exceeded the scope of the eavesdropping warrant. Keller said authorities "failed to take any steps to limit" the extent of the eavesdropping. This failure to set limits was particularly alarming, given that Stacey was working at the time of the electronic surveillance as a secretary for the local Legal Aid office, the very same office that employed defense counsel.

During the hearing, Stacey wore tan jail-issued slacks and a navy shirt. She stared straight ahead and, as would become the norm, displayed no emotion.

14

The Trial

It was front page of the papers in Central New York State, the top story on TV news. After sitting and waiting in jail for more than sixteen months, on Monday morning, January 12, 2009, Stacey Castor's trial was ready to start.

Entering the courthouse, Chuck Keller told reporters, "It's going to be a long trial, and Stacey is looking forward to finally having her side of the story heard."

To those same reporters, William Fitzpatrick refused to comment on the substance of his case, but he did say, "We're going to call about fifty witnesses, and we can't wait to get started."

Stacey's hair had grown long since her arrest, and hung straight down, limp—not a becoming look for a middle-aged woman. Her hair was parted on the left, combed to cover her ear on the right, and back over the ear on the left. She wore a white button-up blouse with a large collar beneath a dark sweater.

As spectators entered the courtroom, the defense table was on the right, prosecution on the left. The spectator section would be filled every day by press and interested citizens alike.

Those who had been subpoenaed to testify were not allowed inside the courtroom, lest they be influenced by the testimony of others. Out in the courthouse hallways, conspiracy theories blossomed. Some thought the defense had purposefully issued superfluous subpoenae just to keep those sympathetic to the victims out of the jury's sight. And, as it turned out, the defense did subpoena more witnesses than it called to the stand.

The bailiff: "All rise, county court judge, the Honorable Joseph E. Fahey, presiding. The court is now in session."

Jury selection was expected to be a lengthy process because of the case's notoriety. Judge Fahey informed the jury pool that the trial was expected to last for several weeks, so they were seeking panelists who could afford to serve for at least that length of time.

As they would be for the entire trial, video cameras from the TV show *20/20* were set up at the back of the courtroom.

Despite the intensity of public scrutiny, jury selection went more smoothly than anticipated. By Monday afternoon, a panel of nine women and three men had been selected. On Tuesday morning, the six alternates were chosen. The jury was sworn in, there was a brief recess, and then Judge Fahey gave an introductory statement to the new panel.

He told them that this was *The People of New York State* v. *Stacey Castor*. He ran down the charges against the defendant, defining each charge as he went, and gave the jury a short course in how trials were conducted: "Trial 101." His job was to determine which laws applied in the case, and to explain those laws to the jury. However, it was *their* responsibility to determine what the facts were in this case, and to apply the law to those facts.

The judge discussed the order of the proceedings. First up were opening statements, in which both sides described the evidence they planned to present. And evidence was all that mattered. They were to base their decision only on the evidence. During opening statements, the jury should keep in mind that what the lawyers said was *not* evidence. The evidence was comprised of the *exhibits*, hard pieces of evidence introduced by each side, and the testimony of the witnesses. Each witness was to be examined and then cross-examined.

Here was a tough part: the jurors were not to, under any circumstances, come to a conclusion regarding the defendant's guilt or innocence before the trial was over. Jurors were not to formulate an opinion until they'd heard and seen *all* of the evidence.

They were not to discuss the case among themselves, the judge said. Or with anyone else, either. If someone persistently tried to talk to them about the case, they were to report it to him via the bailiffs.

The defendant had a right *not* to testify on her own behalf, and should that occur, the jury was not to consider her silence an indication of guilt.

The defense didn't have to prove a thing. It was

the prosecution's job, in fact, to prove the defendant was guilty beyond a reasonable doubt.

The judge explained that sometimes they would have to be out of the room while certain discussions occurred in the courtroom. The jurors had their own room in the building and being ushered from one room to another should be no big deal. He promised that the discussions they weren't supposed to hear were usually pretty boring and almost always concerned points of law.

"I promise you will miss no allowable evidence," Judge Fahey said.

Some of the discussions would be short, with the jury still in their seats. The lawyers would meet up in front by his bench and speak in low voices. These meetings were called sidebars and, again, the jury missed only discussions regarding points of law and no evidence.

Judge Fahey then thanked the jury for doing their duty and being such a large part of the justice process. Because of its nature, he explained, this was going to be a long trial. He urged them to hang in there, and do their best to focus their attentions on the proceedings.

"You should give the evidence on the final day every bit as much weight as first-day evidence," Judge Fahey said.

It was then called to the judge's attention that one of the alternate jurors, a woman named Laura Hand, was a news anchor on WSTM-TV. She was dismissed, as the judge felt she had too great of an opportunity, because of her employment, to learn about the case from sources outside the courtroom. There was discussion of picking a new person from

The single-level house in the town of Clay, where David Castor lived and died. It was a pretty place with a lawn on three sides and a small wishing well. *(Photo courtesy of the Onondaga County District Attorney's Office)*

David Castor's house was near the corner of Wetzel Road and Glenwood Drive. *(Photo courtesy of the Onondaga County District Attorney's Office)*

When Sergeant David Willoughby of the Onondaga County Sheriffs Office kicked in the door to get to David Castor's body, he splintered the door and tore out the lock. *(Photo courtesy of the Onondaga County District Attorney's Office)*

David Castor's body was found lifeless and naked, stretched out sideways across a sheetless bed. *(Photo courtesy of the Onondaga County District Attorney's Office)*

Castor's legs hung over the side of the bed. *(Photo courtesy of the Onondaga County District Attorney's Office)*

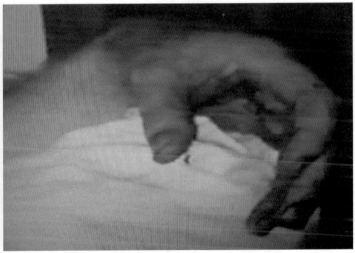

In death, David Castor's left hand was frozen in this position, as if he had died holding a subsequently removed glass. *(Photo courtesy of the Onondaga County District Attorney's Office)*

On the floor beneath David Castor's feet, partially under the bed, was a blue plastic container of Peak anti-freeze. *(Photo courtesy of the Onondaga County District Attorney's Office)*

The sheet that formed a skirt around David Castor's bed, and the shag rug covering the bedroom floor, were stained by a brown matter later identified as vomit. *(Photo courtesy of the Onondaga County District Attorney's Office)*

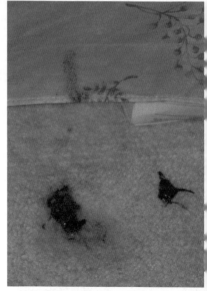

On the night table beside the body were, from left to right, a TV remote, a wireless telephone, a glass containing a bright green fluid, a bottle of Hiram Walker Apricot-Flavored Brandy with its cap off, another glass, an empty bottle of Ocean Spray Cranberry Light, also with its cap off, a wristwatch, and an alarm clock/radio. *(Photo courtesy of the Onondaga County District Attorney's Office)*

The green fluid in this glass was determined to be antifreeze. Three readable prints were lifted from the glass. The early assumption was that they belonged to the victim, but those prints turned out to be Stacey's. *(Photo courtesy of the Onondaga County District Attorney's Office)*

The bathroom next to the room where David Castor died was in disarray. Part of a towel rack was torn off the wall and lay on the floor in front of the toilet. *(Photo courtesy of the Onondaga County District Attorney's Office)*

Although a layer of garbage covered it, Sergeant Willoughby did not have to dig very deep in the kitchen garbage can before discovering a turkey baster, which turned out to be a key clue in the case.
(Photo courtesy of the Onondaga County District Attorney's Office)

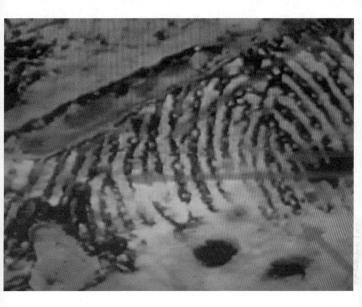

The glass containing antifreeze was dusted for prints. None from the victim were found, but three partial prints were determined to have belonged to Stacey Castor. *(Photo courtesy of the Onondaga County District Attorney's Office)*

Before her arrest, Stacey Castor's appearance was very different. Her face was animated and her eyes seemingly kind. *(Photo courtesy of Linda Foglia, NYS Dept. of Corrections)*

Sex - FEMALE   Race - WHITE   Hair - AUBURN   Eyes - HAZEL   DOB - 7/24/1967
6 TATS

After Judge Fahey sentenced Stacey, she was transferred from the
Onondaga jail to the Bedford Hills Correctional Facility for Women in
Westchester County, the only maximum-security prison for women in
New York State. It would be more than fifty years before she was eligible
for parole. *(Photo courtesy of the New York State Department of Corrections)*

This photo was taken at a time when all the Castor kids had the same
hairstyle. David, Gary, Mike, and Stephen are on the couch, Linda and
Sandra on the floor. *(Photo by Janice Poissant)*

In autumn 1978, David Castor and first wife Janice celebrated the birth of their only child, David Jr. *(Photo by Janice Poissant)*

David Castor shares a tender moment with his young son. *(Photo by Janice Poissant)*

David arrives at work and discovers a birthday surprise from Janice. *(Photo by Janice Poissant)*

01/27/2005

Eight months before David's death, he was on his ex-wife's mind as she took this drive-by photo of the home she'd left. Stacey, we can see, had yet to purchase the pink flamingoes. *(Author photo)*

David stands in the driveway
of his home on Wetzel Road.
(Photo by Janice Poissant)

David's parents, Joyce and Philip Castor. David passed away a month to
the day after his father. *(Photo by Janice Poissant)*

David Wayne Castor

DO HEREBY CERTIFY, th

A handwriting expert determined that the "David Castor" signature on the document purporting to be his will was fake. *(Author photo)*

Just down the road from the Castor house was Liverpool Heating, David's business, which he purchased from his first father-in-law. In the will she forged, Stacey took it for herself. *(Photo by Janice Poissant)*

David Castor, Sr. (right), with his only son, on the occasion of David Jr.'s graduation from U.S. Army basic training, October 2, 1997, at Fort Lee, Virginia. *(Photo by Janice Poissant)*

David Castor Jr. and his mom Janice as they appear today. *(Photo by Janice Poissant)*

Stacey's printer also was covered with a disorganized pile of papers and a pair of sunglasses. Note the bottle caps resting on the paper feed. *(Photo courtesy of the Onondaga County District Attorney's Office)*

When Ashley Wallace arrived at the hospital she had sixty or more pills in her, including some from these bottles, photographed in her bedroom next to her contact lens cleaner. There was an empty bottle of generic Lexapro, a bottle of Amoxicillin with nine pills left, an empty Hydrocodone bottle, and an empty bottle of generic Ritalin. Elsewhere police found an empty bottle of Ambien. *(Photo courtesy of the Onondaga County District Attorney's Office)*

An exhumation of Stacey's first husband Michael Wallace's body proved that he had also been poisoned. *(Photo courtesy of Consumer Programs, Inc.)*

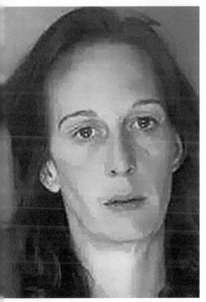

Stacey Castor as she appeared for her mug shot, only hours after her arrest for the murder of David Castor and the attempted murder of Ashley Wallace. *(Photo courtesy of the Onondaga County District Attorney's Office)*

Ashley Wallace, whose mother tried to murder her and frame her for the deaths of her father and stepfather. *(Yearbook Photo)*

the juror pool to fill the sixth alternate spot, but Judge Fahey said this would not be necessary, and that they would proceed with five alternate jurors.

Judge Fahey said, "Now I'd like to call for opening statements. Bill?"

"Thank you, Judge," the DA said, rising to his feet. He began by reiterating what Judge Fahey had earlier told them, that the jurors were to base their eventual verdict on the evidence, and only the evidence, and that the evidence consisted of the testimony of the witnesses and the objects or transcripts marked into evidence during the course of the trial. It did not include any speeches made by any of the several lawyers in the courtroom. He went over with the jury the three crimes the defendant was on trial for—murder in the second degree, attempted murder, and filing a fake will. He added that there was a fourth crime, but her guilt or innocence would not be decided at this trial because it occurred in a different county.

He told the jury that he could give the most eloquent opening statement in the history of law, paint a word-picture masterpiece, and it would make no difference if the evidence did not prove beyond a reasonable doubt that the defendant was guilty of all of the charges against her.

He told the jury that the *overwhelming abundance* of evidence they would see and hear during the trial pointed at Stacey's guilt. He explained to the jury how the authorities had become aware of David Castor's demise, how Stacey Castor had phoned 911 and complained that she was locked out of the master bedroom, how deputies had to break down the door and discovered David Castor naked on the bed, sprawled dead at a forty-five-degree angle.

"There was a significant body of thought at that crime scene that this was a suicide," Bill Fitzpatrick said. On the floor next to the bed was a can of antifreeze. The autopsy later revealed that David had died of antifreeze poisoning.

The defendant told a version of the facts in a way that supported the suicide theory. The widow said she prepared for David an anniversary dinner on the Friday before his death. They fought. He began to drink heavily. David had locked himself in the bedroom. She said that she and David met in the garage of their home on Saturday morning and talked for seven hours. He was down on himself. She worried about him. Later, David lay down and Stacey went to pick up her daughter. When she returned to the home, she discovered David so "out of it" that she had to call for help to get her husband back in bed. She said that this was about seven o'clock Saturday evening, and that when she returned from picking up her daughter, she discovered that David "had collapsed." She said that David was in such bad shape that he didn't even know who he was. She claimed that she last saw her husband alive early on Sunday.

That was her version. It sounded plausible enough, at first. As the evidence came in, however, the Stacey scenario became increasingly porous. The evidence would show that something very different had occurred inside that house.

Fitzpatrick gave the jury a quick lesson in DNA, then drew their attention to the murder scene. The evidence discovered there told a straightforward story. On Castor's nightstand was a bottle of Hiram Walker apricot-flavored brandy, and on it were the defendant's fingerprints. Next to the bottle was an almost-empty glass, and in the glass was antifreeze residue. David Castor's DNA was found on the glass, and Stacey Castor's fingerprints were found on the glass. When David eventually lacked the motor skills to drink out of a glass, she had to find another way. In the kitchen trash can, deputies found a turkey baster. Some murder trials had a gun as a murder weapon. Some had knives. Some had mundane items known in the parlance of law enforcement as "blunt objects." This case wasn't like those, he said. This one had a turkey baster. "The evidence will show that the turkey baster contained traces of antifreeze, the defendant's fingerprints, and the victim's DNA at the tip," Fitzpatrick said.

The DA said that a man on the verge of suicide had his choice as to how to bring down the curtain. Almost everyone chose a method that was free of pain. Yet, this death had been the very opposite, ultimately painful. Death via antifreeze poisoning is a horrible, horrible way to die. Murder, yes. Suicide, no. Who would die of antifreeze poisoning when there was a shotgun under the bed?

The actual drinking of the antifreeze was not that unpleasant. It had a sweet taste. In its initial stages, the symptoms of this type of poisoning mimicked drunkenness. The victim felt woozy and perhaps had difficulty going to the bathroom. Then it got worse, much worse. Liquor, booze, slowed down the poisoning effects of the antifreeze.

"In fact, booze is the antidote," Fitzpatrick said. "If

a person were to walk into the emergency room today and say, 'I just tried to kill myself with ethylene glycol,' they would give him an alcohol drip. When your liver has a choice whether to digest ethylene glycol or Jack Daniel's, your liver picks the Jack Daniel's."

With enough booze in the system, the poison went into the body as ethylene glycol and came out as ethylene glycol. But when it didn't, and the body tried to process that ethylene glycol, a hideously painful series of chemical reactions commenced inside the digestive system. The liver turned the ethylene glycol into glycolic acid, which crystallized in your kidneys, and your brain, and some of your other organs, and it shut them down. Usually, the crystals in the kidneys were the fatal ones, and the victims died of renal failure.

"So you will be asking yourself, 'Why would David Castor lie there, dying, in agony, for three days, when at any second he could have ended his suffering, and his life, with a shotgun blast?'" Fitzpatrick challenged the jury. And mixing the antifreeze with alcohol only made death come slower and more painfully.

The DA then shifted back in time to the death of Stacey's first husband, Michael Wallace, who reportedly had a fatal heart attack on January 11, 2000. It was only years later, after his body was exhumed, that police learned Michael Wallace had died the same way as David Castor, by antifreeze poisoning. The truth could have been discovered years earlier, right after Michael Wallace had died, if his widow, the defendant, had requested an autopsy, but she hadn't done that.

"And, yes, Stacey Castor collected insurance money after her first husband's death," he said.

Fitzpatrick told the story of the attempted murder of Ashley Wallace, how Stacey called 911 and told the dispatcher that her daughter had tried to kill herself with spiked vodka, how she allowed Ashley to sleep for twenty hours without checking on her. In fact, she never did check on her. How it was Ashley's kid sister, Bree, who eventually investigated Ashley's well-being and, finding her in distress, sounded the alarm that resulted in the defendant's 911 call.

Fitzpatrick had had the "suicide note" blown up and mounted on a two-by-three-foot board, which he set on a stand facing the jury. "She forged a suicide note and tried to kill her own daughter," he said. Fitzpatrick called that note the most important piece of evidence in the case. "Somebody tried to dumb down this note. Somebody tried to purposefully mislead the reader as to who the author of this note was." How did he know? Because somebody had done a sloppy job of it. Words were spelled correctly in one part of the note and incorrectly in others. The mistakes were not consistent.

The note's author was preoccupied not only with Ashley's guilt, but with Stacey's innocence as well. He quoted from the note, daring the jurors to identify the author: *No one was ever supposed to know, Mommy. And now they do and they think you did it, but you didn't do it, it was me,*" he read.

Fitzpatrick guessed that the note very well might be one-of-a-kind. Unique. And that was because it wasn't a suicide note at all. It was a forgery, an attempt to make it look like Ashley had confessed to killing Mike and David, and then attempted suicide.

He read the note aloud for the jurors, all seven hundred words. He stopped after reading the note's reference to rat poison. There was the spot where we knew for sure that the note's author had to be the actual killer of Michael Wallace, for only the killer and the authorities knew there had been rat poison found during Mike's autopsy. When he had finished reading the note, he said, "Somebody wrote that letter and it wasn't—ladies and gentlemen, the evidence will show—it wasn't Ashley Wallace," Fitzpatrick said.

Fitzpatrick told the jury that one week before the note was discovered the defendant was interviewed by Detective Spinelli, who heard her use a very unusual word, a word he'd never heard before: "antifree." Spinelli documented that word usage days before the note was found.

"Ask yourselves a question," the DA said. "You've just heard the note. Is it dated? It is." Then reading from the note again, he said, "*When the cops came to my school today.* There's the date. You are going to hear proof that the only time the cops came to Ashley's school, rightfully or wrongfully, was on Wednesday, September 12, 2007." He repeated that date slowly so it would sink in. Ashley had been rushed to the hospital on the morning of September 14.

Fitzpatrick told the jury that they would be hearing from emergency room doctors who treated Ashley for poisoning, and they would testify that never before had they seen such a smorgasbord of chemicals and drugs thrown into one human being's body. The jury would hear about the massive efforts that went into saving her life, how close she came to death, and proof—from the very witnesses who were there—that when Ashley Wallace came to and was able to carry on a coherent conversation, one of the sheriff's detectives there tried to trick her and tried to get her to say that she had written the note and taken the pills. With no guile whatsoever, she looked at him and said, "What note? What pills? Mom gave me an Ambien pill. I didn't write any note. I didn't try to kill myself. I just had my first day of school. Why would I? I have a boyfriend."

Next topic: computers. "We seized the defendant's computer from her home on Wetzel Road. You hit that erase button, folks," Fitzpatrick said, shaking his head. "It don't erase. It goes somewhere. And these computer guys are going to tell you about it, because an amazing discovery was found on the computer." He explained that the note found on Ashley's bed wasn't there, it had been erased, but two "practice notes" were found. The computer experts would prove that the note was generated sometime prior to 2:37 P.M. on Wednesday, September 12, 2007. On the other end of the spectrum, the note had to have been written after 8:40 A.M. on September 12, when Ashley called her mother to tell her she had just been visited by two cops at her school, because there was a reference in the note to that visit. So, while Ashley was at school, someone wrote that note, printed it out, and that someone placed that note in Ashley's bedroom at the appropriate time. Where was Ashley? "She was at school," Fitzpatrick said. "In fact, her own mother will corroborate that." Where was the defendant? "You listen to the proof. We'll show you where she was," the prosecutor said with a knowing smile.

The DA summarized the bogus-will charge and

added, "So there you have it, ladies and gentlemen. The people's case in a nutshell. I apologize for going on so long."

Fitzpatrick asked the jury to give the case a "clear-thinking and careful" consideration. He said he had faith in them. He knew they would scrutinize, analyze, and probe the evidence carefully.

"This is a tale of two women who will be forever tied together by biology and joined inexorably at this trial by murder."

When the jury was through listening to and weighing all of the evidence, Fitzpatrick said, "You will have no choice but to do your duty and stand up and shout as loud as you can, 'Mrs. Castor, you are a murderer and you tried to kill your own daughter, and for that you will pay.' Thank you."

After a ten-minute recess, it was the defense's turn to set out their objectives: "Ladies and gentlemen of the jury, I also want to take a moment before I begin my opening here to thank you for putting in your time and effort. I want to thank you for your attention during jury selection this morning," Charles Keller said.

Keller spoke to the jury with a haunted expression, as if he'd risen up from the bowels of hell to address them. And the horror was, if they didn't do their job the way they should—the way he thought they should—a miscarriage of justice would occur, an innocent woman might be sent away to prison for the rest of her life. If that didn't fill the jury's souls with horror, then they weren't human. That was what Keller's expression said.

He said that often when he spoke to his friends about jury duty, it was their opinion that most people dreaded it, but he found exactly the opposite to be true. Juries he talked to and practiced in front of enjoyed their experience. They relished the opportunity to serve their community in such an important way. And he hoped that this jury would find their experience fulfilling as well.

"Now I am going to ask you for a few things. I know you are going to do a fantastic job. That's why we picked you. If we didn't think you were up to the job, you wouldn't be here today."

He said his first request of the panel was that it be fair, and that it collectively keep an *open mind*. He couldn't stress that enough.

"'Fair' means that the prosecution has to prove all of the elements of these crimes, and they have to prove them all beyond a reasonable doubt. They have to prove that Stacey Castor committed these crimes, and they have to prove it beyond a reasonable doubt."

Keller said that he had listened along with them to Mr. Fitzpatrick's opening statement and he thought "impressive" was the best word to describe it. The defense attorney said he'd done a little research. He'd spoken to a number of lawyers who'd tried cases against this district attorney. They agreed Fitzpatrick was a fantastic lawyer, a great speaker. But, as the DA himself had explained during his opening, what he said was not evidence. By the same token, what Keller said was not evidence. "His words and my words are not proof. They, in fact, do not mean a thing," Keller said.

Though *not evidence,* an opening statement was like

a road map for the jury, so they were not hanging out in space wondering what was going on. Evidence could be complicated, with lots of names and dates and places, and the opening statement, if it did its job, would give the jury context by which to understand the evidence, a skeletal framework upon which to hang the flesh of evidence until the full body of the crime was revealed.

The rules said the defense did not have to give an opening statement.

"But we have decided to give an opening statement, anyway," Keller said. "Do you know why? Because we don't have anything to hide."

They should expect from the prosecution a mountain of evidence. Some of which did not point at Stacey Castor alone. He would be "disingenuous" if he argued that none of this evidence gave anyone any reason to suspect that Stacey Castor had done anything. He wasn't going to suggest that. He suggested, rather, that after the jury heard all of that evidence, there were some things they needed to consider.

"First: opportunity," Keller said. There was opportunity for, actually, three people to have been the person who committed these crimes. "You will hear that two of those persons are the likely suspects. But you will only hear that one of them confessed to it. And the person who confessed to it was Ashley Wallace."

Keller asked the jury to back up for a minute: "Let's talk about Michael Wallace, Stacey's first husband, Ashley's father." The evidence would show that Ashley was there and present and had every opportunity to do to Michael Wallace exactly what she wrote in her suicide note.

Keller had his own visual aid. His needed projecting, so he was working A/V equipment. The note was projected onto a screen.

He said there would be no evidence excluding Ashley. He complained that the case against Stacey was completely circumstantial. The jury again looked at the note.

"I want you to put what the prosecution said about the note out of your minds for a moment and look at it with a fresh point of view," he said. He would show that the note was not written by the defendant, and that it was an actual suicide note. And that Stacey's spoiled and ungrateful daughter, Ashley Wallace, was the one who input it on the family computer.

"We'll talk about when this note could have been written," Keller said. "And whether there are multiple drafts, and whether it was printed or whether it was saved—you'll hear all about that, and you'll hear that the evidence is just not as clear-cut as the people would like you to believe." Ashley, the evidence would show, had "every opportunity" to do all of the things she claimed to have done in her letter.

Keller spoke for a moment about the events at Auburn Memorial Hospital after Mike Wallace had been declared dead there. The DA, he said, was going to show that Stacey Castor didn't want an autopsy.

"Well," Keller added, "what the evidence is actually going to show was that that was not the whole story.

"There are just certain things about this case that don't make sense if Stacey is the killer," he added. "On the flip side of that, you will hear evidence, and when you hear it, you will say that the evidence makes sense only if Ashley Wallace is the killer."

He noted that when Stacey's first husband died, doctors didn't even suspect foul play, so there was no reason for Stacey to suspect it, either, no reason for her to request an autopsy.

He acknowledged that Stacey and David Castor argued during the last days of David's life, but it was nothing earth-shattering, nothing volcanic. "Was it the Mount St. Helens of arguments? No," Keller said.

Stacey's behavior during the last weekend of David's life was consistent with that of an innocent person. The prosecution would ask why, if David was so sick for so long, Stacey had not called 911 earlier. Her answer was simple. She thought the man was drunk, drunk out of his mind, and that he would sleep it off eventually.

She acted, Keller said, like any woman would act after having a fight with her husband. She got away from him so there could be a cooling-off period, and only after she realized that there was something wrong, did she call 911.

"Ladies and gentlemen of the jury, there is nothing about the evidence that shows Stacey killed David Castor," Keller said. "The prosecution's case is circumstantial, an assembly of guesses and theories."

Sure, David Castor took out a life insurance policy and named his wife as the beneficiary. Sure, his business was not doing particularly well. But these just weren't the kinds of things that you kill over.

The police and the district attorney's office, Keller claimed, had their minds made up that Stacey was guilty from the start, and they never adequately considered the alternatives. They had Stacey's phone tapped and they taped her conversations—but did they tape the phone conversations of Ashley Wallace? No, they did not.

He also tried to poke holes in the prosecution's case by denigrating police investigators. After about twenty-five minutes of speaking, Keller concluded with, "You find that none of the evidence in this case was as clear-cut as the people would have you believe. After looking carefully at all of the evidence, I'm certain you will decide that the wrong person is sitting in that chair," Keller predicted. "The guilty person is Ashley Wallace, and not Stacey Castor."

The judge declared that testimony would begin first thing Wednesday morning and ordered all of the parties to be back in the courtroom at that time. With a bang of his gavel, Judge Fahey adjourned court for the day.

15

Ashley on the Hot Seat

On Wednesday, January 14, 2009, everyone dealt with a cold and snowy commute. Now inside and warm from what was a pretty typical Syracuse winter day, there was a problem with a male juror—Juror #12. The morning session began with the jury outside the courtroom.

It came to light over the weekend that Juror #12's wife was a counselor at the county jail. Potentially he could learn information regarding the defendant from sources other than trial testimony. Judge Fahey promptly dismissed the juror, who was replaced by a female alternate. That done, the slightly altered jury was brought in.

"The people may call their first witness," Judge Fahey said.

That witness, as it turned out, was just an appetizer for the main course to follow. "The prosecution calls Kieran Shields to the witness stand," the district attorney said.

Shields testified that he was an employee of Unum Insurance, an Ivy Leaguer (Dartmouth), and a lawyer (University of Maine School of Law).

"Are you familiar with the name Stacey Castor, wife of David Castor?"

"Yes, she took out a policy with the company I work for," Shields said.

"Please tell the jury what type of policy it was," the DA said.

"It was a supplemental life insurance policy for fifty thousand dollars with her group insurance at Rural/Metro," the witness said.

"On whose life did she take out the policy, Mr. Shields?"

"On the life of her husband, David Castor," Shields stated.

"No further questions," Bill Fitzpatrick said.

"Chuck?" Judge Fahey said, looking in the defense table's direction.

"No questions, Judge," Keller said.

And thus the stage was set. The appetizer consumed, Fitzpatrick dished up the entrée.

If the prosecution had a "key witness," it was the tense but determined-looking young woman who now strode through the back doors to the front of the courtroom. Ashley Wallace had her hair pulled back tightly into a bun. Careful observers noticed that Stacey and Ashley were wearing almost identical makeup, eyeliner heavier on the bottom and the same pale pink shade of lipstick. They were in the same room for the first time since the emergency room.

Ashley was wearing a dark blue suit. A brighter blue blouse was visible, covering the top of her chest. As she finished taking the oath, she blew out her cheeks to release some stress and sat, white-knuckling the armrests to the witness chair. With taut muscles and suppressed emotions, Ashley radiated strong-victim vibes.

Fitzpatrick began: "Ashley, did you have a good relationship with your father?"

"Yes. Yes, I did."

"Did you love your father?"

"Absolutely."

Fitzpatrick asked Ashley to describe her last memories of her father.

Ashley said that he was sick on the couch and she was about to leave to pick up her little sister at school. "I saw him move his arm and take a breath, and he didn't move again after that, so I thought he was just sleeping," Ashley sobbed.

"How old were you when your father died, Ashley?"

"I—I was twelve," she replied.

"Okay, now let's switch subjects—shall we—to your stepfather, David Castor. Do you remember meeting David for the first time?"

"Yes."

"What was your opinion of him when you met him?"

"I didn't like him very much."

Ashley said she cut David some slack, even though she didn't like him, because he wanted to be with her mom and that meant "he wanted to be a part of my life as well."

During the last weekend of David Castor's life, Ashley said, she was working most of the time. She was in the house a few times that weekend, was aware that her stepfather was ill, but at no time was she ever alone with him.

"During the times you were home that weekend, did you even see your stepfather?" Fitzpatrick asked.

"No," Ashley replied.

Ashley testified that while at work on the Monday of her stepfather's death, she had repeatedly tried to phone her mother. A few times, someone answered her mother's phone, but it was always a friend, who would never explain what was going on, only that her mother couldn't come to the phone right then. Finally she called and Stacey answered.

"My mom gets on the phone and she sounds like she is crying. And I go, 'What's wrong?' She goes, 'I have to tell you something, but I don't want you to get upset because I am not there to comfort you.' I said, 'What's wrong?' And she said, 'I have to tell you that David killed himself.'"

"And what did you do then?" Fitzpatrick asked.

"I just broke down," Ashley replied.

Fitzpatrick then told Ashley to move ahead in time and focus on occurrences starting a few days before she was poisoned.

"A few days before it [her poisoning] happened, two detectives came to my school," she said. She was just starting college, she explained.

She arrived at school and was signing in on a sign-in sheet when a lady from the school's administration came and got her and took her to the detectives.

The witness didn't have to explain. The jury understood that the embarrassment was extreme: to go to a new school and then be publicly separated from the other students because the cops wanted to talk to her.

"What did the detectives say to you?"

"They asked me questions about the deaths of my father and stepfather."

Content in the belief that her father died of a heart attack and her stepfather of suicide—after all, that was what the death certificates said—she was stunned to realize that police now believed both men had been murdered.

She had only recently learned that her father's body had been exhumed, and that had angered her, disturbing a man she loved who was resting at peace. She knew police thought her mom did it, which only made her mom seem like a victim and the cops like bullies, as far as she was concerned. She testified that she had called her mother and told her about the detectives, and later that day her mother came and got her.

At that point, there was a break in the testimony as some audio equipment was set up. A tape was played of Ashley's phone conversation with her mother after police came to Ashley's school to talk to her.

Although the tape was recorded by a police wiretap, its quality was poor and it was difficult for spectators in the courtroom to understand what was being said.

But the jury got the gist of it. Ashley complained that the cops had interrogated her, when all she wanted to do was sign in for her class. Stacey was sympathetic.

When Stacey had Ashley home, the mother did

something very strange—something she'd never done before. It came out of left field.

"What did your mother do?"

Ashley explained that her mother suggested that, since they both had been under such stress and were suffering from such a level of anxiety, they should both get drunk.

"What were her actual words?"

"She said, 'Let's get drunk because we've had a hard day.'"

She explained that this was something new. Her mother had allowed her to drink "like, one beer" in the past, but then she had hovered over and watched her drink it. This was something else. Ashley's mom went to the store and bought a six-pack of Smirnoff Ice and pushed to get her daughter drunk. Ashley remembered that the first drink was prepared by her mother and was served in a glass.

"Did you have a drink?"

"Yes."

"Did it taste normal to you?"

"No. It had just a weird taste. I said, 'Mom, this doesn't taste right.'"

"What did she say?"

"She goes, 'Oh, that must just be the watermelon flavoring in it.'"

After the first drink, Ashley testified, she was allowed to drink the Smirnoff Ice straight out of the twelve-ounce bottle. After drinking for a while, Ashley began to feel sick and went to lie down.

"I was light-headed and I threw up," she testified. Her mother gave her a pill to take and explained to her that it would "help her sleep it off."

Although this incident might have been a murder attempt, with Ashley saving herself by promptly vomiting, that wasn't the only explanation. The prosecution made it clear this event could have been a "trial run" for the actual murder attempt to come.

Stacey, the prosecution inferred, was perhaps attempting to gauge the level of Ashley's compliance, to determine if she would drink something her mother told her to drink, even if it didn't taste good.

Ashley testified that she woke up in the morning after getting drunk with her mother for the first time, and although she didn't feel her best, she made it to school for her one morning class that day, then returned home.

"What did your mother say to you when you got home, Ashley?" Fitzpatrick asked.

"She said, 'Let's get drunk. Let's just get totally drunk,'" Ashley testified.

"Did she give a specific reason for why she wanted to get drunk?"

"She said, 'Let's celebrate your twenty-first birthday because I might not be around for it.'" When Ashley asked her what she meant by that, Stacey said that she might be in jail by the time her oldest daughter turned twenty-one.

Ashley testified that she was shocked by her mother's suggestion.

"Did it ever occur to you that any of this would be bad for you?"

"No. I was a teenager and my mother was allowing me to drink alcohol," Ashley said, although she was actually twenty at the time. How cool was that? What teenager would have refused such an offer?

Her mother went to the liquor store and bought

real vodka this time. Though Ashley did not accompany her mother to the store, a surveillance camera confirmed that Stacey was at the store buying the vodka at the time Ashley said she did. On the second day, Stacey once again fixed Ashley's first drink for her.

"Did she tell you what was in the drink?" Fitzpatrick inquired.

"Yes. She said it had vodka, orange juice, and Sprite," Ashley testified.

"What container was the drink in?"

"A big cup with a spoon and a straw." She described the drink as looking "chalky."

"What did you do next?"

"I took a sip, and thought it tasted horrible. Not bad. *Horrible.* I told her, 'I can't drink this.'"

"Could you describe the taste?"

"No. I just know it made me gag."

"What did you say?"

"I said, 'Mom, this doesn't taste good.'"

"What did she say?"

"She goes, 'There's probably just too much vodka in it.'"

Ashley testified that Stacey had an idea to get Ashley to drink it, even though it didn't taste right.

"'I'm going to teach you a little trick,'" Ashley quoted her mother as saying. "She said it was a trick she had learned when she was a kid and she had to drink something she hated the flavor of."

So Ashley did as she was told. She pushed the straw deep into her mouth, down toward her throat, behind her tongue, and drank as she slowly counted to ten.

"Did you continue to drink?"

"Yes."

"Did you finish everything in the cup?"

"Yes."

"Ashley, I want you to explain to the jury. If the liquid in the cup tasted so bad, why did you drink it?" the district attorney inquired.

"Because I *trusted* her!" Ashley said.

"How did you feel after you drank the drink your mother had given you?"

"I felt terrible. I felt like I was in a tunnel," Ashley said. As she had done the day before, she went into her bedroom and stretched out on her bed.

"What is the next thing you recall?"

"I woke up in the hospital and there were detectives there." She could hear questions being shouted at her. They were right in her face, booming voices.

By this time, the jury could hear that Ashley's emotions were affecting her voice. Her jaw was set defiantly and her back was straight with the strength of her will. There would be no collapse on the stand for Ashley. But her voice continued to rise in pitch and volume. It swelled with anger into an alto whine. Emotionally, she regressed.

At one point, she was unable to continue, and Fitzpatrick gave her a moment to compose herself. He handed her a Kleenex. She used it to dab at her face a few times; then she held it crumpled in a clenched fist.

"What did the detectives say to you?" Fitzpatrick queried.

Ashley's voice lowered and she tried to sound gruff in imitation of those voices: "'What did you do? What did you take? What did you write in that note?'" Then she returned to her own voice and added, "But I didn't know what they were talking about, because I didn't write a note."

Fitzpatrick handed her a copy of the note. It was typed and on two pages, stapled together.

"Do you recognize the note?"

"No."

"Had you ever seen the note before?"

"No."

"Did you write the note?"

"No!"

Ashley dabbed at her upper lip and nose with the crumpled facial tissue.

"You are absolutely sure?"

"I am one hundred percent positive that I did not write the note."

"When you lived with your mother, your step-father, and your sister, there was a computer in the house?"

"Yes."

"During the days before your overdose, did you see anyone using that computer?"

"Yes, I saw my mother typing on it."

"Did you attempt suicide?"

"No."

"Did you poison your father with antifreeze?" Fitzpatrick asked.

"No, I did not!"

There were tears in the witness's eyes. The crumpled Kleenex now dabbed at the outside corner of her left eye.

"Did you poison your stepfather with antifreeze?"

"No, I did not!"

"No further questions, Your Honor."

* * *

For three hours she'd been on the stand, stretched to the limit, yet holding together, near hysteria but getting the job done. For the entire three hours, Ashley and Stacey never made eye contact.

There is perhaps a chance that Ashley snuck a quick peek in her mother's direction, but Stacey never looked back. Stacey sat at her desk impassively, eyes downward, never looking up, occasionally resting her head on her hand.

As Ashley testified, her maternal grandmother sat in the back row of the spectator section, teeth clenched, not believing a word the girl uttered.

Ashley would have the world believe she was some sort of robot, who followed commands without thinking, when in reality—and you only had to know Ashley for a short time to figure this out—Ashley was an extremely contrary person.

"I don't believe that Stacey ever put anything in a drink," Ashley's grandmother would later say. "If you are twenty years old and the drink tastes bad, it doesn't make any difference if your mother tells you to drink it. You are not going to drink it. Not if it really tasted that bad."

Anticipating a lengthy cross-examination, the judge recessed court for the lunch break. After eating, everyone returned to the courtroom, and Ashley was cross-examined by Keller.

For the remainder of the court day, Chuck Keller tried to pick apart Ashley's version of the events surrounding the murders of her father and stepfather, as well as her version of the day she ingested poison.

"You were aware that your father used drugs, correct?" Keller asked.

"Yes."

"How did you know?"

"I told my mother that I smelled a smell I hadn't smelled before. She told me what it was."

Ashley was asked about the day of Michael Wallace's death, how she had been the last to see him alive, how she saw him moving his arms in an unusual way, and making faces while lying on the living-room couch, and how she had done nothing to help him because she had to leave and pick up her little sister, Bree, at school. That was the version she had given to investigators, but earlier, when asked by hospital personnel if her father showed any signs of illness, Ashley had said that he had not, and that he was just snoring when she left to get Bree.

"Your memory changes over time," Keller noted. "It doesn't stay the same."

Keller asked the witness if her father, Michael Wallace, ever abused her physically, and she said that he had spanked her three times in her whole life for being bad, and that was it.

Keller asked Ashley if she got along with David Castor, and she said she did not.

"Did you ever hear your mother and your stepfather arguing behind closed doors?"

"Yes."

"Did you ever hear him make any comments regarding his role in your life as a dad?"

"Yes. He said that he didn't want to get to know

me, that he was not my father, and he didn't want to be my father."

"Did you ever tell any of your relatives that David Castor had touched you inappropriately?"

"No."

Keller showed Ashley a letter and asked if she had written it. She said she had. It was a letter from Ashley to a former boyfriend in which she complained about David Castor, and that, because of him, she didn't think she could live at home for much longer. The day she moved out her mother "would be sorry."

"The note says, *Sometimes he is so lucky I can't punch him in the face.* Did you write that, Ashley?"

"Yes."

"And you were referring to your stepfather, David Castor, weren't you? It was his face you wanted to punch, correct?"

"Yes." She kept her chin high. She'd already admitted she didn't like the guy.

Keller then played a tape recording for the court, a wiretap of a phone conversation between Ashley and yet another former boyfriend. On the tape, Ashley could be heard complaining about police thinking her mother was a murderer.

"It's not fair," Ashley said on the tape. "She didn't do anything. That asshole killed himself."

Moving to the time of Ashley's OD, Keller asked, "Did you argue with your mother about getting drunk before noon?"

"Yeah, for, like, five seconds."

Keller moved to Ashley's near-death experience.

"So you woke up one morning and you were in the hospital, right?" Keller inquired.

"Yeah," Ashley said.

The please-help-me tone she had emoted under direct examination was now tamped down and infused with indignation. *This is contrary Ashley,* Judi thought in the back row. *For all to see.*

Keller attempted to get Ashley to nail down just how many vodka mixers she had drunk before she was found near death from poisoning. Ashley, of course, maintained that she'd drunk far fewer than Stacey said she had.

During the back-and-forth about numbers, Judge Fahey, looking for a laugh, interjected, "You're making me thirsty."

Not long afterward, Judge Fahey got a signal from one of the jurors and declared a ten-minute recess.

"Members of various law enforcement agencies, did they ask you if you'd ever hurt yourself before?" Keller asked when court was back in session.

"Yes."

"Members of the district attorney's office, did they ask you if you'd thought about hurting yourself before?"

"Yes."

"Do you remember what you told them?"

"I told them that there might be a note." She was referring to a note she'd written to a boy. In that note, Ashley discussed a certain fascination with dying and death. Ashley knew the defense team had possession of the note, so there was no point in denying it.

She said yes, she'd written the note on a day when she was feeling bad because her dad died. Keller asked her if she wanted to give a quick read of the note on the copy she'd been provided, to refresh her recollection as to what it said. Ashley said that wouldn't be necessary.

"The note you hold in your hand, to whom was it intended?" Keller asked.

"I had wrote a note to an ex-boyfriend," Ashley replied.

"And isn't it true in this note, you admitted to two previous suicide attempts?"

Ashley now took a moment to look at the typed copy she held in her hands. Regarding suicide, the note said, *I almost tried to do it twice but each time I thought about my sister and how I couldn't have her here without someone to protect her, or someone for her to look up to sometimes.* She glanced ever so quickly at the top page, flipped it, and then glanced ever more quickly at the second page.

"Yes," she said softly.

Keller then drew Ashley's attention to the suicide note found at the head of the bed soon after Ashley was discovered poisoned. Keller suggested that since Ashley admitted to writing about suicide before, she might have written the other note as well.

"In fact, you had tried to commit suicide before, hadn't you?" Keller said.

"Yes," Ashley admitted.

"How many times?"

"Twice, but there was no third time, and I didn't write that note."

Having induced Ashley to admit that her relationship with her stepfather was wholly adversarial, the defense attorney smelled blood and moved on to an even more sensitive subject: "Your father, he had a pet name for your sister, Bree, didn't he?"

"Yes."

"Your father called your sister 'Princess,' didn't he?" Keller asked.

"Yes," Ashley concurred.

"Did your father have a nickname for you?"

"Not that I recall."

Keller couldn't stand still during his cross. He paced behind his lectern, his head still, his deep-set eyes wide and always on Ashley.

"Did it bother you that your father had a pet name for Bree, but not for you?"

"No."

"You were sexually assaulted by David Castor when you were thirteen, weren't you?"

"No."

And with that thought in the jurors' heads, Chuck Keller called it quits with Ashley. He'd established his points. She had the motive, and the opportunity to commit murder—plus, a history of feeling suicidal.

On the other side, Bill Fitzpatrick was likewise feeling good about Ashley's appearance on the stand. She had been absolutely believable. He saw no reason why the jury would turn on her.

The day was not through. After Ashley left the witness stand, there was a short break and the people continued with their case, presenting a Mike Wallace witness questioned by Christine Garvey.

Ian Trainor, an EMT from Weedsport, New York, discussed Wallace's death, establishing for the jury that Stacey had a history of husbands dropping dead from antifreeze poisoning. Wallace's drool had contained a brown powdery substance, which, at first, reminded him of coffee grounds, but turned out actually to be blood.

"In the course of your duties, you have seen patients having heart attacks?"

"Yes."

"Dying of heart attacks?"

"Yes."

"Did Michael Wallace appear to you to be a man dying of a heart attack?"

"No, he did not."

The prosecution completed the first day of testimony by presenting two more witnesses connected with Michael Wallace. But these were not technicians. In fact, their testimony could not have been more personal.

The first was Michael Wallace's sister, Rosemary Corbett, who testified about the day in 2000 when her brother had died. Rosemary said she'd been close to her brother, Michael, and saw him frequently, including during the weeks before his death. His appearance changed during that time, she said. He grew puffy, and his respiratory system audibly deteriorated. He was short of breath and had developed a chronic, hacking cough.

After Michael died, Rosemary talked with Stacey. Their relationship was close as well—Rosemary and Stacey's. Still, in the hospital, Rosemary asked Stacey if she was going to request an autopsy for Michael. Stacey said no.

Michael's mom was also asked, and she said she didn't think an autopsy was necessary. Both women said that the doctor said it must have been a heart attack, and that was good enough for them.

* * *

During cross-examination, Keller made Rosemary admit that brother Michael was no angel. Hardly. He smoked pot.

"Had Michael Wallace ever been in prison?"

"Yes."

"On what charge was he convicted?"

"Driving while intoxicated."

Rosemary said that she had been close to her brother during his first marriage as well, before he was married to Stacey. She admitted that she'd heard her brother abused his first wife, but had no firsthand knowledge of that.

The last witness of the day was Stacey's former sister-in-law Melanne Keim, who took the stand and repeated much of Rosemary's testimony. Questioned by Garvey, she admitted that Michael Wallace did not have a healthy lifestyle, and everyone who knew him well knew it. That was the reason no one jumped to the conclusion that foul play had anything to do with his death. He seemed like a likely candidate to drop dead, and that, everyone assumed, was precisely what had happened. She also repeated for the jury that both Stacey and Michael's mother had said no to an autopsy and had believed, without question, that Michael had died of a heart attack.

Nervous enough about testifying without the whole world watching, Keim requested that the courtroom cameras be turned off during her testimony. Judge Fahey granted her wishes.

16

Parade of Law

On Thursday, January 15, the prosecution presented a series of law enforcement officials and employees, each of whom described his or her role in developing the case against Stacey Castor.

The morning's testimony began with John Deisz, an Onondaga County 911 dispatcher, who established for the prosecution a chain of evidence for tapes that would be played for the jury.

Deisz testified that he personally provided the police with audiotapes of Stacey making emergency phone calls on August 22, 2005, regarding David Castor, and on September 14, 2007, regarding Ashley Wallace's overdose.

Sergeant Robert Willoughby testified that he was the officer who first responded to the scene of David Castor's death. Willoughby was aware at first of the courtroom cameras, but he soon discovered that testifying demanded full concentration. He didn't want to screw up his testimony, and there was no time to worry about being on national TV. "I thought the cameras were going to bother me more than they did," the sergeant recalled.

During direct examination conducted by the ADA, Willoughby related how the 911 operator received a distress call from a home on Wetzel Road in the town of Clay, and how, after talking to the woman making the call, he went to the scene. It was he who discovered David Castor's body.

He said that when he arrived at the scene in his patrol car, the defendant was sitting outside on a folding lawn chair. She told him that her husband, David, was in the locked master bedroom and that he was not responding. Willoughby entered the house and knocked on the door to the master bedroom several times and heard nothing.

Christine Garvey asked if the defendant was sticking close to him as he did this. He said she was not, that she didn't enter the house at all when he first went inside, and even when she did, she only made it as far as the kitchen. He tried to open the door and verified that it was locked. After circling the house in a vain attempt to see in the bedroom window, he reentered the house.

"Did the defendant follow you inside this time?"

"No."

"What did she do?"

"She went into the garage," Willoughby testified. "I kicked the bedroom door open."

"What did you find inside the bedroom, Sergeant Willoughby?" Fitzpatrick asked.

"I saw David Castor lying across the bed. He was deceased," the witness said.

"In what position was David Castor's body?"

"Facedown on the bed. There was a nightstand right next to the bed. There was a bottle of brandy on it. There was also a pair of drinking glasses, one empty, one partially full."

"What was in the partially full glass?"

"Some sort of green liquid."

"What else did you find during your initial search of the bedroom?"

"I discovered a jug of antifreeze on the floor next to the bed," Willoughby said.

"Sergeant Willoughby, after you made these observations, did you make notifications?" Garvey asked.

"Yes. When I realized we had more than a simple death, I backed out of the room, notified my lieutenant, and made notifications for detectives and evidence technicians."

When they arrived, Willoughby testified, he followed orders. "I was told to search a trash container in the kitchen," he said.

"What were you supposed to be looking for?"

"A receipt for some purchases that the defendant said she made at Wal-Mart."

"What, if anything, did you find in the kitchen garbage can?"

"I found a turkey baster."

"Where in the basket was the baster? Did you have to move a lot of items to discover it?"

"No, I only had to move a couple of things. It was close to the top. I started digging through, looking at all of the papers on top, checking for the receipt I'd been told to look for."

"And it [the turkey baster] caught your eye?"

"Yes, it struck me as odd that it was in the trash," Willoughby said.

"Why odd?" Garvey asked.

"Well, there didn't seem to be anything wrong with it," the witness answered. "Usually, when you throw a turkey baster away, it's because the bulb is rotten, or you left it on the stove and the plastic melted. This one, though, looked brand-new, so that caught my attention."

"Other than its seeming newness, did you observe anything else about the turkey baster?"

"Yes, I could see that there were small droplets of a liquid inside of it."

"After first observing the turkey baster, what did you do, Sergeant Willoughby?"

"I asked that it be photographed in the position I found it, and, that done, I picked it up, pulled off the rubber bulb, and gave it a sniff."

"What, if anything, did you smell?"

"I could smell some sort of alcohol in it," Willoughby said.

On cross-examination, Chuck Keller made it clear that he felt Willoughby's interpretation of Stacey's behavior at the scene of David's death was ill-considered. Yes, she had stayed outside when Willoughby first went inside the house, and she stood in the garage when he kicked the door open. Didn't he want her to stay back? After all, she'd said there was a shotgun under the bed. Wasn't he concerned that her life might be in danger?

"She didn't say that to me," Willoughby said. "She made no mention of a shotgun to me."

* * *

Deputy Lawrence Knapp testified that he was the crime scene photographer who had created images of David Castor's death scene, and he had taken the photos of the turkey baster in the kitchen trash basket in the position in which Sergeant Willoughby had found it.

As photos of Castor's body sprawled across the bed were shown in open court, Knapp testified as to what the photos depicted. The photos were in color. The deceased's extremities were starting to purple. The vomit was dark brown.

In addition to taking photos, Knapp also recovered evidence from the crime scene. He testified that it was he who had confiscated the drinking glass that had the defendant's fingerprints on it and contained antifreeze, and the jug of antifreeze that was found on the floor of the bedroom underneath David Castor's overhanging feet.

Knapp testified that during the initial hours of the investigation, the prime theory among investigators was that David Castor had committed suicide.

His testimony was interrupted when the back doors of the courtroom burst open and a force of security people ran in, causing much confusion. When it was sorted out, Judge Fahey announced that it was a false alarm, that somebody in the courtroom had hit the "silent alarm" button by mistake.

Detective Diane Leshinski testified that she had a master's degree in criminal justice from SUNY at Albany, that before becoming a detective in the Felony Crimes Unit of the Onondaga Sheriff's Criminal Investigation Division, she had been a road patrol deputy for the sheriff, and before that had been a police officer with the Mohawk Police Department (MPD).

Under direct examination, Leshinski described her conversations with the defendant on the day of and the day after David Castor's death. The first took place at a neighbor's house, only minutes after David was declared dead. Leshinski said that the widow seemed sincerely distraught over her husband's death, but calm enough to give a coherent statement.

That initial interview with Mrs. Castor went well. Leshinski had been in similar situations with new widows, and getting information out of them was a struggle, but that wasn't the case with Stacey. She was clear and concise.

Leshinski described for the court how the defendant had discussed her marital woes, how David was jealous of Stacey's kids and all of the attention she paid them. Stacey had said that she was afraid of David. The fights they'd had were repetitive and got worse when David drank, as he'd been doing that weekend.

The defendant had been specific when describing her final argument with her husband. She had not wanted to go on a vacation because she didn't want to leave her youngest daughter home alone.

During that same conversation, Leshinski said, Stacy had described the scene on Saturday when she found her husband kneeling naked next to the bed, covered in vomit, and how she'd gotten him to his feet, only to have him reel and fall, hitting his head on one of the night tables. She said she'd taken him into the bathroom, where he'd reeled again, this time ripping part of a towel rack out of the wall. She struggled to keep him on his hands and knees, with his head over the tub, and somehow she managed to wash his hair. After pulling the vomit-covered sheets off the bed, Stacey said she'd tried to get him back into bed. But it was a struggle, and there was no way she could do it solo. So she elicited the aid of her friend Michael Colman. Together, they got him back up on the bed. Stacey covered him with a blanket before leaving.

Leshinski testified that it had been Stacey who'd first brought up the TV show she claimed to have watched with her husband, watched it twice, in fact, about the woman who'd poisoned two of her husbands with antifreeze. The witness emphasized that it was the defendant who first mentioned the subject, and she had not been prompted by a leading question.

"No further questions," Christine Garvey said.

On cross-examination, Chuck Keller asked: "Did you, or anyone else, inform Stacey of her Miranda rights before taking down her statement?"

"No."

"Why not?"

"Because it was not a criminal investigation, it was a suspicious-death investigation," she said. She explained that suspicious-death investigations usually do not warrant the administration of Miranda rights before taking a statement.

Keller asked her what police thought as they first observed the scene. Leshinski admitted that the consensus at the time was that David Castor had committed suicide.

"And when you changed your minds and decided

David Castor had been murdered, was Stacey the only suspect?" Keller asked.

Leshinski admitted that she was not. There had been two suspects at first, the other being Ashley Wallace.

Lieutenant Craig Costanzo testified that he was the executive officer of criminal investigations in 2005 when David Castor's body was discovered. Stacey had volunteered in his presence that her fingerprints might be on the brandy bottle, thus trying to account for evidence even before it had even been hinted that a crime was committed.

Costanzo had also reported to the Castor home in 2007 on the occasion of Ashley's poisoning. At that time, he was the officer to secure the would-be suicide note, along with the drinking glasses, empty bottle of vodka, and pill bottles confiscated from Ashley's room.

Following the Thursday lunch break, the case's top cop testified. Detective Dominick Spinelli said he was the lead investigator into the suspicious death, then the murder, of David Castor. He described how he had interviewed Stacey Castor at the Onondaga County Sheriff's Office headquarters many months after the murder and had noticed contradictions between her statements at that time and those she made to Detective Leshinski following her second husband's death.

Spinelli testified that a great bulk of the investigation was done between the time in 2005 when David Castor was murdered and 2007 when Ashley overdosed. The fingerprint and DNA evidence was all in place by the time Ashley OD'd. Indeed, the defendant would have been arrested eventually, anyway, for the murder of David Castor, but the arrest happened when it did because Ashley had almost died, and police wanted to prevent anyone else from getting hurt.

"Let's get the time frame of this interview straight," DA Bill Fitzpatrick said. "Your interview of the defendant at the police station came after the body of Michael Wallace was exhumed?"

"Yes, two days after."

"That would place the interview in September 2007, correct?"

"Correct. September the seventh."

"Was she emotional?"

"She cried."

"What were the discrepancies between what she said during [your] interview and the one she'd given immediately following David Castor's death?"

"During the September 2007 interview, the defendant told me that she did not check in at her Wetzel Road home before calling 911 to have police check on her husband. But the first officer on the scene on August 22, 2005, reported that the defendant told him she had called the emergency number only after going to the house and being unable to get a response from the victim.

"Also she told me that she had called her home every thirty to forty-five minutes that morning after her husband failed to show up for work. I confronted her with telephone records [that] indicated she had only called once."

"Those records showed she'd only called her residence once on the day she called 911?"

"Yes."

"At what time was that call made?"

"Twelve fifty-four in the afternoon."

Another discrepancy, Spinelli testified, was noted when the defendant told him that on the Saturday before her husband's body was found, she had been in the residence, specifically in the living room, when she heard her husband fall to the floor in the bedroom. She said that she immediately called her friend Michael Colman to come over and help get David back into bed. This disagreed in several ways with the eight-page written statement she had given Detective Diane Leshinski in 2005, in which she said she was helping her husband back to bed from the bathroom when he fell and couldn't get up.

"What did she say in the previous statement?" Fitzpatrick asked.

"At that time, she said, she'd been trying to help her husband get back into bed when he fell to the floor and couldn't get up. She also said that she'd waited more than two hours before asking a friend to come over and help."

Spinelli described a moment during that subsequent interview when the defendant committed a Freudian slip. He'd handed her a photo of the crime scene that showed the nightstand next to the bed. On it were two glasses.

"Stacey had earlier told me that she had poured a glass of water for her husband. I asked her which glass was the one she had poured. She said, 'When I poured the antifree, I mean, the cranberry juice— you're confusing me.'"

Then she stopped, realizing what she had said, and claimed she misspoke because she'd been flustered.

"Let me get this straight," Fitzpatrick said. "The defendant did not say 'antifreeze,' correct? She said the word 'antifree'?"

"Yes."

"Not 'antifreeze'?"

"No, she distinctly said 'antifree.'"

"Are you aware that the word 'antifree' appears several times in the confession/suicide note supposedly written by Ashley Wallace?"

"Yes, sir."

Attempting to take advantage of Stacey's flustered state, Spinelli testified, he had asked the defendant if she was aware that the glass containing the antifreeze only yielded one set of fingerprints, and they were hers.

"How did she respond to that?" Fitzpatrick inquired.

"She said she wanted to execute her right to stop the questioning," Spinelli testified.

"Thank you, Detective Spinelli," Fitzpatrick said respectfully. "No further questions."

"Chuck?" Judge Fahey said.

On cross-examination, Chuck Keller established that his client wasn't alone in getting confused. "Stacey Castor was not the only one who couldn't keep her facts straight," he said.

Keller induced Detective Spinelli to admit that during his testimony before a grand jury in this case, a recess had to be called when Spinelli became confused.

"You needed to review your written reports, didn't you, Detective Spinelli?"

"Yes."

"You could not continue without refreshing your recollection, right?"

"Yes."

"Do you recall testifying at a pretrial suppression hearing last year?"

"I do."

"During that testimony, did you need to pause to refresh your recollection?"

"Yes, sir."

"How many times?"

"I don't know."

"By count, you needed to refresh you recollection by reviewing your written reports thirty-two separate times during that pretrial suppression hearing, correct?"

"If you say so."

Keller shifted gears.

"You were aware of the details of David Castor's life insurance policy?"

"Yes."

"Was Stacey Castor the lone beneficiary of that policy?"

"No, Castor also left money to his first wife."

Keller emphasized this point for the jury by repeating it. He then sought to highlight the OCSO's tunnel vision. He got Spinelli to admit that Ashley Wallace was never considered by him to be a serious suspect in the murder of David Castor.

When he asked if Spinelli, being the lead investigator in the case, had ever been approached by any one of the other detectives with a lead that might have pointed toward Ashley instead of Stacey, Spinelli said he didn't remember that happening. Yet, Spinelli admitted, Stacey was scrutinized.

Keller framed that scrutiny as wildly invasive. A camera had been installed out in front of the Castor home to capture Stacey Castor's comings and goings, wasn't that right? A wiretap had been placed on the defendant's phone to record all of her conversations, right? Yet, her daughter was not subject to this sort of scrutiny, was she? Detective Spinelli admitted that he had searched through Stacey Castor's multiple statements to the police in search of inconsistencies, indications that she had changed her story over time. But he had never compared Ashley Wallace's statements side by side to see if her story had changed.

He made Spinelli admit, even though he had been among the first people to read the would-be suicide note found on Ashley's bed, he had never considered the possibility that it might be genuine or that Ashley Wallace was even a suspect in her stepfather's murder. This, despite the testimony earlier in the day by Detective Leshinski that initial information pointed to both Stacey and Ashley.

The prosecution's next two witnesses—Patrick Smith, a retail sales manager from AT&T, and Ann Donahue, from Verizon—testified that despite Stacey Castor's claims, which were made immediately following the discovery of her second husband's body, that she had called the house every half hour, forty-five minutes, to see if David was finally up and about, phone records contradicted these claims.

Smith and Donahue both testified that according to their records, only one phone call had been made from Stacey's cell phone to the residence on the day David Castor's body was found, and that call had been made at six minutes before one o'clock in the afternoon.

"Did your records show that calls had been made to other numbers earlier that day?" Christine Garvey asked Smith.

"No, ma'am."

"No calls at all?"

"No, there had been no activity whatsoever on the defendant's cell phone for three days before the twelve fifty-four call to her home."

Thursday's last witness was Michael Colman, the friend who had helped Stacey Castor get her sick husband, David Castor, back into bed when Castor was desperately ill. Colman testified that David Castor had seemed drunk and incoherent.

"Did you think that it was alcohol causing David Castor's problems?" William Fitzpatrick asked.

"Yes."

"Just alcohol?"

"Well, it occurred to me that it might be alcohol and something else," that the victim might have voluntarily taken some sort of drug, in addition to being blotto drunk.

"Why was that?"

"His condition seemed too intense to be just from alcohol," Mike Colman said.

* * *

On cross-examination, Chuck Keller asked if there had been any discussion of getting medical attention.

"Yes, Stacey asked me if she should call an ambulance."

"What did you say to that?"

"I said, no, just let him sleep it off."

"You gave a statement to the police soon after David Castor's body was found, correct?"

"Yes."

"In that statement, did you mention that Stacey had suggested calling an ambulance?"

"No."

"You also testified before the grand jury in this case, didn't you?"

"Yes."

"Before the grand jury, did you mention that Stacey asked if an ambulance should be called, and you said 'no, let him sleep it off'?"

"No."

"You were close enough to the Castor family to know how they all got along?" Keller asked.

"Yes."

"And how would you characterize the relationship between Castor and Stacey's two daughters?"

"Ashley and Bree did not like David Castor too much," Colman said.

That concluded the day's testimony. One reporter described the day as "overwhelming." The prosecution called eleven witnesses that Thursday, and testimony ranged from the most technical to the most emotional.

17

The First Friday

On the afternoon of Friday, January 16, the first witness of the day was Dani Colman, Stacey's good friend, and the wife of the man who had helped Stacey put David Castor to bed.

"I show you now an empty pill bottle," William Fitzpatrick said. "Do you recognize it?"

"No, I do not," Dani said.

"Sidebar, Judge," Keller said.

"All right," Judge Fahey said, and called the attorneys up to his bench.

After a brief discussion, the jurors were told to leave the courtroom. There was more discussion, and when the jurors were called back into the courtroom, they were informed that Dani Colman's testimony regarding a pill bottle had been stipulated. The witness was dismissed.

* * *

"I call Mark Mills to the stand," William Fitzpatrick said.

An OCSO fingerprint expert, Mills was a bespectacled gentleman who testified that it had been his job to analyze the fingerprints found on the glass on the night table at David Castor's death scene, the glass that contained the green substance.

"I am going to hand you a glass now, and I would like you to look at it," Christine Garvey said.

"All right," Mills answered, and pulled on a pair of blue rubber gloves.

The ADA handed the witness a drinking glass in a sealed bag. At Garvey's suggestion, Mills opened the bag and removed the glass.

"Is this the glass that you examined?" Garvey asked. "The glass that was found on the nightstand next to the deceased?"

"Yes," Mills replied. The chain of evidence was clear.

"Did you find any identifiable fingerprints on the glass?"

"Yes, three," Mills said.

"[Were] you able to identify those three fingerprints?"

"Yes."

"To whom did they belong?"

"Those fingerprints matched the prints of the defendant, Stacey Castor."

"Did you also dust the brandy bottle for fingerprints?"

"I did. I found one print, also belonging to the defendant."

Garvey showed Mills the suicide note and asked if he recognized it. He said he did, and, yes, he had tested it for fingerprints.

"Did you find the fingerprints of Bree Wallace on the note?"

"I did."

"And did you find the defendant's fingerprints on this paper?"

"Yes, sir."

"And did you find the fingerprints of Ashley Wallace on the suicide note?"

"No, I did not."

"What other items were dusted for prints, Mr. Mills?"

"A container of antifreeze, a turkey baster, and a bottle of Ambien."

"Were any identifiable fingerprints found on those three items?"

"No."

"Thank you, no further questions," Garvey said.

During cross-examination, Chuck Keller established for the jury that it only stood to reason that Bree and Stacey's fingerprints were found on the suicide note, since both admitted touching the note after it was discovered on Ashley's bed. The fingerprint expert acknowledged that, despite the fact that no identifiable print belonging to Ashley was found on the note, there were some additional "ridge details" found that were insufficient to test for identification purposes.

He also admitted during cross-examination that even though Stacey's prints were found on the glass and the brandy bottle, there was no way to determine scientifically *when* those prints were made.

* * *

Kathleen Hum, an Asian American with shortly cropped hair parted on the left, testified she was a "bio-fluid" expert, aka a DNA expert. As had Mills before her, Hum donned blue latex gloves before touching the exhibits she discussed.

Hum said she was a forensic scientist. It was her job to analyze the items of evidence confiscated at the David Castor crime scene. DNA evidence was found on both the glass found on the nightstand and the tip of the turkey baster.

"How did you go about examining the turkey baster?" William Fitzpatrick asked.

"I started at the tip and worked back," she said. She made swabs from material found both outside and inside the baster. "I believe I swabbed the last one-and-a-half to two inches of the turkey baster for the purpose of DNA." She'd also examined the rubber bulb at the other end of the turkey baster. "Unfortunately, there was an insufficient amount of DNA on the bulb, and therefore we did not obtain a DNA profile from there," she explained.

"Were you able to obtain a DNA profile from the tip of the baster?"

"Yes."

"What did that profile reveal?"

"A DNA profile was obtained from the swabbing taken at the tip of the turkey baster, and this profile was a match with the DNA profile of David Castor." The DNA found on the glass also matched that of the deceased, Hum testified.

* * *

On cross-examination, Chuck Keller established that the turkey baster was hardly the only evidence in this case. There were other items discovered at the scene of David's death, and items from the scene of Ashley's overdose—pill bottles and an empty vodka bottle—were discovered at the scene of Ashley Wallace's apparent suicide attempt. Swabs had been taken from those items for possible future testing. That testing, Keller demonstrated, was never done.

18

"Sissy, are you okay?"

Bree Wallace swore to tell the truth, the whole truth, and nothing but the truth, then described the morning in September 2007 when her sister, Ashley, got sick.

The testimony didn't go smoothly as Bree, as had her sister earlier, became emotional while on the witness stand. Bree repeatedly broke down, and there were breaks in her testimony for her to wipe away tears and sip water to compose herself.

Bree said she noticed that Ashley had been in her room for a long time. She'd originally wanted to wake her sister up the previous evening, but Stacey told her to leave her sister alone. She'd opened the door to Ashley's room and looked in, but her mother shooed her away.

"She's fine. Leave her alone. I want her to sleep through, until morning," Bree quoted her mother as saying.

In the morning, Bree eventually investigated,

anyway. That was because she heard something that demanded investigation.

"I was in the hallway and I heard a noise," she said. At Bill Fitzpatrick's invitation, Bree imitated the sound, sort of a gasping and moaning sound. She took shallow breaths and made the noise with each rapid exhale.

Bree quickly became uncomfortable and stopped making the noise. Instead, she summed up, "It was a high-pitched kind of noise."

At first, she thought the sound might be coming from her mother's room. She listened at her mother's door for a moment, then moved to her sister's door. It was Ashley.

"I opened the door to Ashley's room and I saw her lying at the foot of the bed," she testified. With the door open, the sound was much louder, so loud that it upset her. Ashley was in distress.

"I walked into the room, and there were pillows on Ashley's head," Bree said. "I took one pillow off her head, and there was another one, so I took the other pillow off her head, and I could see that her head was facing toward the window. She didn't have any clothes on, and her eyes were wide open. They were all glassy and red, and she had thrown up." Bree sniffled and sobbed, and was temporarily unable to continue.

"It's okay," the district attorney reassured the witness.

Bree continued, "I called out for my mom, I didn't know what to do. I called out, 'Sissy, are you okay?' But she didn't answer me. She was making that noise, where she was breathing out. So I ran and called for my mom. And I opened the door and I said, 'Mommy, there's something wrong with Ashley.' And

my mom came out and said, 'What's wrong with her?'
I said, 'I don't know!'"

Bree testified that she and her mother were in
Ashley's room for a few minutes, she didn't know exactly how long, trying to snap Ashley out of her
seizure, but it didn't work.

"And so my mom got on the phone and called
911," Bree testified. She heard her mother on the
phone and went into her sister's bedroom for a
second time.

"I noticed something at the head of the bed. It was
a piece of paper, so I grabbed it and opened it, and I
said, 'Look, it's a note.' And my mom took it from me."

Fitzpatrick asked, "Bree, when you were in the
room earlier, did you see that note?"

"I didn't notice it, no."

"You left?"

"Yes."

"Came back?"

"Yes."

"How soon did you notice the note when you
came into the room the second time?"

"Almost immediately."

"And your mom took the note away from you?"

"Yes."

"What happened next?"

"Then I found the vodka bottle that was laying
there in front of me. My mother took the bottle and
placed it on the dresser."

"Did you ever try to hug your mom, or say anything to her?"

"She was sitting at the kitchen table with her knees
pulled up, and she was holding on to her knees.

When I went to give her a hug, she told me to get the eff away from her."

Fitzpatrick repeated the alleged remark for the jury's benefit: "She told you to 'get the eff away from her.' And then what happened, Bree?"

Again, Bree had trouble spitting out the words: "I went into the living room and I stayed there for a few minutes. And she came in after a few minutes and said, 'I'm sorry, I'm sorry. I didn't mean it.'"

"Bree, had you ever seen your sister take a seventeen-hour nap?"

"No."

After police arrived at the house, she again tried to read the note, but her mother asked an officer to take the note away from her.

Fitzpatrick asked Bree about David Castor's condition during the weekend before his death.

"He was either sick or sleeping," Bree said. Although it was her understanding that David really was locked inside the bedroom, as her mother had said, there was no reason for the police officer to break the door down. Stacey had a key to that bedroom door, Bree testified, and had used it at least twice to open the door over the course of the weekend.

"Are you certain she used the key to open the door, Bree?"

"Yes. One time, I was asking her if David was okay, so she opened the door and let me look in," Bree replied.

The DA paused and let that sink in. Stacey was unlocking—and apparently locking—the door to David's room with a key as he lay dying.

The district attorney asked Bree about things that occurred before Ashley's poisoning. Bree testified that although she loved her father, Michael Wallace, very much, she "didn't particularly care for" David Castor.

She recalled David's illness and said that she had been watching when Michael Colman came over and helped her mother lift David and put him back in bed.

Asked how she felt about the situation, Bree said that she was worried about her stepfather because days had gone past and he hadn't left his room. She asked her mother about David's condition and Stacey said he was "just sleeping."

That morning, the prosecution played for the jury the tape of the 911 call from the defendant regarding her daughter's illness, so the jury still had it fresh in their minds. They recalled vividly how Stacey had reported that her daughter had drunk a full bottle of vodka and had taken sleeping pills.

After more than an hour of testifying, the defendant's youngest daughter was allowed to step down.

OCSO deputy Michael Graham told the jury that he had been a first responder to the scene of Ashley Wallace's poisoning, and that it was he who recovered the would-be suicide note.

"Who was in possession of the note when you first saw it?"

"The victim's sister, Bree, had it."

"Did Mrs. Castor instruct you to take the note away from her daughter?"

"Yes."

Detective Valerie Brogan also was among the first responders to the scene of Ashley's poisoning, and was subsequently assigned as lead detective into the attempted murder of Ashley Wallace.

"How would you describe the nature of the scene when you arrived?"

"It was chaotic," Detective Brogan replied.

As the jury would not be allowed to tour the house in person and to see where both the murder and attempted murder occurred, a slide show would have to be the next best thing. Using a slide projector, William Fitzpatrick showed the courtroom a series of police photographs of the Castor house, he had Detective Brogan give a walking tour of the home.

"How would you describe the defendant's demeanor at the scene of Ashley Wallace's poisoning?"

"I would say that she was being difficult."

"How so?"

"I was having trouble establishing any kind of truth with her. It was clear that she did not trust the police."

"No further questions, Your Honor," Fitzpatrick said.

"In that case, let's take our lunch break," Judge Fahey said.

That afternoon, Chuck Keller cross-examined Brogan.

"Were you aware of Ashley Wallace's history when you reported to the house on Wetzel Road?"

"No."

"You didn't know at that time that she had a history of trying to hurt herself?"

"No, I didn't."

"No further questions," Keller said.

* * *

Detective Brogan was allowed to step down and she was replaced on the witness stand by Detective Bob Pitman, who briefly testifed that after reporting to the scene of Ashley Wallace's poisoning, he discovered and confiscated several bottles of pills.

Detective Keith Hall testified that he also recovered pill bottles at the Castor house after Ashley was rushed to the hospital. In addition, it was he who discovered a life insurance policy check to Stacey Castor.

"For what dollar amount was that check?"

"It was made out for $45,200.13."

Deputy Brian Phelps testified that he had observed Ashley Wallace in the hospital, incoherent.

"In that condition, could you trust the accuracy of any statements she made?"

"No."

"Would she be able to accurately estimate time, the day and time?"

"Not at all."

"Deputy Phelps, you took a statement from the defendant soon after Ashley was rushed to the hospital, is that correct?"

"Yes."

William Fitzpatrick produced the next people's exhibit, a transcript of a police interrogation. Phelps positively identified the document as a transcript of the statement he had taken from the defendant when her daughter was poisoned.

The DA then asked the witness to verify for the court that the transcript was accurate at a couple of key points. One: yes, the defendant said that her daughter Bree found the note under Ashley's pillow and subsequently gave it to her. And two: the defendant told Phelps that she didn't know why Ashley would try to commit suicide, or why she would admit to killing her father and stepfather.

Sergeant Michael Norton testified that he, too, had been at the hospital and was among the first cops to talk to Ashley after she regained coherence. He'd tried to trick Ashley into admitting that she'd taken an overdose of pills, but she wouldn't do it. In fact, on the contrary, she told him she'd taken no pills and certainly did not want to kill herself. Norton found her manner consistent with someone telling the truth.

Matthew Gandino testified that he was Ashley Wallace's boyfriend. They'd been going together for about two years.

He described repeatedly calling Ashley on the afternoon and evening before her hospitalization. He was unable to get in touch with her.

"There was no answer to any of your calls?"

"My last call was answered."

"By whom?"

"Ashley's mother."

"The defendant answered Ashley's phone?"

"Yes."

"Had the defendant ever answered Ashley's phone before when you called?"

"No, that was the first and only time that ever happened," the boyfriend said.

What, if anything, had Stacey Castor said to him?

"She said Ashley was asleep and couldn't be disturbed." Stacey, he said, seemed to be trying to prevent him from contacting Ashley. "She said Ashley was very tired and was taking a nap."

Gandino testified that during that phone call, he asked Stacey if she could retrieve an item for him that he'd left in Ashley's room the previous day.

"What was the item?"

"My ATM card."

"Did she do that for you?"

"No, she did not. She said she had looked for the item but couldn't find it, but I knew that wasn't the truth."

"How did you know?"

"I was standing outside the house at the time, and the light in Ashley's room didn't go on."

"Did you visit Ashley after she was hospitalized?"

"Yes."

"Did she seem drunk to you?"

"No, she was more loopy than drunk."

Gandino testified that Ashley, to his knowledge, had never considered committing suicide. He said that he and Ashley had discussed suicide about a month before her overdose and had agreed that it was selfish and unfair to the friends and loved ones you would leave behind.

That concluded the first week of the trial. Judge Fahey reminded everyone that the upcoming Monday was Martin Luther King Day and that court was adjourned until Tuesday morning.

19

Day Four

Following the three-day weekend, testimony restarted on Tuesday morning, January 20. With the jury outside the courtroom, Fitzpatrick informed Judge Fahey that he had planned a full day of technical testimony.

This announcement resulted in Charles Keller calling for a mistrial. Much of the technical evidence to be presented by the prosecution, he said, was based on what the defense attorney termed "experiments."

Since the defense had not had an opportunity to replicate those experiments, a mistrial was in order, Keller said.

Keller argued: "I am not saying that the people were intentionally trying to sandbag us. But our inability to replicate prosecution experiments when it comes to their so-called computer forensic evidence has hampered our ability to present a defense."

This was particularly true when it came to evidence regarding Stacey's fraud charge, Keller argued. The prosecution had been allowed to analyze the will, looking for signs of forgery, yet the defense hadn't had an opportunity to gather evidence supporting the document's authenticity.

"The prosecution is going to claim that David Castor's name was forged, but the defense has had no opportunity to properly study that signature," Keller said.

Fitzpatrick argued in return that the case he was presenting was basically the same as that which he had set forth during preliminary hearings.

"Not that much has changed, Judge," Fitzpatrick said. "We are not bringing in anything that is going to be a surprise to the defense."

Judge Fahey agreed with the prosecution, noting that the authenticity of the signature of David Castor's disputed will had been known to the defense for at least fourteen months, ever since the time the charge first appeared on an indictment, so the defense had had plenty of opportunity to examine the document in question.

Keller's motion for a mistrial was denied, Judge Fahey ordered the jury brought into the courtroom, and Fitzpatrick called his first witness of the day.

Dr. Daniel Olsson was an emergency physician working at University Hospital and had been on duty on September 14, 2007, when Ashley Wallace was brought in by ambulance.

"Was Ashley Wallace conscious when she arrived at the emergency room?" Garvey asked.

"She was conscious but incoherent," Dr. Olsson replied crisply. It was only later that Dr. Olsson learned that Ashley had morphine and codeine in her system.

"Did you test her blood-alcohol level?" Garvey asked.

"Yes."

"What was the result of that test?"

"She had a blood-alcohol content of zero-point-fourteen percent," Dr. Olsson said. To put that into context, a level of 0.08 was enough to warrant a charge of drunk driving.

The doctor explained that he'd also measured the rate of Ashley's heartbeat and discovered that it was dangerously fast.

"What do you mean by 'dangerously'?"

"I mean potentially fatal."

Olsson testified that the mother was present in the ER and insisted her daughter was sick from a combination of alcohol and sleeping pills, but he could tell by the patient's symptoms that this could not be entirely correct.

"I could tell that there was some other poison at work," Dr. Olsson said.

"Without receiving medical attention when she did, what would have happened to Ashley Wallace?" Garvey asked.

"She would have died."

"No further questions, Judge," Garvey said.

"Chuck?" Judge Fahey said.

* * *

Charles Keller said, "It is your testimony that Ashley Wallace had been drinking before she arrived in the ER, is that correct, Dr. Olsson?"

"Yes."

"You mentioned a blood-alcohol figure. How much would a person of Ashley Wallace's height and weight have to drink to achieve such a level?"

"She would have to drink a lot."

Detective Gerald Mancill was a forensic computer expert who worked at the Onondaga County Center for Forensic Sciences. Mancill testified that after Ashley's poisoning, he secured and analyzed the Castor family computers. He determined that the "suicide note" was written on Stacey's computer.

That computer and its accouterment of hardware were positively identified by the witness and then marked into evidence. The hard drive of that computer, Mancill said, contained several versions of the note.

"Did this computer have a method of timing and dating its activities?"

"Yes, it used a BIOS chip, sort of an internal clock that times and dates all nondeleted data." (BIOS stands for Basic Input/Output System.)

"Did you check the computer's BIOS to see if it was in sync with our time here in the Eastern time zone?"

"Yes, it was reasonably accurate—twelve seconds off the official time."

* * *

Frank Brackin was a computer expert. He had determined that the suicide note was written on Stacey Castor's computer.

"Were you able to determine which user account the note fragments were found in?" Christine Garvey asked.

"The fragments were found in the Stacey Castor account," Brackin replied.

"In the defendant's account?"

"That's right."

"Mr. Brackin, did you review and compare the two fragments of notes?"

"Yes, I did."

"Were there any differences in spelling, language, and sentence structure?"

"There were a number of differences," the computer expert said. He went through the changes one by one. An "is" became an "I did." A word spelled r-e-l-e became r-e-a-l-y, and so on. Most of the changes were minor. "In one spot, an entire sentence had been deleted."

"You examined Ashley Wallace's computer profile as well, Mr. Brackin?" Garvey asked.

"Yes, I did."

"Could the letter have been written on Ashley's computer profile?"

"It could not."

"And why is that?"

"I found that Microsoft Word, the program used to write the note, was not fully loaded and running on Ashley Wallace's computer."

"And Microsoft Word was fully loaded and running on Stacey Castor's computer?"

"Yes."

"How many profiles were there on that computer?"

"There were three, one for the defendant and one for each of her daughters."

"And only the defendant's profile had Microsoft Word operating?"

"That's correct."

Garvey asked how this could be determined beyond doubt and Brackin explained in simple terms how computers work, that they tend to remember everything that was ever saved, and everything not deleted is saved.

"When using Microsoft Word, the computer automatically saves what was written, even if the document is not manually saved by the user," Brackin said. In fact, that was the case here. Fragments of the document had been saved a couple of times automatically.

"Could you determine when the fragment of the would-be suicide note was accessed on Stacey Castor's computer?" Garvey inquired.

"Yes," Brackin replied. "It was last accessed on Wednesday, September twelfth." That was a day and a half before a printed copy of the note was found on Ashley's bed.

That was not long after Ashley had called her mother and complained that policemen had come to her school with questions about poison and murder. In fact, the incident was mentioned in the letter, and referred to as happening "today."

Brackin said that although the fragments from the note were available on the hard drive, the entire text of the note, as it appeared on paper, wasn't

there, probably because it had been deleted after
it was printed.

On cross-examination, Chuck Keller induced
Brackin to admit that although he could tell when
the letter fragments were last accessed on Stacey
Castor's computer, there was no way to tell when the
final version of the letter was printed.

"We do know that each note fragment had to have
been written before it was last accessed, is that correct, Mr. Brackin?"

"Yes."

"Given that, what time restraints can we put on
when those note fragments were written?"

"One note fragment had to have been written
before three thirty-four P.M. on September eleventh,
and the other had to have been written before two
twenty-seven P.M. on September 12, 2007."

Both note fragments, Brackin testified, bore significant differences in wording, punctuation, and
grammar from the finished edition that appeared
on Ashley's bed.

As it was approaching noon, Judge Fahey interrupted Keller's cross-examination and declared
the lunch recess, ordering everyone to be back by
one-fifteen.

That afternoon, Chuck Keller resumed cross-
examination by establishing that even if one could
prove that the letter was written on Stacey Castor's
computer, there was no way to say for certain if
Stacey Castor had written it.

"I'd like to make one thing perfectly clear," Keller said to the witness. "Although there were passwords on this computer, you didn't need a password to access any particular user account, isn't that right?"

"Uh, that's two questions," the witness said.

"Let me put it this way—the computer had a password, did it not?"

"I didn't find any," the witness said.

"Okay, well, that kind of answers my question, then," Keller said. "If I were to go up to this computer and turn it on, whatever user account it happened to be in, I could just open it up and type a document without any problems, right?"

"That is correct."

"All right," Keller said. "So anyone with access to the computer could have written those note fragments, is that correct?"

"Yes."

On redirect, Christine Garvey established that even though the note fragments could not be dated, they nonetheless defined a creative process that lasted over a stretch of time. That evidence proved the note was written in stages and was revised.

Perhaps a juror or two looked at this and thought, how odd it would be for Ashley Wallace to use the house computer to write and rewrite a suicide note, then go to school and begin her college career. One act was so filled with hope, the other with despair. Could both activities coexist in a young woman's ultimate itinerary?

* * *

Mark Rathbun testified he was an investigator, an electronics surveillance specialist, working for the Onondaga County District Attorney's Office. "The wiretap was working from September 4 through 14, 2007," he said. He'd helped wiretap Stacey Castor's phone. The defendant's phone conversations were taped starting soon after it was learned that Michael Wallace had been murdered. Electronic surveillance continued until after Ashley's hospitalization, right up until the moment of the defendant's arrest.

The prosecution played a series of twelve taped conversations, all featuring Stacey Castor. Rathbun identified each tape as one that had been recorded by his wiretap. Although eleven days' worth of conversations had been recorded, all of the exchanges entered as evidence were recorded during one 48-hour span. Each tape, it was noted, was made on either September 12 or 13.

Among the tapes played was one recorded conversation between the defendant and Ashley's boyfriend, taped on September 13, the night that, according to the prosecution, Stacey began poisoning her daughter. Ashley said that she'd gotten ill the night before because her mother made her drink lousy-tasting watermelon-flavored vodka ices. According to this conversation, however, Stacey took none of the blame.

"Poor baby, she's exhausted. What were you doing with her last night?" Stacey said to Ashley's boyfriend, Matthew.

"I wasn't doing anything, she just sort of passed out," the young man replied.

"When she wakes up, if she wakes up before I go to bed, I'll tell her to give you a call, okay?"

During this same conversation, Matthew asked Stacey to look in Ashley's room for his ATM card, and he caught her in a lie when the light in Ashley's room never went on. It was from this wiretap that a recording was made during which Stacey sounded to be talking and typing simultaneously.

When Rathbun's testimony was finished, Judge Fahey noted that the trial was ahead of schedule and adjourned court early.

20

Day Five

On Wednesday morning, January 21, 2009, the prosecution called the Honorable Franklin A. Josef to the stand. Judge Josef explained that he was the town justice in nearby Manlius. Back in 1989, though, Frank Josef had been the practicing attorney who'd helped David Castor prepare his first will.

That will, Judge Josef said, bequeathed everything to his first wife, Janice, and, in case of her death, to his son.

Under cross-examination, Josef said that when David Castor divorced his first wife, the 1989 will may have become null and void.

The prosecution called Connie Jordan, who testified that in 2000 she was a clerk in a Skaneateles, New York, doctor's office, where Michael Wallace received treatment.

The prosecution read a document from the doctor's

office detailing an office visit Michael Wallace had made several months before his death, during which time he complained of and was treated for dizziness and confusion.

Dwayne Wisbey grew up in Amherst, New York, and earned his Bachelor of Science degree in geology at SUNY at Geneseo, class of 1985. Since July 1999, he had been employed as a forensic document examiner at the Onondaga County Center for Forensic Sciences, Wisbey testified.

"As a document expert, are you considered an expert in handwriting as well?" Christine Garvey asked.

"Signatures, yes."

"You can verify if a signature is genuine or forged, correct?"

"Yes."

Wisbey testified that during the course of his duties for the county, he had compared the signature of David Castor that appeared on the 2003 will—the will the prosecution contended was forged—with a variety of earlier verified-as-genuine David Castor signatures.

Garvey made it clear to the jury that the will dated 2003 was different and separate from the 1989 will that Franklin Josef had testified about earlier in the day.

"How many genuine David Castor signatures did you examine?"

"Many." Janice Poissant had supplied the genuine signatures, from papers she had or had access to. Others of the real signatures were discovered during police searches of the Castor home, and all had an established chain of evidence.

"And can you give the jury examples of where those signatures were found?"

"The genuine signatures came from various documents, deeds to his house, and so on."

To help demonstrate his analytic techniques to the jury, blowups of three signatures had been made and were now placed one above the other on a demonstration board. The signature from the disputed will was on the top, the other two were David Castor signatures stipulated as genuine.

The witness stood next to the board with a pointer in his hand. He noted initially that all three signatures on the board had "pictorial similarities." That is, at first glance, the top signature looked pretty much like the other two.

Upon a closer examination, the differences became obvious, Wisbey said. A careful look at the top signature revealed many aspects of it that were awkward.

"It isn't as pleasant to the eye, like the others," the witness noted. "The questioned signature was not as pleasant to the eye because it was written *much more slowly.*"

Slow writing, he added, was a symptom of forgery. Real signatures tend to be done very quickly. Forgeries were written slowly, as the forger was far more careful and tentative than would be someone scribbling down his or her own signature.

"When you are signing your own name, your hand knows where it is going and does not need to slow down," the expert testified.

The lines in the top signature were less fluid

because the pen moved at an inconsistent speed. The lines were wavy and not smooth, and it appeared that the signer had gone back and had tried to retouch the signature to make it look more like the genuine article. The line wavered, he added, and real signatures rarely wavered.

"What do you mean by 'waver'?" Christine Garvey asked.

"It is not straight. Not like the ones below," Wisbey replied.

Maybe sometimes there was wavering in the signatures of ill or very old persons, Wisbey said, but David Castor was young and healthy when he purportedly signed the will. He was a man fresh from the altar, embarking on his honeymoon.

Another difference between real and forged was how lines ended. Real signatures had lines that tapered off to a stop. Forgery lines ended bluntly. The questioned signature featured blunt line endings, an indicator of an uncertain and hesitant hand. The genuine signatures had tapered line endings.

Garvey sought to sum it up: "After your examination, to a reasonable degree of scientific certainty, do you have an opinion regarding the questioned signature?"

Wisbey replied, "It is my opinion that this is a simulated David Castor signature."

Following Wisbey's testimony, Judge Fahey called for a half-hour morning break.

Lynn Pulaski testified that she had been the defendant's friend for eighteen years. After some preliminaries, William Fitzpatrick got down to the crux of the matter. He asked if there came a time after David Castor's death when Stacey Castor came to her with a will.

"Yes, Stacey contacted me and asked if I could do her a favor. She told me she had David's will and asked if my husband and I would witness it."

"Where, if anywhere, did she suggest you meet?" the DA asked.

"She said she would come to our home. She came over and she had one of her daughters with her. I can't remember if she had both of her girls with her. We just went into the kitchen and we were talking. She was thanking us for helping her out. She presented me with a folder with a document in it. I opened it up and looked at it. I did not read it. I looked at the second page and it showed a signature on the document that I believed was David's."

"You then signed as a witness to this document?"

"Yes, I did. I was told that I would receive something in the mail from an attorney's office, which I signed, had notarized, and returned."

"And, Lynn, you know I am not trying to embarrass you, but the document you signed wasn't true, was it?"

"No, it was not."

"And would it be fair to say that you did not witness David Castor's signature on the will?"

"Yes."

"The document is dated August 17, 2003. How did that date come to be on the will?"

"When we signed the document, I did notice that it wasn't dated. I had asked Stacey, you know, 'What do we do about this?' It was just decided at that time that we would date it the day after their wedding. If anyone were to ask us, we would say that they were on their way to their honeymoon and asked us to witness the document before they left."

Chuck Keller sat out the cross-examination of this witness. Instead, Stacey's second-chair defense attorney, Todd Smith, questioned Lynn Pulaski.

"When agreeing to witness this document," Smith said, "Stacey told you she had some bills that were coming due?"

DA Fitzpatrick reacted immediately: "Objection, Your Honor." He didn't specify a reason.

"I'll sustain," Judge Fahey said.

"What was the nature of that discussion?" Smith asked.

"Same objection, Your Honor," Fitzpatrick said, and again the judge sustained.

"Did Stacey and David fight a lot?" Smith asked.

"Not in front of me," the witness replied. "I was not aware of any major problems in the marriage, no."

"Did it appear to be a loving relationship to you?" Smith asked.

That question was objected to and sustained. So far, Smith had asked four questions, and only one had resulted in an answer. His luck didn't improve much as he tried yet again.

"Did you know Michael Wallace?"

"Yes."

"You had seen Michael and Stacey together?"

"Objection!"

"Sustained."

There was a pause as Smith and Keller had a short

private conference behind the defense table. Lifting his head, Smith said, "No further questions, Your Honor."

It's hard to say what the defense hoped to accomplish with their cross-examination of Lynn Pulaski. Apparently, it had hoped to use her to establish Stacey's love for both of her husbands. Trouble was, no questions on those subjects had been asked during Bill Fitzpatrick's direct examination, so it was all improper cross.

The next prosecution witness was Gerald LaPorte, a member of the U.S. Secret Service. Because of the potential that the witness was or would be undercover someday as an agent of the Treasury Department, all cameras were turned off during his testimony.

LaPorte testified that he was an office machinery expert and that tiny imperfections in the print revealed that Ashley's suicide note was most likely printed on the Castor family printer.

Following the agent's testimony, the prosecution announced that they were out of available witnesses. The judge excused the jury for the remainder of the day.

"How many witnesses do you have remaining to be called?" Judge Fahey asked.

"Seven," Fitzpatrick replied. The DA then noted that he had prior commitments for the remainder of the week. Since things were proceeding efficiently, Judge Fahey adjourned court until the following Monday.

21

Day Six

On Monday morning, January 26, 2009, after four days off, with the attorneys in the courtroom and the jury out, Judge Fahey asked for duration-of-trial estimates from both sides. Fitzpatrick said he intended to finish his case in one day. Taking the DA's estimate into consideration, Keller told the judge that he'd be finished by the end of the week. They were beginning the sixth day of testimony and could see light at the end of the tunnel. There might be deliberations by Friday.

The state's first witness of the morning was Laura LaBay, a forensic toxicology expert employed by National Medical Services, a private lab in Pennsylvania. She testified that in 2007 she studied brain and liver tissue from Michael Wallace's exhumed remains. The tests she performed revealed the presence of ethylene glycol in both organs.

* * *

Christine Garvey called Raymond Van Orden, a trial veteran who had testified under oath hundreds of times—but this one was different. The courtroom was packed. SRO. Cameras everywhere, cameras you couldn't see. "It was pretty big. I was shocked—and nervous," Van Orden recalled. Once he took the oath and started his testimony, he smoothed out, but his heart was racing when he first entered the courtroom.

Van Orden testified that he was a former Onondaga County crime lab chemist. Technically, he had been a sworn deputy's sheriff, but his job was in forensics. Since his work on this case, he had retired from the sheriff's office and had moved to Mesa, Arizona, where he worked in a similar capacity. Now he did purely toxicology work, testing blood and urine samples for alcohol and drugs of abuse.

Not that the weather in Mesa wasn't great, but the harsh Syracuse winters had nothing to do with the move, which occurred so he and his wife could be close to his in-laws. He'd received a subpoena, and the prosecution had flown him into Syracuse for three days.

To establish him as a local boy for the obviously local jury, Van Orden testified that he was a former chemistry professor at Cayuga Community College.

Yes, he'd run tests in connection with evidence in this case. Specifically, he was the guy who had tested the fluid found inside the turkey baster.

"What did the liquid look like?"

"It was a green liquid."

"Did you identify the substance?"

"Yes. It was antifreeze."

Following Van Orden's brief testimony, Judge

Fahey called a recess. He informed the court that "everything didn't stop" just because there was a murder trial going on, and he needed to tend to his morning schedule.

The trial resumed that afternoon and the convoy of experts continued. Jeff Hackett was another former Onondaga County crime lab technician. Unlike the somewhat dry testimony of the morning, Hackett's contribution to the record had a bit of a kick.

He testified that he had analyzed a sample of David Castor's blood following David's death.

"Did you test David Castor's blood-alcohol level?"

"I did."

"What did he register?"

"Zero."

"Zero! You mean there was no alcohol in David Castor's bloodstream at the time of his death?"

"That is correct."

Carol Schulz testified that she was a toxicology expert and an employee of Strong Memorial Hospital in Rochester, New York.

"Did you analyze a sample of David Castor's blood following his death?"

"Yes."

"And what did you discover?"

"I discovered evidence of antifreeze poisoning, the presence of ethylene glycol," Schulz testified.

The jury's focus was just starting to wane. They got the idea. David Castor died because he drank antifreeze—probably at first out of a glass and then later, when he was groggy or paralyzed, by having it squirted down his throat with a turkey baster. It wasn't suicide, and the fact that there was no alcohol in his bloodstream at the time of his death flew in the face of Stacey Castor's scenario. While the jury's minds might have wandered with the steady flow of somewhat redundant expert testimony, they didn't wander into sympathetic territory for Stacey. Dry or not, the evidence Christine Garvey presented was damning to the defendant. Some courtroom spectators, veterans of many trials, thought the jury had it easy. Garvey was pleasant, presented the evidence crisply, and didn't drone and repeat like some lawyers.

Dr. Thomas G. Rosano testified that he was vice chairman and professor of pathology and laboratory medicine at the Albany Medical Center College and Hospital, in Albany, New York. He added that he was an expert in forensic toxicology and chemical pathology, had been an expert for twenty-three years, and frequently testified in criminal, civil, and family court proceedings on a broad range of toxicology issues. He assisted pathologists, attorneys, and law enforcement with toxicological issues in deaths involving drugs and chemical poisons. Regarding this case, he analyzed a sample of David Castor's blood and discovered glycolic acid, which he said was a by-product of ethylene glycol.

* * *

On cross-examination, Chuck Keller asked if the level of ethylene glycol in David Castor's remains could be quantified. Dr. Rosano said it could not.

"Why is that?" Keller asked.

"Because it was too small to quantify," Rosano replied.

Dr. Karla J. Walker testified that she had a doctorate in pharmacy from the University of Minnesota. She earned her Bachelor of Science degree at the same school after first attending Mankato State University. Her professional experience included being a diplomate of the American Board of Clinical Chemistry in 1998, and a fellow of the National Academy of Clinical Biochemistry in 2000. She was employed by MEDTOX, where she first worked in 1985 as a medical technologist. She left MEDTOX for a few years and returned in 1993 with her doctorate and a two-year research fellowship in pharmacokinetics under her belt. Dr. Walker's current position entailed the review, release, and interpretation of laboratory results.

"You are a toxicology lab director, is that correct, Dr. Walker?"

"Yes."

"And during the course of your duties, you made tests that involved this case?"

"Yes. I studied urine samples of Ashley Wallace, following her poisoning in September of 2007."

"Did you determine what caused her illness?" Christine Garvey asked.

"Yes, it was a combination of pain relievers, antidepressants, sleeping pills, and other drugs. There were eight different drugs all ingested in various quantities." These included sleeping aids, antidepressants, antibiotics, painkillers, and Ashley's attention-deficit medication. It appeared that every prescription drug in the house had been blended into a potentially fatal formula.

In that cocktail, Dr. Walker detected both codeine and morphine. What's more, because of the state of the breakdown of those chemicals in Ashley's body at the time the sample was taken, she could confidently testify that Ashley *must have been unconscious at the time most of the drugs were ingested.* Getting even more specific, she estimated that some of the drugs were ingested only ninety minutes before the sample was taken. Since Bree discovered her sister in a sorry state at approximately six-thirty in the morning, Ashley was still getting dosed during the early-morning hours, perhaps as late as four-thirty to five o'clock. She could not have been ambulatory at that point. So she must have ingested the drugs *against her will.*

The afternoon began with Dr. Christine Stork testifying that she was an employee of the Clay, New York, local poison-control center. She had a doctor of pharmacy degree from St. John's University College of Pharmacy and Allied Professions, a Bachelor of Science degree from the Albany College of Pharmacy of Union University, and had studied the medical and autopsy records of both of the defendant's husbands. Plus, she had studied the complete medical history of Ashley Wallace. Indeed, by the time Ashley overdosed, Dr. Stork was already familiar with Stacey Castor as being the wife of two men who had died from ethylene glycol poisoning.

"For an average-sized man, how much antifreeze would need to be ingested for the poison to be fatal?" Christine Garvey asked.

"If the patient went untreated, a very small amount could prove fatal," Dr. Stork said. "About three fluid ounces. That would be the equivalent of three shot glasses full."

"Three shots of antifreeze would be fatal?"

"Probably, yes."

"Four?"

"Four would be most certainly fatal. Yes."

She explained that those quantities assumed that the antifreeze was ingested all at once. If it were ingested over a long period of time, the victim would be in great discomfort as organs in his body shut down, but it would take more than four shots of antifreeze to kill him.

Stork opined that David Castor was poisoned with ethylene glycol sometime on Saturday—between Friday night and Saturday night—and that he didn't die until Monday—a long and torturous way to go.

Garvey then shifted the topic to Stacey Castor's first husband. "Was antifreeze residue the only poison found in Michael Wallace's body?" she asked.

"No, there were also measurable amounts of rat poison in his tissue as well."

"Does rat poison kill the same way as antifreeze, by shutting down the organs?"

"No, it kills by depriving the blood of its ability to clot," Stork replied.

Again, the topic shifted, now to the defendant's eldest daughter. She testified that Ashley was "critically ill" when she was brought to the emergency room at University Hospital, and that a "host of drugs" was found in her system.

Under cross-examination, the witness admitted that there were aspects of Ashley's version of what happened that didn't fit the facts. If Ashley had only had one drink seventeen hours before she showed up in the emergency room, then her blood-alcohol level would have been zero. She must have digested alcohol in large quantities sometime over the weekend for it to register as it did in blood samples taken in the hospital.

Based on the quantity of drugs found in Ashley's system, she would not have been able to move around as she had. "If she had had any more drugs on board," Dr. Stork said, "she would not have been breathing." The same was true with the amount of time she'd had the drugs in her system. If it had been longer, she would have died. Because of this, Dr. Stork came to the conclusion that at least some of the drugs had been ingested less than two hours before she was discovered by Bree.

The story of what happened, according to Ashley, was "incomplete," the witness said. Alcohol and drugs were ingested soon before her sister found her, yet no one's version of the facts accounted for that.

Dr. Stork was briefly and, according to her, "lightly" cross-examined by Chuck Keller. The defense was not entirely displeased with Dr. Stork's testimony, and after inducing her to reiterate some of the key points of her testimony, he let her go.

* * *

The prosecution's final witness was Dr. Robert Stoppacher, David Castor's (and Michael Wallace's) autopsy surgeon.

"What is your current title, Dr. Stoppacher?" Christine Garvey inquired.

"I am the acting chief medical examiner for Onondaga County."

"During your autopsy of David Castor, what, if any, evidence of disease did you find?"

"I found none."

"Any evidence of chronic illness?"

"No," Dr. Stoppacher said. The only thing wrong with David Castor was the antifreeze in his system, and that was what had killed him.

"We have witnesses that say David Castor appeared drunk during the days before his death. Does that observation agree with your conclusion?"

"Absolutely. Antifreeze poisoning will first affect the brain and the nervous system. During that time, the victim may very well appear drunk."

Dr. Stoppacher told the court that the second stage of antifreeze poisoning affects the circulatory and respiratory systems. The blood vessels contract. The victim loses the ability to breathe.

Christine Garvey's voice emoted sympathy for the victim's suffering. "And about how long would that second suffocating phase of the poisoning last?" she asked.

"There is a broad range. In a healthy adult male, such as David Castor, the respiratory failure could go on for anywhere from twelve to twenty-four hours," Dr. Stoppacher said.

There was a third stage as well, the medical examiner pointed out. It affected the kidneys and caused acute kidney failure. The third stage could last from one to three days, and ended with death.

He said his best guess was that David Castor passed away sometime between four o'clock on Sunday afternoon and four o'clock in the morning on Monday. Urged to be more specific about the time of death, Dr. Stoppacher said, "It's impossible to say."

"No further questions, Your Honor."

"Chuck?"

Under Chuck Keller's cross-examination, Dr. Stoppacher testified that combining antifreeze with liquor would slow the poisoning process. A smart killer would not purposefully combine an alcoholic beverage with the antifreeze because the combination decreased rather than increased the chances that the poison would be deadly. The alcohol, he testified, prevented the antifreeze from breaking down into its lethal chemical components.

"The prosecution rests," Fitzpatrick said.

Judge Fahey asked if Charles Keller was prepared to begin his case.

"I am, Your Honor."

The judge declared a ten-minute recess, after which Keller would call his first witness.

22

The Defense's Case

After court, on the days when the prosecution was presenting their case, Chuck Keller was having long, sometimes all-night, sessions with his client. The question was, should Stacey testify on her own behalf? It was risky. But possibly necessary.

If the jury didn't find Stacey a credible witness, they were sunk. Of course, they might be sunk, anyway. Juries did not like it when defendants did not testify. Even though the law was clear that choosing *not* to testify was *not* an indication of guilt, juries were human beings and saw not testifying as a sign of something to hide.

So Keller spent many hours alone in a room with Stacey. They practiced cross-examination. Keller tried to anticipate the types of questions Fitzpatrick might ask. He would switch up, ask questions softly, and then become more firm. He'd ask many questions on one subject, and then abruptly switch topics. And throughout it all, Stacey was a rock. She was unflappable. Keller told Stacey the decision was up to her. Stacey didn't give him the green light until hours before the defense was scheduled to start its case.

The first defense witness was Dr. John Roy, a Brooklyn College linguistics professor. He refused to testify with television cameras rolling, so the cameras were turned off.

Dr. Roy told the jury he was an "authorial attribution" expert. Based on syntax, spelling, punctuation, etc., he could determine whether or not an individual was the actual author of a written piece.

"Dr. Roy, did you have any contact with the defendant before this trial?" Keller asked.

"No, I never spoke to or met Stacey Castor before this trial," Dr. Roy replied.

Dr. Roy said he had compared the language of the "suicide note" to writing samples by both Ashley Wallace and Stacey Castor.

Before getting an opportunity to offer an opinion, the district attorney popped to his feet and eagerly asked to question the witness regarding his credentials as an expert.

Fitzpatrick knew forensics and knew that "authorial attribution" was not what he would later describe as an "authorized beast" within the forensics community.

The DA knew there were some qualified people who could do authorial attribution, first and foremost Jim Fitzgerald, a former FBI agent who was down in Virginia now. He was good. But regarding this defense witness, Fitzpatrick had his doubts.

Under Fitzpatrick's grilling, the doctor admitted that, no, he had never been published as an expert, and, no, he wasn't a member of the International Association of Forensic Linguists.

While it was true that Dr. Roy testified in court twenty times before, his true expertise was in Creole and Caribbean dialects, obviously not relevant here.

With Dr. Roy's credentials as an expert shaken, Fitzpatrick turned the witness back over to Chuck Keller, who rapidly switched the subject: "Who wrote the note?"

Dr. Roy broke down his methodology. He'd analyzed the note in terms of grammar, punctuation, spelling, and syntax. The note had little or no punctuation. He had to use his best judgment—his ear—just to break it up into sentences. He imagined the words spoken aloud and thus determined where the breaks should be. He said that he had examined writing samples of Stacey Castor and she always used proper punctuation. Her use of periods and commas was precise and accurate. That discrepancy was a strong indication that the defendant was not the note's author. In the note, when punctuation was present, it was often wrong. "Commas, when present, were misplaced," Dr. Roy testified. Not that Stacey's writing was perfect. Her imperfect writing style was subconscious and a matter of habit. Stacey almost always had the wrong subject-verb agreement. Yet, the suicide note, despite its faulty-when-present punctuation, had correct subject-verb agreement. Obviously, if the defendant wrote the note in a purposefully camouflaged style, it would be much easier to mess up the things she usually did correctly than to correct things she usually got wrong.

"You also compared the note to material written by Ashley?"

"I did. I compared the note to between thirty and forty letters Ashley wrote."

"How did you find the spelling in the note, Dr. Roy?"

"The note had many, many spelling errors."

"Did you compare those spelling errors to the writings of both women?"

"Yes."

"And what was your conclusion?"

"I found that the spelling errors were more consistent with Ashley's writing than with Stacey's."

"Could you give examples of similarities between Ashley's writing and the suicide note?"

"Yes, silent *e*'s tended to be dropped from the ends of words: *e-l-s* for else. *P-r-o-m-i-s* for promise. That was present in the note, and in Ashley's writing samples."

"But not in Stacey's writing?"

"That's correct."

"So, of the two, which do you think wrote the note?" Keller asked.

"I believe Ashley Wallace wrote the note," the linguist replied.

"No further questions, Judge," Keller said.

Fitzpatrick rose to cross-examine, but Judge Fahey put up his hand. The hour was getting late.

23

Fitzpatrick
Turns Up the Volume

On Tuesday morning, January 27, 2009, Dr. Roy returned to the witness stand, reminded by Judge Fahey that he was still under oath, and the jurors got their first taste of Bill Fitzpatrick as a cross-examiner. The whole tone of the trial changed dramatically.

The prosecution had presented its case in a normal tone of voice. Now that it was the defense's turn, the jury learned, there was going to be a lot of anger, squabbling, and yelling.

Fitzpatrick designed his cross-examination to discredit Dr. Roy, who still refused to be photographed or videotaped.

Many, many of Fitzpatrick's questions were objected to on the grounds that they were argumentative. Judge Fahey overruled almost all of them.

At one point, Chuck Keller asked if he could speak.

"Actually, you cannot," Fitzpatrick snapped.

The witness said he'd never met Stacey Castor before the trial and had been involved in the case only since August 2008.

For more than an hour, Fitzpatrick picked at Dr. Roy's direct testimony, going point by point over the so-called suicide note and samples of Stacey Castor's writing. Wasn't this a similarity? Wasn't that a similarity? The witness refused to give a straight answer, which frustrated and angered the prosecutor.

The witness tended to give long answers to questions that called for short ones. No matter how many times Fitzpatrick told the witness to answer yes or no, the witness couldn't do it. When the doctor did answer a question yes or no, Fitzpatrick was not above making a snide comment. "At last, a straight answer," the DA said at one point.

"Objection, Your Honor. He can cross-examine without obnoxious editorializing," assistant defense counsel Todd Smith said.

"Overruled," Judge Fahey said.

The objections were flying from the defense table—sometimes from Keller, sometimes Smith, sometimes both men rose to shout out in unison. Although a couple of the objections were sustained, Fitzpatrick got most of the testimony he wanted onto the record. To Keller's frustration, by the time Dr. Roy left the stand, the jury thought there was evidence of authorial attribution pointing both toward Stacey and Ashley.

Charles Kurtz testified that he was a tax specialist, and the man who'd prepared David Castor's taxes. He had received a subpoena in the mail from the defense.

"I was Castor's tax guy for years—somewhere in the neighborhood of fifteen years," Kurtz said. He'd known David before David knew Stacey, back when he was still with Janice. He wouldn't call David Castor a friend, although they were friendly. He was a client, a "good acquaintance."

The prosecution wanted the jury to believe that Stacey killed David for money. Chuck Keller planned on giving them a reality check. Kurtz testified that Castor's business *lost* $5,000 the year before his death.

During cross-examination, Kurtz admitted that the loss was atypical and was in part due to a one-time write-off. As a rule, he said, the company was profitable.

Chuck Keller called a series of Stacey's friends, some of whom had also testified for the prosecution.

Robert Ross testified that he had been a friend of David Castor's for thirty years. He managed to testify that it was he who had suggested Stacey get out of the house on the last weekend of David's life, but when he tried to explain why, his testimony was hindered and then halted altogether by hearsay concerns. The jury got the idea that Stacey and David had an argument, but not much else.

Dani Colman was recalled as a defense witness and said that David Castor's death had brought Stacey and Ashley closer together, in essence that Ashley's domestic situation improved with her stepfather out of the picture.

Dani's husband, Michael Colman, was also recalled and testified briefly for the defense. His testimony was meant to be a bit longer, but Chuck Keller had earlier lost a ruling regarding Colman's testimony.

With the jury out, Keller had told Judge Fahey that Ashley had made incriminating statements about herself in the hospital the day after her overdose. Keller asked Judge Fahey to allow the testimony, stating that the testimony was not bound by hearsay rules. He told the judge he planned to ask both Michael and Dani Colman questions regarding the statements they heard Ashley make on Saturday, the day after she went to the hospital. "My understanding from these witnesses is that the sum and substance of those statements was 'Sorry, Aunt Dani, I am sorry, please forgive me.'"

Judge Fahey ruled against Keller. He would not allow either of the Colmans to testify in front of the jury about what they had heard Ashley say in the hospital. Keller complained that the judge was not allowing him an opportunity to refute allegations against his client that she had tried to poison her daughter. If the daughter was heard apologizing for her suicide attempt, then that would do the trick. But Judge Fahey's ruling stood. The judge noted that Ashley Wallace had been a prosecution witness at the trial two weeks before, and Keller had every opportunity during his cross-examination to ask if she had said those things, but he chose not to. That would have been the time to bring it up, and now the moment was past, and he would not allow Keller to introduce the topic at this time.

So Michael Colman's testimony for the defense was limited. He described how he helped move the seemingly inebriated David Castor. Stacey, he said, had suggested that maybe they ought to call an ambulance, and he'd replied, no, he didn't think that was necessary. All David needed was a chance to sleep it off.

"Did you go to David's funeral?" Chuck Keller asked Stacey's friend.

"Yes, I did," Michael Colman replied.

"What was Stacey's demeanor that day?"

"Umm," the witness said, thinking a moment. "Very upset. Very shaky. Distraught."

"Do you recall seeing Ashley Wallace at David Castor's funeral?"

"I do."

"How would you describe her demeanor on that occasion?"

"It was more of going to the prom," the witness said.

"Objection, Your Honor," Fitzpatrick said.

Judge Fahey paused before saying, "I am going to sustain it."

"Can you be more specific?" Chuck Keller asked the witness.

"It wasn't more of a funeral atmosphere," the witness said. "It was more of like going to a regular social gathering."

"Objection," Fitzpatrick said, now sounding angered. "I move that that nonsense be stricken."

"No, I'll let it stand," Judge Fahey said; then to Keller, he added, "Go on."

"Without giving us a summary, can you point to specifically what happened or what you saw that made you think that?" Keller asked.

"Well, everybody else was upset. Bree was crying. Stacey was a nervous wreck. Dani (the witness's wife) was a nervous wreck. But, remembering back, Ashley just didn't seem to be (at) all upset, in my opinion."

On cross-examination, Bill Fitzpatrick attacked Michael Colman's credibility on various fronts. He held up a document and saw the witness's eyes focus on it. The document was "People's Exhibit 123," an affidavit the witness now verified he had signed in August of 2005.

"Would you agree with me that in this affidavit there is no mention of speaking with the defendant about getting medical treatment? Is that true?"

"Not in the written statement," Colman said.

Fitzpatrick spoke rapidly, a machine-gun cadence: "So, when you were talking with the police, you were anxious to tell them, but they just forgot to put it in the affidavit, is that your testimony?"

"Well—"

"Yes or no?" the DA said abruptly, dripping impatience.

Keller objected to the tone, but Judge Fahey all but ignored him, and the cadence of the cross-examination continued without interruption.

"What it was—was . . . ," the witness stammered.

"Yes or no, sir?" Fitzpatrick said, even more urgently now.

"I told the officer, yes. And I—"

"You told them, but they didn't put it in the affidavit? So you said, 'I wanted that put in there.' Is that what you told them?"

"That—that isn't what happened. I—"

"You read over the written statement, didn't you?"

"I looked over the statement and I—"

"And you made some corrections, didn't you?"

"Objection," Keller said.

"You have to let him finish the answer," Judge Fahey told the DA.

"No further questions, Your Honor," Fitzpatrick said disgustedly.

The court took its lunch break. Following lunch, the defense called Norman Chirco, a lawyer practicing out of the nearby town of Auburn. He testified that he helped Stacey probate David's estate, which included large business debts and other legal issues. The point here was that Stacey really didn't gain anything financially by David's death.

Under cross, the lawyer said the will Stacey brought to him had not been composed by a lawyer. As executed, Stacey received approximately $70,000 from David Castor's estate.

The defendant's mother, Judi Eaton, was immaculately coifed on the stand, a gray-haired woman who emanated a cool and stubborn mindset. Her take on the case was simple: her daughter was innocent; her granddaughter Ashley was guilty.

In order to believe this, she conceded, one had to be able to envision a twelve-year-old Ashley killing her own father. Eaton had no trouble with that.

Lending coherent voice to the Oedipal portion of the defense's case, she testified that when Bree was born, the younger sister instantly became her daddy's favorite, and that Ashley was all but ignored.

"Did Michael Wallace, to your direct knowledge, physically abuse his daughter Ashley?"

"Yes. He whipped Ashley severely. It was so bad that I spoke to him about it."

"What did you say to him?"

"I told him that he should treat Ashley better."

The subject moved to David Castor and his hostile relationship with his stepdaughters. Eaton recalled a celebration dinner in honor of the girls during which David Castor stormed out, slamming the door behind him, rather than participate.

Eaton testified that her granddaughter Ashley had told her that David Castor, at times, had touched her inappropriately, and she hadn't liked it.

"Objection, Your Honor. Hearsay," Fitzpatrick said.

"Sustained," Judge Fahey said. "Jury will disregard the statement from the witness about inappropriate touching."

"Was Ashley upset about her stepfather's death?"

"Not about his death. She was upset that she had to go to his funeral."

"Why was that?"

"Ashley hated David," Eaton said.

"Objection!" Fitzpatrick said.

"Sustained," Judge Fahey said. "Jury will disregard the witness's last statement."

"Ashley did not want to go to David Castor's funeral?"

"Not at all."

"No further questions," Chuck Keller said.

"Cross?" Judge Fahey said.

The DA knew it was bad form to intensely cross-examine a woman with gray hair—plus, he wasn't convinced that Mrs. Eaton had damaged his case. She didn't come off as a woman with inside info regarding the case, but rather—at best—as a family member with a firmly held, but baseless, opinion.

"No questions, Judge," Fitzpatrick said, and Eaton was allowed to sit in the spectator section.

OCSO detective William Naughton testified that he was among those who investigated the Castor house following Ashley's overdose. He said he recovered three straws from the home at that time. One of them was protruding from the plastic lid on a fast-food soft-drink container. According to later lab reports, none of them had DNA from Ashley Wallace on them. This would enable Chuck Keller to argue later that if Ashley was telling the truth and used a straw to drink the foul-tasting beverage her mother had prepared, then where was the straw that must have had poison on the inside and Ashley's spit on the outside? As far as anyone could tell, the straw didn't exist, Keller would be able to say.

* * *

Mark Czapranski (pseudonym), Ashley's ex-boyfriend, was next up. Chuck Keller wasn't sure how this guy was going to come off in front of the jury, but he had to take the chance. If he could get Czapranski's story on the record, it would be worth it.

Keller's anxiety was based on the fact that the witness—although twenty-two years old, and old enough to know better—still boasted the teenage affectations of "gangsta." He came off like a man with some growing up still to do. A check of his page on a well-known social-networking website showed him about to light up an elaborate marijuana pipe. On that same page, he gave his address as *Bitchville in da three-one-five,* a reference to the town of Bald-winsville and the Onondaga County area code. A check of his criminal record showed that he'd been popped for carrying a pot pipe in 2006, when he was still a teenager. He was a big kid, six-two, one-eighty, and—no stranger to the weight room—he was pumped.

As soon as Czapranski was called to the stand, Bill Fitzpatrick rose to his feet and objected: "This witness should not be allowed to testify."

Judge Fahey ordered the jury out of the room, and Czapranski testified at first for the judge only. Hearing his story, Judge Fahey overruled Fitzpatrick's objection. The jury was brought back in.

The witness said his name, spelled it for the benefit of the court reporter, and gave his address. He explained his connection to the case. He was Ashley's ex-boyfriend, and he noted that during the time they were going out Ashley communicated through letters and phone conversations that she had contemplated suicide.

As it turned out, Keller would be thrilled with this witness. The hearsay rule was waived because Ashley's statements could be shown to refute the charges against his client. Ashley testified earlier that she had mentioned suicide in a letter once, but that it was only an abstract notion, something she had just *thought* about. And those thoughts were something that had occurred earlier in her life. According to previous evidence, her depression had been caused by the death of her father in 2000.

What her ex-boyfriend was now saying was quite different.

"Did you ever talk to Ashley about her suicidal feelings?" Keller asked.

"Yes."

"When did these conversations take place?"

"Best I can remember, sometime fall of 2004."

"And this was after she wrote you the letter in which she said she had contemplated suicide?"

"Yes, sir. We talked about her suicide attempts. She said she couldn't deal with life anymore, and that she didn't want to be alive."

"Did she give you any reasons for her suicidal feelings?"

"Yes. She wasn't doing well in school and she had family problems."

"Was she specific about these family problems?"

"Yes, she said that she was having a hard time getting along with her stepfather."

"What did you do in response to that?" Chuck Keller asked.

"I told her not to do it," Czapranski replied.

* * *

DA William Fitzpatrick hoped the jury would think it through. This was not evidence that Ashley's overdose had been a suicide attempt. This was evidence that showed why Stacey thought she could get away with framing her daughter's death as a suicide. It was because of Ashley's depression, for which she was being medically treated, that her mother figured everyone would be quick to believe she purposefully OD'd.

Feeling good that the "boyfriend" section of his presentation was going well so far, Chuck Keller called Stacey Castor's fiancé, Michael Overstreet, to the stand. Feel-good time for the defense was over. In retrospect, Keller may have wished he hadn't called Overstreet at all.

Sure, Keller induced Overstreet to say that, yes, he had been with the defendant during the time period when she was supposed to have been attempting to murder her daughter, and she couldn't have done what the prosecution said because she'd only been out of his sight once.

"When was that?"

"She went to the bathroom."

There was no way she could have force-fed her daughter all of that alcohol and all of those pills without him knowing about it.

"Was there, to your knowledge, a bottle of vodka in the house the evening before Ashley was taken to the hospital?"

"Yes, there was."

"Was it empty, partially full, or full?"

"It was full."

"Where was that bottle?"

"In the freezer."

"Could Ashley have gotten out of bed, gotten the bottle of vodka out of the freezer, and returned to her room without you knowing about it?"

"Sure."

"No further questions."

So far, so good, Chuck Keller thought. But Keller's optimism waned almost immediately as Bill Fitzpatrick took the reins. Keller knew by the second or third question in the prosecution's cross-examination that this was what the jury would remember best about the defendant's fiancé. Fitzpatrick had studied Overstreet's previous statements under oath, including his testimony before the grand jury. The DA tried to get Overstreet to admit he lied, that he lied all the time, that he lied when he wasn't under oath, when he was under oath, whenever. The witness tried to represent his false statements as "misunderstandings" and "misspeaking," but Fitzpatrick used the word "lie" in just about every question he asked. Why had Overstreet not mentioned the full bottle of vodka in the freezer in any of his previous statements to authorities, including his testimony to two grand juries?

During his direct testimony, Overstreet had given Stacey an alibi. She couldn't have tried to kill Ashley. He was with her every second, all except for that time she went to the bathroom. In earlier statements, however, Overstreet said Stacey was out of his sight several times during that night because she'd gone to Ashley's room to check on her sleeping daughter.

Fitzpatrick asked Overstreet if he and Stacey had ever had a conversation during the hours and days following Ashley's overdose about not mentioning a pill bottle that had been discovered in Stacey's closet. Overstreet said no such conversation had ever taken place. Fitzpatrick played a taped conversation between Stacey and Overstreet in which the defendant's boyfriend had informed her that he had discovered a pill bottle in her closet. "Don't give that to anybody," she replied on the tape.

The jury understood what was happening here. Overstreet was in love with the defendant and would say whatever he thought was best to get her acquitted. Therefore, you couldn't believe a word he said. Alibi denied.

But Fitzpatrick wasn't done. Now that he had caught the defendant lying under oath, his ire swelled, and the volume of his voice grew in anger.

"Mr. Overstreet, when you testified before the grand jury, you raised your right hand, you put your hand on that Bible, and took the oath—just like you did today, correct?"

"Correct."

"And then you *lied* to that grand jury, didn't you?"

"I told them the truth."

"The truth?" Fitzpatrick said incredulously.

"Yes, I did."

"And you were asked about the pill bottle on December 15, 2008?" Fitzpatrick asked, referring to the date of Overstreet's grand jury testimony.

"Yes, I was."

"And didn't you, at that time, deny any knowledge of that pill bottle?"

"I didn't deny any knowledge of it," the witness replied stubbornly.

Fitzpatrick had a transcript of Overstreet's testimony before the grand jury in his hand and he waved it in the air for a moment before reading the Q and A aloud from it: *"Question—Now did there come a time when either Michael or Dani Colman located a pill bottle?"*

The DA didn't have a chance to read the answer before the witness said, "I didn't deny any knowledge of it, I just said that I didn't find it."

Fitzpatrick continued reading, informing the jury of the witness's previous answer to the same question: *"Answer—The only thing I can recollect being found on the floor was a pill.* Were you asked that question, and did you give that answer?"

"I gave that answer, but I also said that Dani Colman found a pill bottle."

"Excuse me, sir."

"Yes."

"Were you asked that question, and did you give that answer?"

"That I found a pill on the floor, yes."

"Was the answer you gave to the grand jury correct, that the only thing you could recollect being found on the floor was a pill?"

"I, uh—"

"Did you give that answer?"

"Yeah."

"Was it true?"

"No."

Fitzpatrick's chest puffed out. The witness had again confessed to perjury.

The DA read more questions and answers from the grand jury transcript. Overstreet had been asked if he recalled seeing a Lexapro bottle that day. The witness, at that time, said he did not recall seeing such a bottle.

"Were you asked that question, and did you give that answer?"

"Yes."

"Now, when you told this jury a few minutes ago that you had not lied to the grand jury, was that answer true?" Fitzpatrick inquired.

"Objection, Your Honor," Keller said.

"Overruled," Judge Fahey quickly chimed in.

"Yeah, I guess it was not true," Overstreet said.

The DA now erupted with fury. "So you lied to *these people*!" he hollered, gesturing broadly, but mostly in the direction of the jury.

"No," the witness said, "I told you that day there were circumstances—"

"You told these people just a few minutes ago that you told nothing but the truth to the grand jury?"

"Yes."

"And that was a lie!"

"There are underlying circumstances," the witness said. His hesitant and meek voice was in sharp contrast to the DA's bark.

Fitzpatrick's voice now echoed off the courtroom walls as he boomed, "Oh, I'm sorry. I forgot!"

"Objection."

"Sustained," Judge Fahey said, and then to Fitzpatrick, "Go on."

"So whether or not you tell the truth depends on the circumstances, right?" Fitzpatrick asked.

"No, I was doing it to protect Stacey," Overstreet said, now finding his footing a bit—but not for long.

The DA again erupted, now with near-hysteria, deeply angered by this liar—this perjurer. "I didn't ask you anything about that today! Listen to my questions! Listen to my questions!"

"Okay."

"You lied to this jury a few minutes ago!" Fitzpatrick didn't even attempt to make this sound like a question. It was a flat-out statement.

Since no question had been asked, the witness struggled formulating a response. "I . . . Could you repeat . . . ? I'm not following you."

"You. Lied. To this jury. Minutes ago. In this courtroom." It was how one might speak to a small child or to a person who didn't speak the language well.

"That I didn't recollect finding the pill bottle?" The only one asking questions now was the witness.

"No." the DA said. "I asked you if you lied to the grand jury in December '08, and you told this jury, 'No, I didn't lie to the grand jury.'"

"Okay, I misspoke. I apologize," Overstreet said.

"Is there any reason you can think of that anyone should believe you, Mr. Overstreet?"

"Objection," Keller said.

"Overruled," the judge said, again deciding almost instantly so as not to interrupt the rapid rhythm of Fitzpatrick's cross-examination.

"Yeah," the witness said, answering the question. "Because I'm telling the truth."

"Right now?"

"Yes."

"Okay," Fitzpatrick said.

Fitzpatrick now attacked Overstreet's credibility from a different angle. "When you went over there on Thursday night, on the night the people allege the defendant tried to kill her daughter, you never saw Ashley that night, did you?"

"No, I did not."

"The defendant told you that she was just sleeping normally, didn't she?"

"Yup."

"From one-thirty in the afternoon to six-thirty in the morning, right? Just like good old Dave, just hanging out like normal, right? Is that what you are telling us?"

"I wasn't there at one-thirty (in the afternoon), so I couldn't tell you if she was in bed."

At one point, Fitzpatrick's attack could not have been more personal. He asked Overstreet if he was the one on a recorded phone conversation with Stacey, the one who made casual comments about drinking heavily and regularly, the one who made a racist joke about President Barack Obama.

Now the DA erupted anew. "You are a drunk! You are a racist! You are a perjurer!" Fitzpatrick yelled. Why, Fitzpatrick asked, should the jury "ever believe anything you say?"

Keller rose to his feet. "Objection!"

"Sustained," Judge Fahey said calmly.

But the intensity remained in Fitzpatrick's eyes. His point had been made. "Nothing further with this guy," Fitzpatrick said, spitting disdain.

"Any redirect?" Judge Fahey asked the defense table.

"No further questions, Your Honor," Keller replied.

"You may step down," Judge Fahey informed the thoroughly grilled witness, and Overstreet breathed a visible sigh of relief.

That concluded the first day of testimony for the defense. Perhaps just to give the prosecution something to think and worry about, Chuck Keller announced at the end of the day that he planned to call Ashley Wallace. The judge wanted to know what the subject matter would be, and Keller explained he hoped to quiz Ashley in front of the jury regarding her animosity toward her mother's boyfriends, a pattern that he believed couldn't be more relevant to this case. Keller reminded the judge that he hadn't wanted to ask these questions to Ashley in the form of cross-examination when she was on the stand as part of the prosecution's case, and because the subject had not been brought up during direct examination, the judge had ruled that it was not proper cross-examination. Now Judge Fahey ruled that if the defense wanted to call Ashley as their own witness, he would allow those questions to be asked.

The defense was ready to start right back in the next morning, but they encountered problems.

24

Whiteout Conditions

As was customary during these courtroom proceedings, on Wednesday morning, January 28, 2009, the judge and counsel from either side began their morning's work with the jury outside. Business that the jury did not need to hear was, when possible, taken care of first, so the panel wouldn't have to be ushered back and forth from the jury room. On this morning, that early-morning business ended up negating the entire day.

Before a word was spoken, nerves were already on edge. Outside, Syracuse was getting blasted with a snowstorm. With the exception of the defendant, everyone had to battle whiteout conditions on the roads just to be in attendance. No one was frazzled—these were all local people who handled the grueling winter well—but there was just a touch of that got-out-of-the-wrong-side-of-the-bed feeling.

First subject: Chuck Keller said he wanted to call

Lynn Pulaski to the stand as a defense witness. He planned to ask her why the will she signed had been backdated two years. The prosecution objected to the whole idea, because the witness would have no way of knowing for sure why this was done, that even if Pulaski had some understanding as to the motive for the backdating, at best she was basing it on hearsay. She only "knew" what Stacey had told her to be true, and anything Stacey had said to her friend was apt to be so self-serving as to be useless. The judge ruled that Lynn Pulaski should not be called by the defense for that purpose.

Keller wasn't done. He announced that he only planned to call one new witness that day, a computer expert. A summary of the expert's testimony had been given to the prosecution only minutes before.

"Talk about coming out of the blue," Bill Fitzpatrick complained. The DA vigorously objected to the planned testimony. It was based on an expert's findings. "We haven't had adequate time to study those findings," he said, adding that he felt "ambushed" by the defense.

Keller replied that he wasn't ambushing anyone. He had given the prosecution almost as long to look at his expert's results as he himself had. "I received this report via e-mail at two o'clock this morning," Keller said.

Judge Fahey lent a sympathetic ear to Fitzpatrick's objections and declared that no witnesses would be called on this day, and the time should be used for the people to familiarize themselves with the computer expert's findings and prepare cross-examination.

Keller had another issue to take up, and he sounded testy this time. He asked Judge Fahey to admonish Fitzpatrick for comments he made "during yesterday's testimony," comments made during the cross-examination of Michael Overstreet that the defense felt were "disrespectful and unprofessional."

"This is the way I behave in trials," Fitzpatrick said. "I don't need lectures from defense counsel."

Judge Fahey said, "Everyone, take a step back. Let's do it professionally and politely. Let's just leave it at that."

Fitzpatrick wondered aloud why the defense didn't fill the day by putting the defendant on the stand. Keller, hot under the collar at this suggestion, replied that he didn't feel he had to change the order of his witnesses just because the people said so. Judge Fahey agreed.

When the jury was called back into the courtroom at 9:24 A.M., it was only so Judge Fahey could apologize three times for bringing them all the way into court during a snowstorm, only to send them right back home again.

25

Defense Experts

Almost twenty-four hours later, on Thursday morning, January 29, they tried again. The weather was much improved and sunglasses were in order because of the brilliance of the sun's reflection off the snow. After all the fuss the day before regarding the computer expert, Keller did not call him as his first witness. Instead, he called Dr. Francis Gengo.

"I'm a pharmacologist employed by the University of Buffalo," Dr. Gengo said. He was also an associate professor of pharmacy and neurology and a clinical assistant professor of neurosurgery at the SUNYAB School of Medicine. He'd received his B.S. at Buffalo and his Doctor of Pharmacy degree at the Philadelphia College of Pharmacy and Science, which happened to be the oldest pharmacy school in the United States. The school had undergone a name change, but for the life of him, he couldn't recall what the new name was. (The answer turned out to be the University of the Sciences in Philadelphia.)

He'd spend approximately six to nine months in the classroom, and the rest of the time was spent on clinical rotations at the Hospital of the University of Pennsylvania, Thomas Jefferson Hospital, and the Children's Hospital of Philadelphia. He explained that he had also completed a postdoctoral fellowship in pharmacokinetics and biopharmaceutics at Buffalo. And that he had also, since 1982, been a member of the Dent Neurologic Institute in Amherst, New York, where he had been recruited to initiate and develop a research program in clinical neuropharmacology. That program became so successful that Dr. Gengo was awarded the 1993 George Thorn Award, given to superior researchers under the age of forty by the University of Buffalo Alumni Association. He was currently the Dent Institute's director of clinical research. Over the years, he had published a number of papers on the effects of various drugs on the central nervous system, and his research entailed significant abstraction and statistical analysis of data acquired from several modalities.

"In simple terms, tell the jury what it is that you do," Chuck Keller said.

"I study drug concentrations in the human body," the witness replied.

Dr. Gengo's job as far as Keller was concerned was to make Ashley Wallace look like a liar, to cast suspicion on her story that she took only one drink the afternoon before her hospitalization.

"During the course of your duties, did you study the prosecution's medical and toxicology reports based on a blood sample taken from Ashley Wallace while in University Hospital, Dr. Gengo?" Keller asked.

"I did."

"And, based on those medical and toxicology reports, did you come to a conclusion as to how long before her hospitalization she'd last had a drink of alcohol?"

"Yes. I determined that she'd had her last drink at about midnight on the night before her hospitalization," the witness replied.

"Is it possible that she drank after midnight?"

"Yes, but she couldn't have had more than one drink after midnight."

"How do you know that?"

"Because, with the concentration of drugs in her body, another drink would have been fatal."

"One more drink would have killed her?"

"Yes."

"Okay, let's discuss the quantity of drugs in her system," the defense attorney said. Ashley, the jury recalled, claimed she ingested the drugs through a straw, as they had been mixed into a foul-tasting drink. "When, according to your tests, had Ashley last ingested drugs?"

"In order for Ashley to have the concentrations found in her blood, she had to have taken drugs during the early-morning hours of the day of her hospitalization."

"I see. It is impossible for her to have ingested all of the drugs she took on the afternoon before?"

"Oh yes."

"And how much drugs are we talking about? How many pills approximately?"

"There were upward of sixty pills' worth of drugs in her system," Dr. Gengo said.

"No further questions."

"Bill?" Judge Fahey said.

"No questions, Your Honor."
"Call your next witness, Chuck."

Gerald Grant was the defense's computer expert whose job it was to refute the testimony of Frank Brackin—i.e., that the suicide note had to have been written on Stacey's computer. Grant testified that he was the owner and a consultant at JR Computer Consulting, of Rochester, New York. He was the computer systems administrator for the Western District of New York Federal Public Defender's Office. As a consultant, he specialized in computer forensics, system installation, and training. He lectured and conducted training programs for many large groups at various companies, and was a graduate of Bryant & Stratton Business Institute (the same school Ashley attended) with an A.S. in computer programming. Grant had extensive knowledge of PCs and had been involved in forensic computer examinations, cell site analysis, cell phone forensics, and litigation support for many federal cases. He was a certified access data forensic examiner.

"Let's talk about the computer on which the suicide note was written," Chuck Keller said. "You performed tests on that computer, am I right?"

"Yes. I examined the computer's activity on the days the prosecution expert ignored, days near the time when the note was written."

"What did you find?"

"I discovered that even though there were copies of fragments of drafts of the note on the computer's hard drive, there were no fragments saved of the final version." His conclusion: "I do not agree that any forensic expert can determine from examining that hard drive when the final draft of the suicide note was written."

"Not with any accuracy?"

"Not with any accuracy or specificity," the defense witness said.

The prosecution had tried to show the jury that the so-called suicide note had to have been written when Ashley was not home—and therefore had to have been written by Stacey. This witness said it was impossible to come to that conclusion.

26

In Her Own Defense

"The defense calls Stacey Castor to the stand."

Ready for her close-up, Stacey's hair was shiny and didn't hang as limp as it had on previous days. It had been washed, conditioned, and brushed. Her hair remained parted on the right, and a gray streak in the brown ran down the left side of her face. That gray streak went well with the shades-of-gray-plaid jacket she wore. The jacket had large shoulder pads that made Stacey's upper frame look three feet wide. The jacket was over a black shirt and black pants. Chuck Keller designed the outfit. It completely lacked color. This was not a murderous woman taking the stand. This was a widow—a *grieving* widow.

Stacey walked slowly, her chin high, from behind the defense table to the front of the courtroom. She took the oath and sat on the witness stand.

"Stacey, did you kill Michael (Wallace)?" Keller asked right off the bat.

"No."

Stacey was noticeably heavier than when she was arrested.

"Did you love Michael?" Keller asked.

"With all of my heart," Stacey replied. "I still do."

Like the woman herself, Stacey's voice was swimming with contradictions—deep yet soft, emotional yet calm. Her voice was normally soothing, and it retained some of that quality, even as she sat in that chair, all eyes upon her, executing what must have been one of the more nerve-wracking tasks of her life. That soothing quality to Stacey's intonations was in sharp contrast to her daughter's much edgier voice. Ashley's feelings had spilled forth as she testified. Whatever emotions Stacey was going to feel on the witness stand were going to remain hidden, where the jury would not be able to see or hear them.

"But Michael Wallace was not a perfect human being, was he?" Keller asked.

"No."

"What were some of his faults, as far as you, his wife, were concerned?"

"Well, he smoked like a chimney, for one thing."

"Tobacco or marijuana?"

"Both. Michael did drugs after I got pregnant, while we were dating," the defendant said.

"Did you take drugs as well?"

"No, I always chose not to partake in that lifestyle," she said.

Stacey said that during her first pregnancy and the birth of Ashley, Michael Wallace did not seem to engage himself in the role of father. He was still the wild guy whom she had fallen in love with. When it came time to settle down, he didn't, and when his baby was delivered, he lacked paternal instinct.

Michael was part of the problem, for sure. He just wasn't stepping up. But part also was logistics. Stacey admitted that she broke up with Michael while pregnant with Ashley.

"When did you get back together?"

"In 1990, the year we were married." That would have been when Ashley was still a baby.

But all of that fear-of-fatherhood stuff went right out the window when Bree came along. He was there every step of the way for his second daughter.

"She was the light of his life," Stacey said.

"Your first husband treated his daughters differently?"

"Oh yes."

"He disciplined them differently?"

"Yes. Michael would spank Ashley—but never Bree."

"Did Ashley have an easy childhood?"

"No. She struggled in elementary school. I was always screaming at her and she would always cry. We took her to see a doctor. He said she had ADD."

"Attention-deficit disorder?"

"Yes."

"Did you and your husband have arguments?"

"Yes. We fought about the kids sometimes."

"Ever fight about money?"

"Not money. We never fought about money. That was because we didn't have any."

"Why wasn't there more money?"

"Well"—Stacey paused—"Michael's past had a way of catching up with him. He had unpaid legal fees and other problems."

During the hours before his death, did he seem particularly ill to her? He was on the couch, but that was normal. She used that word: "normal."

Keller now asked Stacey to discuss her relationship with some of her friends, friends who had testified against her for the prosecution.

About Lynn Pulaski, who testified that Stacey had forged a will leaving David Castor's money to her following his death: "I was almost like sisters with Lynn. She is not the 'party friend.' She is the 'cry-on-her-shoulder friend.'"

About Dani Colman: "She is my best friend. We hung out at work, smoked, and partied together."

"Dani is quite the partyer, right?"

"She can keep up with the best of them," the defendant replied.

"There came a time during January of 2000 when Michael Wallace got sick, correct?"

"Yes, I took him to see the doctor once and he got some medication. I made another appointment for him to see the doctor, but he died before the appointment."

Stacey discussed the night before Michael died. "He was sick, lying on the couch, and he had no appetite. He didn't eat dinner."

Stacey then described the time when she came home from work, the girls were home and Michael was motionless on the couch. She remembered standing on the porch and opening the front door. When you first entered the house, the couch was right in front of the door, so the first thing she saw was Michael on the couch. She knew that something was seriously wrong, so she told the girls to leave the room and called an ambulance.

"Do you know about how long it took an ambulance to get there?"

"It felt like years but it was five to seven minutes before the first responders arrived."

"What were you doing during those five to seven minutes? What was going on?"

"I shook Mike. I was trying to wake him up. I was trying to talk to him."

"And after the ambulance arrived?"

"When the responders came in, they told me to go out onto the porch."

"And there came a time when the ambulance left for the hospital?"

"Yes."

"How long was it before that happened?"

"I have no idea how long that was. I rode in the ambulance with Mike to the hospital."

"To which hospital did you go?"

"Auburn Memorial."

"And how long did it take to get there?"

"I have no idea."

"All right. What was going on in the ambulance at that time?"

"They were trying to resuscitate Mike," Stacey said, her voice quavering. She was not enjoying the memories. She gestured to her own throat with her fingers. "They were putting an airway in," she said, referring to a tracheotomy. "They had IVs in. They were doing CPR."

"What were you doing at this time?"

"I was sitting in the front with the driver."

"Were you watching all of this?"

"Yes, I was."

"What happened after the ambulance arrived at Auburn Memorial?"

"We backed into the ambulance bay and they took

Michael out the back. One of the nurses came out and held the door and brought me into the treatment room, where he was. In the ambulance, he had slid off the stretcher and it dislodged his airway." Again, she gestured to her own throat with her fingers. "So they had to retube him in the emergency room. When I walked in, they had his head bent back as far as they could so they could get the tube back in. They set me in a chair in the corner so I would be out of the way. Shortly after that, my mom showed up."

"Was she in the same room?"

"Yes, she stood right behind me."

"You were all together in the same room with the doctors and Michael?"

"Yes."

"What happened next? What did you do? What did you see? What were the doctors doing?"

"There were doctors and nurses and hospital people all over the place. There was a person performing CPR. There were people taking blood pressure. They were giving him IVs with different medications. They were trying to save his life."

"There came a time when Michael died. What do you remember of that?"

"I don't know the exact time, it felt like forever, but there came a time when they decided there was no point in continuing. He didn't even have a shockable heart rate, so there was nothing they could do for him, and the doctor declared him dead."

"Where were you when this happened?"

"In the room with him."

"What did you do?"

"I fell apart," Stacey said. "I wanted to die right

along with him at that point. The doctors and nurses left me alone with him, and I leaned on his chest and cried."

Stacey described how Ashley and Bree came to the hospital and were allowed to come into their father's hospital room to "say good-bye." They were extremely distraught, Stacey testified, and did not remain in the room for long.

"Did there come a time when there came a discussion about whether there should be an autopsy?"

"After they declared Mike dead, our family doctor came, and he met with the emergency room doctors. They discussed what they thought had happened."

"Did they come and talk to you at all?"

"Yes."

"Is that when the discussion of the autopsy happened?"

"Yes."

"Was there a final decision at that time about whether there'd be an autopsy?"

"My family doctor, Dr. Allen, was speaking to me and he said they had pretty much determined that Mike had died of a heart attack, that that was the general opinion between the three doctors."

"Do you know who made the final determination over whether or not there would be an autopsy?"

"The doctors did."

"Did you have some say in it?"

"They asked me. They said they didn't think it was necessary, but if I wanted one done, they would do it."

"What was your decision?"

"I said no."

"Were you the only one there who did not want an autopsy?"

"No, Michael's mother did not want an autopsy, either."

"Why didn't you want him to have an autopsy?"

"I sat in that room for over an hour and watched them try to save his life, somebody jumping up and down on his chest, someone sticking him with needles, and I just wanted him to rest at peace at that point."

"Let me turn your attention to your first husband's funeral for a moment. Both of your daughters were there?"

"Yes."

"How was their demeanor?"

"Ashley was stoic. Bree was distraught and repeated again and again that it was going to be okay."

"Did you collect any money from Michael's life insurance policy?"

"Yes, I collected fifty thousand dollars."

"How did you spend that money?"

"I spent thirteen thousand five hundred on Mike's funeral and burial. I paid off car loans, and I took the girls on vacation," Stacey said.

"Stacey, did you continue to wear your wedding ring after Michael's death?"

"Yes, I wore it for a year. After that, I put the ring on a necklace."

"How long after Michael's death did you meet David Castor?"

"Almost two years. I met David during the fall of 2001, in November."

"How old were your daughters when you met David?"

"Fourteen and ten."

"Just like Michael before him, David wasn't perfect, correct?"

"Correct."

His flaws?

"Well—he snored like a chain saw," she said.

At that point, Judge Fahey interrupted, noting that the noon hour was upon them and it was time for lunch. He called the midday recess and ordered everyone back at 1:20 P.M.

After the break, Chuck Keller picked up right where he'd left off. He asked if Stacey recalled the last weekend of David's life and she said she did. They'd had a fight. He wanted to go away for the weekend, just the two of them, but Stacey thought Bree was too young to be home without adult supervision, and Ashley did *not* count as an adult. She had left the house, but returned on a number of occasions to check on him. David was making a pig of himself. Because he was pissed off, he was determined to drink his way through the weekend. He was going to drink and drink and strip off his clothes and throw up all over the place and be belligerent and generally make a pain in the ass out of himself. She tried to help him a couple of times, and she even called a friend of theirs over to help him, but he didn't want to be helped. No matter what she said or did, David was determined to perpetuate his sad state.

Under Keller's careful direct examination, Stacey told the jury about her last attempt to talk sense to David. She tried, but he was still angry with her. Hostility was now the only emotion David could muster.

She stood outside the bedroom for a moment and then opened the door.

"What did you see when you opened the bedroom door?" Keller asked.

"When I opened the door, David looked up at me and said, 'Get away from me and leave me alone.'"

"What happened next?"

"I backed out of the bedroom and closed the door behind me."

"Stacey, were you the only one with access to David Castor that weekend?"

"No."

"Who else?"

Stacey thought about the question as if she'd never thought of it before. Her eyes searched the ceiling of the courtroom, and then she said, "Ashley, for a while."

"Ashley had an opportunity to be with her stepfather alone that weekend?"

"Yes."

"When was that?"

"When I went to the post office, Ashley and David were in the house alone."

"You went to the post office alone?"

"Yes."

"And when you got back, who was home?"

"Just David and Ashley."

"How long had you been gone, from the time you left until the time you got back?"

"I would say about an hour."

On the other side of the courtroom, Bill Fitzpatrick straightened up a bit in his seat. The post office trip was mentioned in the note, but—in all of the statements Stacey had made to authorities since David Castor's death—she had never before mentioned the trip to the post office or the fact that Ashley and her stepfather were left alone in the house during his final weekend.

"Tell me now about the day that David Castor died."

"I woke up at my friend's house and went to work. David did not show up for work. I gave him the morning, but at one-thirty in the afternoon, I called police."

"What did the police say to you?"

"They told me to go to the house and meet them there. That was what I did."

"You went inside the house and waited?"

"Well, no. I opened the garage door and sat outside until police arrived."

"How did you react when you were told David was dead?"

"I pretty much freaked out and lost it," the defendant said.

"Did you give police a statement during the first hours, after you learned that David had passed away?"

"Yes, I did."

"Was it a complete and thorough statement?"

"No, I was in no condition to give a complete and thorough statement. I told them that I wasn't telling them everything and that I was leaving things out. Police told me that that was okay, that they didn't need every detail."

"At David's funeral, what was your daughter Ashley's demeanor?"

"She didn't seem very upset, but that didn't surprise me really."

"Why not?"

"They were not that close."

"Following David's death, did his business thrive?"

"No, David's business pretty much died when he died."

"So you were out of a job following David's death?"

"Yes, I had to go on assistance for a time," she replied.

"Did you get any money from David's life insurance?"

"Yes. I got forty-two thousand dollars."

"And how was that money spent?"

"It went toward David's funeral and burial, to settle his estate and for other expenses."

In addition to the charge that she had murdered David Castor and attempted to murder Ashley Wallace, Stacey Castor was also charged with forging her late husband's will. Chuck Keller now briefly addressed that subject.

"During your marriage to David Castor, did the subject of a will come up?"

"Yes, it was one of the first things we talked about after we got married. Just before we left on our honeymoon, David mentioned that he wanted a will."

"Was that will ever written?"

"We never got a lawyer to help, and we never signed a will at that time."

"Did you have a friend sign a will after David's death?"

Stacey admitted that she had, and Keller inquired as to her motives.

"It needed to be done," Stacey said matter-of-factly, as if her attorney had just asked her why she went grocery shopping or cleaned the house.

"Please explain."

"I needed to be able to take care of David's things," Stacey replied. "I could never have anticipated in a million years that I would be widowed after two years of marriage. David's estate needed to be settled. I needed money to pay taxes, so I asked friends to witness David's will after his death."

"And what did you get?"

"I got the car and the house, the rest of David's estate. His company and the building were sold to pay off his debts."

"Any money?"

"I received about sixty thousand dollars."

"Did you get a new job?"

"Yes, I became employed at Hiscock Legal Aid." It was noted for the record that this was the organization that also employed Stacey's defense attorney, Chuck Keller.

"Were you questioned again by sheriff's deputies about David Castor's death, in 2007?"

"Yes, I was."

"The prosecution has noted so-called discrepancies between your answers during this interview and what you said when interviewed immediately following David's death. How do you explain those differences?"

"As I said before, the first statement wasn't complete, and I admitted at the time it wasn't complete, and they said that they didn't need a complete statement."

"Did the sheriff's deputies show you your answers

from the first statement when interviewing you again two years later?"

"No, they did not."

"You have read the transcript to that 2007 interview, have you not?"

"Yes, I have."

"The prosecution has noted that you used the word 'antifree,' correct?"

"Yes."

"Did you use that word?"

"No. I started to say 'antifreeze,' then stopped myself before I finished saying the word, so I said 'antifree.' I did not use 'antifree' as a word during interrogation."

Chuck Keller then drew Stacey Castor's attention to the events that preceded Ashley's suicide attempt. Did she remember how Ashley was feeling?

"Ashley was extremely angry that police had dug up her father's body."

"You have heard your daughter Ashley testify that before becoming ill, you gave her a drink, correct?"

"Yes."

"Was her testimony an accurate depiction of what occurred?"

"No."

"How did it differ from your recollection of events?"

"I gave Ashley one vodka mixer to celebrate her first day of college."

"How much did Ashley drink at that time, to the best of your recollection?"

"Ashley drank five and a half mixers total."

"Did you at any time serve her a drink in a pink cup?"

"I did not."

"Did she become ill?"

"Yes, she got sick that night. I told her she probably drank too much, too fast, and she went to bed."

"Did you give your daughter any medication at that time?"

"No."

"Not an Ambien tablet?"

"No," Stacey said firmly. "I didn't give her a sleeping pill or any other kind of drugs."

According to Ashley's testimony, Stacey had suggested they get drunk together again the next night, and it was on this occasion that Ashley became severely ill. Stacey said that this never occurred. There was no second time. Whatever Ashley ingested to make her so ill, she had done on her own, without Stacey's cooperation or approval.

Keller asked Stacey if she remembered the day that she'd found her daughter Ashley seriously ill, near death from an intake of pills and alcohol. Stacey said of course she did.

"You say that Ashley went to her room at about one-thirty in the afternoon?"

"Yes."

"Did you see her come out of her room for the rest of the afternoon?"

"No."

"Was that unusual in any way? Was there anything strange about that?"

"No."

"Why not?"

"Ashley could come home at nine-thirty on a Friday

night and sleep until two Saturday afternoon—if she didn't have to get up."

Perhaps some of the jury picked up on the psychological point being made by this statement. Excessive hours of sleep, a reluctance to join the waking world, could indicate angst or depression.

"What were you doing on the night that Ashley became so ill?"

"I was watching TV with my boyfriend."

"Did you check on her at all that evening?"

"Yes, I checked on her once when her cell phone went off. I answered the phone."

"Who was calling?"

"It was Ashley's boyfriend."

"What did you say to him?"

"I told him Ashley couldn't come to the phone, she was sleeping."

"How did you learn that Ashley was ill?"

"It happened the next morning when I woke up to the sounds of my younger daughter screaming. I woke when I heard her screaming, 'Mommy, there is something wrong with Sis.' I got up and went into Ashley's bedroom. I called out her name. I tried to shake her [awake] and she didn't give any response. She was making a gurgling noise. Bree handed me an empty bottle of Absolut Vodka that was on Ashley's bed. I put the bottle on the nightstand. There was a bottle of Ambien on the bed. I put it on the dining-room table. My younger daughter found what I believe to be Ashley's suicide note." Throwing a thumb to one side like a hitchhiker, the defendant added, "So I immediately went to the phone and called 911."

"What did you say to the 911 operator?" Keller asked.

"I said I needed an ambulance and I gave the address on Wetzel Road."

"What did you say was the reason for your call?"

"I said that my daughter had taken some pills."

"And what were you thinking at that moment, Stacey?"

"I was thinking that this was the most devastating thing that had ever happened to me."

That was Stacey's closing note for the day. Judge Fahey recessed court.

The following morning, January 30, 2009, Stacey Castor wore a solid blue jacket. This one, too, had shoulder pads, but not as large as those in the gray-plaid jacket. Under the jacket, she wore a white turtleneck sweater, the collar of which came almost to her chin, perhaps to protect her jugular.

Chuck Keller asked his client a flat-out question: "Did you kill David Castor by poisoning him with antifreeze?"

"No, I did not." She was firm, calm, and confident. She exuded innocence. Stacey was a woman who always kept the best intentions of others in mind. She was always on the side of good. However, she did not display much emotion—not for a woman who'd lost two husbands and almost one daughter to poisoning.

Bill Fitzpatrick was not displeased by the way the defendant's direct examination had gone. There was a good chance that the jury had already pegged her as cold, unflappable, in sharp contrast to her daughter's anxiety. There were only two viable suspects in this case, and, of the two, Ashley seemed by far the most distressed over the events that had occurred.

"Did you try to kill your daughter and *frame* her for the murders of Michael Wallace and David Castor?"

"Absolutely no. I did not."

"No further questions, Judge."

Judge Fahey turned toward the district attorney, who was licking his chops.

"Cross?" the judge said.

27

The Cross-Examination of Stacey Castor

William Fitzpatrick began on the one point he found most perplexing regarding Stacey Castor's version of the whole truth.

"Why would your daughter Ashley, at twelve years old, want to kill her own father?" Fitzpatrick asked. Would Stacey throw her first husband's reputation under a bus, the reputation of a man she claimed to have loved, and still loved?

"I can't give you a reason for that. I don't know why," Stacey replied.

"Ashley knew where in the house the antifreeze was kept?"

"Yes."

"And she knew how to get her hands on some rat poison, too, I'll bet."

"Yes."

"And it is your belief that Ashley killed Michael (Wallace), correct?"

"Umm." Stacey again paused to consider the matter. Perhaps it was only the wording of her response that she needed to contemplate, but the pause came off as insincere. "Yes," she eventually said.

"And it is your opinion that Ashley killed David Castor, correct?"

"Yes."

"Were there any behavioral problems in Ashley that might indicate she was capable of murdering two grown men?"

"Well, she set our bathroom on fire when she threw a cigarette butt in the trash."

"She set the bathroom on fire on purpose?"

"I don't know. I don't know if it was an accident or not."

"A twelve-year-old who kills her father with antifreeze and then gives him rat poison because he's not dying quick enough, would it be fair to characterize that person as a psychotic monster?"

"I would not define anyone with a mental illness as a psychotic monster."

"All right, would you characterize a twelve-year-old who could kill her father as a psychotic monster?"

"That's not how I would put it."

"How would you put it, Mrs. Castor?"

"I'd say it's a person who has some problems."

The district attorney then ran off a checklist of Ashley's worst deeds, according to her mother. Stacey acknowledged that they were killing her father, killing her stepfather, and trying to frame her mother for those crimes.

"How old is Ashley now?"

"She is twenty-one."

"Does she exhibit signs of mental illness now?"

"No."

"Have you ever sought psychiatric counseling for Ashley?"

"No."

"Did she display signs of mental illness during the days and weeks before David Castor's murder?"

"No."

"I hold in my hand a transcript of the *four-thousand-word statement* that you gave to police the day after David Castor was found dead. Did you mention in this statement that your daughter Ashley had been home alone with her stepfather during the period of time when he must have been poisoned?"

"I don't remember. No, I don't think so."

"Isn't it true that the first time you ever said that was during your testimony at this trial?"

"It might have been. . . ."

"Isn't it true that in your *four-thousand-word statement* you said that you were home alone with David from about four in the afternoon on Friday, until eleven in the morning, Saturday?"

Stacey said she didn't recall, but the transcript indicated she had said it. "I must have forgotten to say the part about Ashley or maybe they forgot to write it down."

"Why did you sign this statement if there were inaccuracies and omissions?"

"I didn't notice that."

"You did not ask for an autopsy when Michael Wallace died, right?"

"I trusted doctors. They said he died of a heart attack. That's why I didn't ask for an autopsy."

"You told police that you called David Castor several times when he was sick?"

"I thought I had called David more than once, but it was only once," she said.

Fitzpatrick, without missing a beat, forged into the area of money. He drew out the fact that Stacey had somewhat understated the financial gain she'd enjoyed following David Castor's murder.

Stacey admitted that she received $19,000 from David's IRA, $16,000 from selling one of his cars, and $30,000 from an auction. That was all in addition to the $60,000 she received through her second husband's estate.

Castor gave the defendant an opportunity to testify as to mistakes her daughters might have made when testifying for the prosecution.

She said that there was one major flaw in Bree's depiction of events, and that was that Stacey's youngest daughter last saw her stepfather alive on Sunday, rather than Saturday.

Judge Fahey called the morning break, and the action heated up upon Stacey Castor's return to the witness stand.

"Isn't it true that you had spent years working for a paramedics company?"

"Yes."

"In that case, I am puzzled by your inaction when David was stricken with his fatal affliction. He's having difficulty talking and standing. He's staggering, he's vomiting. He can't stand in the bathtub. He collapses on the floor and couldn't get back into bed by himself—and you said he looked okay?

What's your definition of '*not* okay'? What would he have to be doing before you say, 'Holy moly, he's sick'?

"You were present in this courtroom when the expert testified what it was like to die from drinking antifreeze. It is a slow, agonizing death that takes place over long hours, yet that Monday morning, you didn't know he was so sick that he needed hospitalization?"

"He was talking to me before I left that morning," the defendant insisted.

Through expertly crafted cross-examination, Bill Fitzpatrick gave the jury a summary of the evidence against the defendant—and he made her confirm it all, point by point: She understood that Michael Wallace's body was exhumed? Crystals were found in the remains of his kidneys? Those crystals were found to be the residue of antifreeze, which was the same chemical that had killed David Castor? She understood all that, right? Yes. Yes. Yes. And . . . yes.

The summary, in the form of questions, continued. The police were closing in on her. A court order was acquired and Stacey Castor's phone tapped. During one recorded phone conversation, there could be heard in the background a tippy-tapping sound. The tape was played for the jury, so they could hear the sound. It sounded like typing.

"Were you typing when you had that phone conversation?" Fitzpatrick asked.

"No, I was not."

"You were typing the suicide note, weren't you?

We caught you, Mrs. Castor, didn't we? With that little *click, click, click.*"

"No."

"Well, then, what were you doing?"

"I don't remember, but I know I wasn't typing."

"You just remember that you weren't typing, right?"

"Yes."

Fitzpatrick's voice rose suddenly to a shout, startling in its intensity. Jurors and spectators jumped in their seats—but Stacey could have been made of marble. She didn't budge. The DA bellowed: "You were typing a suicide note to frame your daughter, weren't you, Mrs. Castor?"

"No, sir," Stacey replied firmly, slowly turning her head from side to side. Fitzpatrick's sudden burst of heat brought further attention to the defendant's chilliness.

The DA was pacing. Now he walked toward the back of the courtroom for three steps, then whirled around to face the witness. Fitzpatrick pointed at Stacey and said, "And we *caught* you at it, didn't we, Mrs. Castor?"

"No, you didn't."

"Just with that little phone call!" Fitzpatrick's voice boomed off the walls of the courtroom. His was a thunderous shout—but now his words came slower, clipped and drenched with contempt. "We caught you with that little *click, click, click.*" The DA's fingers pantomimed typing; one by one, his fingers stabbing downward angrily. Then, with mocking intonations, he quoted from the suicide note: *"Mommy, please don't hate me."* His disgust was twofold. It wasn't just that she had done these horrible things, but also that she was so stupid that she thought the world would believe Ashley did them. "We caught you. Right, Mrs. Castor? We caught you."

"No," Stacey said. The DA was throwing his best shots at her, and it seemed like she hadn't blinked once.

He tried to get her to admit that she knew David Castor's death was being considered suspicious. After all, police were investigating the death and continued to investigate months after. She reiterated that while some of her friends might have known David's death was under investigation, she herself did not. She might have expected that one of them would tell her—they being her friends and all—but none did. She insisted that she never had the slightest inkling about David's death being suspicious.

"You eventually *figured out* that David's death was being investigated, right?"

"Yes, two years later," she said—when they exhumed Mike. Only then was she told that there was an issue with David as well.

Fitzpatrick made the defendant verify a statement she made to police immediately following David's death. She said he had problems coping with life during his last days. He'd been feeling depressed. Inadequate, even. He might have been showing signs of despair, signs of being suicidal. And yet, when Ashley was ill, she discovered a typed note that proved he'd been murdered.

"What were the chances? What were the chances that David was suicidal and being murdered at the same time?"

Stacey was silent.

"What are the odds of that, Mrs. Castor?"

"I don't know," she said.

Fitzpatrick mentioned the "antifree" coincidence. The word appeared that way in the suicide note, and in a verbal statement she made to police.

Stacey replied that the slip of the tongue was the most ridiculous evidence of all. She didn't say "antifree." She had started to say "antifreeze" but stopped midword and said cranberry juice. That's all. Antifree! It was ludicrous. She was a grown woman. She knew the word.

Stacey told the prosecutor that she did not see the suicide note, but that when informed of its existence, she assumed that Ashley must have written it.

"Didn't read it at all?"

"Hardly any of it."

"How much did you read?"

"I skimmed the first few lines, that's all," Stacey said.

"At the hospital, a policeman asked you straight out what you thought happened to your first husband, do you recall that?"

"I was asked a lot of questions."

"You said you thought maybe Ashley had poisoned Mike, poisoned him by putting antifreeze in his Gatorade. Do you remember saying that?"

"I might have."

"As far as I can tell, the only mention of Gatorade at any time in any place in this case is in that note. That note is about seven hundred fifty words long and Gatorade is perhaps the five hundredth word." (Actually, it was word 440.) "How did you know it said Gatorade if you only skimmed the first few lines of the note?"

Stacey had no answer to that.

"Let me make sure I've got this straight," Fitzpatrick said, rubbing his forehead. "It is your testimony that Ashley went to bed at one-thirty in the afternoon and nobody checked on her until six-thirty the next morning? Is that correct?"

"Yes."

"Seventeen hours!"

"Yes."

"For seventeen hours, Ashley was napping, and the next time you saw her conscious was when she was being carted out by ambulance attendants on Friday morning."

Stacey looked upward as she thought. "Yes," she replied.

"During that time, you told Ashley's boyfriend she couldn't come to the phone. She was asleep and drooling, right?"

"Yes."

"You've lost two husbands to poisoning, and you're not concerned that your daughter is laying in bed drooling? And this is *normal*, right, Mrs. Castor?" Fitzpatrick said, his voice again rising in intensity. He looked and sounded on the edge of losing control, literally spitting mad, synchronized accusations and saliva spraying in the defendant's direction. He could not have created a more awkward and hostile atmosphere for the witness.

Stacey remained of stone and didn't squirm.

"Objection, Judge," Chuck Keller said, rising to his feet. "He's screaming at the witness."

"Overruled," Judge Fahey said. The defense attorney sat back down and the DA continued the cross without lowering his voice a decibel.

"This is what you consider normal, is that right, Mrs. Castor?"

"For Ashley to be in her bedroom for seventeen hours? Sure it is."

"Sure it is! Sure it is! Sure, it's normal. And she was drooling, wasn't she! She was drooling! Was she drooling normally, Mrs. Castor?"

"Objection, Judge," Keller said, rising.

"Overruled," Judge Fahey repeated. "Witness may answer the question."

"Was she?" Fitzpatrick said.

Again, Stacey paused to think before giving her response. "I don't know," she said.

"My God!" Fitzpatrick screamed, now pounding a fist on the prosecution table. "You lost two husbands. Your daughter has just learned that her father was dug up out of his grave. And for seventeen hours, your daughter is in her room drooling normally. My God! Is that your testimony?"

"Yes, it is," she said.

Fitzpatrick concluded his cross-examination with a seemingly minor point. He made the defendant acknowledge that in the so-called suicide note, there was the phrase *but it did it*. This was an error. The writer meant to type *but I did it*.

"Now I direct your attention to this," Fitzpatrick said. It was a letter that Stacey admitted she'd written to a friend. She had written it in her jail cell while awaiting trial. In the letter, there was the phrase *but it didn't do it*, instead of *but I didn't do it*.

"Mrs. Castor, isn't it true that 'it' did do this?" the DA asked.

"Sure, I'll answer that. No," she replied—and that concluded Fitzpatrick's cross.

"No further questions," Fitzpatrick said, spitting the words.

On redirect, Chuck Keller established that the reason Stacey Castor allowed her daughter to sleep for seventeen hours was that Ashley did that sometimes, and Stacey had no reason to suspect Ashley was suicidal.

"Recross?" Judge Fahey asked the district attorney.

"No, Judge," Bill Fitzpatrick said.

"Call your next witness, Chuck," the judge said.

Keller moved for a mistrial because of the zealous prosecutor's wild-eyed manner. Judge Fahey denied the defense motion with a small wiggling of the fingers.

"The defense rests, Judge," Keller said.

"Very well, jury is dismissed for the week. We'll resume Monday morning with the closing arguments."

28

Keller's Closing Argument

On Monday morning, February 2, 2009, all the parties were back in their places. Some might have been a tad bleary from the previous day's Super Bowl parties, but Chuck Keller was not one of them. He was alert but nervous as a network TV cameraman shadowed him into the courthouse.

The defense gave its argument first. Keller began his presentation with a Super Bowl joke designed to dissipate the tension. The technique was only marginally successful. A woman's life was on the line.

Keller said that this was a circumstantial case, that no one saw Stacey Castor do anything to harm her second husband or her daughter. There was a reason for that. She didn't do it.

There was no proof as to how these things happened, no way to tell how David Castor died or Ashley Wallace became ill, Keller added. These things remained *mysteries*. Police never considered alternatives to their Stacey-did-it scenario. Cops were stubborn. When a husband was poisoned, the wife did it. That was the way they thought.

Keller invited the jury to look with him at the forensic evidence. He reminded them of Ashley's testimony, and made a laundry list of ways in which the evidence did not fit the testimony.

"Remember, Ashley said that on Wednesday, her mother allegedly tried to poison her, giving her Smirnoff Watermelon to drink. Then on Thursday, she gets the even-more-horrible drink of vodka and orange juice."

Keller asked the jury to recall the many forensic scientists and experts the prosecution had put on the stand. Did any of them at any time say that a glass had been found with residue of vodka and orange juice in it? Was there a glass introduced that carried residue of Smirnoff Ice watermelon flavored? Did they find any glasses at the scene of Ashley's overdose with residue of drugs in them?

"I sure haven't seen them," Keller said.

There was more. Ashley vividly described her mother giving her a straw that she put deep into her mouth so she could get the foul drink past her taste buds and down her throat without gagging. But where was that straw? Where did it go?

They had heard from one police officer that among the items searched for in the immediate aftermath of Ashley's illness were straws. Straws were confiscated. Yet, police found no straws containing vodka, orange juice, Smirnoff Ice, or drugs.

"Where was the DNA testing on the straw to back up Ashley's testimony?" Keller asked. "Where is the toxicology on those straws? Where is it? Why isn't it here? Because no one wants to know—because the answers might be frightening to the prosecution. That's why."

Among the other pieces of evidence that were missing from the people's case was a DNA test on the empty Absolut Vodka bottle. What about DNA from the confiscated pill bottles?

"You heard Miss Hum from the forensic lab say she swabbed the vodka bottle, she swabbed a bunch of things, but she never tested them. They have it. They collected it. They've never tested it," Keller said.

The reason? They were afraid of what they would find. What if Ashley's DNA had been found on the mouth of that vodka bottle? That might have drastically altered how they looked at this case. If Ashley's DNA was found on the mouth of those pill bottles, Keller explained, that would have gone a long way toward helping everyone understand what really happened.

Those tests were not done because the prosecution didn't want to *look*. They were arrogant and felt they didn't *need* to look because they already *knew*. Keller paused, circled his lectern once, seemingly in thought, and then took a swig of water from a paper cup.

Keller asked the jury to look at the prosecution's case as a whole, as one piece. Didn't it reveal a stubborn mind-set? Wasn't it tunnel-visioned? It was like they were looking at the world through one of those straws. How could justice be served when their point of view was so narrow?

He further poked at the holes in the prosecution's evidence. How come Stacey's fingerprints weren't on the turkey baster? To take a logical look at the prosecution's case, we were supposed to believe she wiped her fingerprints off the baster, but she didn't wash the antifreeze from inside it, and she "threw it out" in a place where it was sure to be immediately found.

"Why weren't Stacey's fingerprints on the antifreeze jug?" Keller asked the jury. "They didn't try to find the killer because they knew Stacey was the killer. Mr. Fitzpatrick started looking at the evidence, and once he found something that said Stacey did it, he stopped. He's not trying to prove who did it. He is trying to prove Stacey did it."

That, Keller said, was simply not the way an investigation was run. In a justice-seeking investigation, detectives and scientists would look at everything, not just the stuff that backed up their theory.

"That's how it should have been done. If they found something that didn't point at Stacey, then absolutely they would run it down. If they found something that indicated David Castor was actually feeling suicidal, then, absolutely, they would run it down," Keller said.

It was a well-known fact that Ashley didn't get along with David Castor. In a fair investigation, the police would have looked into that thoroughly. They would have exhausted the possibilities.

Keller asked, "Do you remember when Detective Spinelli was on the stand, the lead investigator, and I asked him if any one of the other detectives investigating the case had given him a lead that might have pointed at Ashley? What did he say? He said, 'Uh, I don't know.' He's the lead detective?"

And what about Detective Leshinski, whose job it had been to interview friends of Stacey Castor's?

One of the leads she developed had pointed at Ashley. "Did you hear anything about police interviewing friends of Ashley's to find out if they should include her or eliminate her as a suspect in this case? No, you didn't. Not a word," Keller said. "Because they didn't do it."

He reminded the jury that he had asked Detective Spinelli if he knew about the "big problems" David Castor was having with Ashley. Spinelli had replied, "Yeah, I heard about them." Keller asked him what he did about that, whom did he talk to about that.

"He said, 'I talked to Ashley Wallace.' He didn't talk to anyone else about it. He didn't talk to her boyfriend. He didn't talk to her friends. He didn't wiretap her phone!" Keller exclaimed. "Detective Spinelli had already made up his mind (about) what happened, and he ignored everything that might indicate he was wrong."

Even the suicide note couldn't tell investigators who did it. The jury heard the computer forensics expert. The date that the suicide note was written *could not be determined*. It was a *mystery*!

Just in case some jurors had trouble believing a twelve-year-old could kill her father—well, it *was* possible, and, often the culmination of abuse, it happened more frequently than we would like to think.

Keller said the last thing Michael Wallace saw was his daughter Ashley walking out the door, doing nothing to help him. She had to pick up Bree at school. Bye.

Keller poked at misinterpretations of the evidence. It was Ashley who wrote that note, and that proved she had knowledge of the murders that only the killer would have.

He pointed out apparent hypocrisies in the case against Stacey. The people wanted to make a mountain out of a molehill. So what if Stacey's facts didn't quite match in interviews she gave two years apart. Yet—yet!—they didn't want you to think at all about Detective Spinelli, who couldn't even keep the facts straight during his own grand jury testimony.

"Let's take a look at Detective Spinelli. Let's examine his work. He had the audacity—the audacity!—to point an accusing finger at Stacey because she gave a statement in 2005 immediately following David Castor's death and then two years later her version isn't quite the same as it was in her written affidavit."

Keller didn't want the jury to think that because he was a defense attorney that it was his habit to question the investigatory prowess of a lead detective. "Hey, my whole family is cops," he said. "But I am pointing the finger at him. Why? Remember when he was on the stand and he was saying how Stacey had told the story of David falling down in two different ways? The second version was a little bit different—she had the order of events a little bit off from when she'd told the same story two years before?" For one thing, he said, two years had passed. For another thing, Stacey never got a copy of her written affidavit when she was being questioned on the same events two years later. Spinelli had a copy of the document. Stacey did not. That wasn't fair.

"You wonder why I say the audacity. Do you remember what happened to him when he testified before the grand jury? At one point, it got so bad that he had to stop his presentation and go get his written report," Keller said. "It's outrageous."

Did the jury think that Spinelli didn't have access to his written report before he testified before the grand jury? Did they think he didn't know ahead of time that he was going to testify, that he had no opportunity to prepare? "Do you think it was like a birthday surprise—'Surprise, Detective! You're testifying today.' Of course not. He did, he knew, and he had plenty of preparation time. Yet, he still couldn't keep his facts straight," Keller said. This, despite the fact that it was only a couple of months later, and he was a trained professional, yet he pointed a finger at an untrained Stacey for doing the same thing two years later when she had no access to the written report. Under Spinelli's intense interrogation, she mixed up a couple of details, and he tried to make a big deal out of that. It was flabbergasting in its audacity.

And Spinelli's difficulty keeping the facts straight was not limited to his grand jury testimony. Keller had been meticulous in his investigation of Spinelli's statements over time. He had gone over the transcripts. He counted the number of times Spinelli couldn't remember details while talking about the case against Stacey Castor. Including the trial and the preliminary hearings at which Spinelli had testified, the detective referred to his notes thirty-two times in order to refresh his recollection. "He had all of the reports, and if you think he didn't read over his reports before he testified, then I don't know what to tell you," Keller said. It wasn't unreasonable to hope he would have had some of the facts memorized, that some of the details would have sunk in, perhaps by osmosis. Spinelli, he said, was the man who didn't take any notes during his 2007 interrogation of Stacey, and then summarized what she said from memory.

"What memory?" Keller asked.

The detective, Keller noted, pointed an accusatory finger at Stacey for mixing up a small detail, when he revealed, during his testimony, that "he didn't know anything about this case."

Keller remembered asking Spinelli about the antifreeze can. There was a print on that can, a palm print. It wasn't Stacey's. That much they knew. Keller asked him if he knew whose palm print it was; he said he didn't know. Keller asked if the palm print belonged to Stacey; he said he didn't know.

"How could he not know?" an exasperated Keller said, holding his arms out to his sides. "This was the biggest murder investigation of his career. How could he not know whose fingerprints were on what? I asked him, did he test this or this? What were the results? He kept saying, 'I don't know.' We're supposed to trust his word?"

Keller continued to criticize Spinelli's work. Noting some temporary confusion Spinelli once displayed while testifying about phone records, Keller said he wasn't at all surprised that Spinelli didn't know how a phone bill worked. "When he was interrogating her, he screwed it up."

Keller asked the jury to imagine the scene. Spinelli, as they now knew, had not been reading the phone bill correctly, yet he was in Stacey's grill about it. He was pounding his fist on the table as he asked his questions, anything to make her fluster and increase the likelihood that she'd utter something he could use against her.

"'Mrs. Castor! Mrs. Castor! I have the records that

prove you wrong!'" the defense attorney quoted the lead detective as saying. "But he was the one who screwed it up. He was the one who had it wrong.

"Let's talk a little bit about that interrogation," Keller said. Could the jury imagine what that must have been like? Hour after hour alone in a room. And not a nice room. There was nothing pleasant about the room. This was a classic interrogation room. Metal desk, chairs, that window where you couldn't see out, but you knew others could see in.

According to Stacey, sometimes Spinelli would speak very softly, Keller explained, lowering his own volume as he said this. "And sometimes he would shout!" he yelled, demonstrating how disconcerting such neurolinguistics could be. Sometimes he talked slow, other times fast. Some questions he asked while up close to her; for others he moved back. He was pacing. He was all over the place.

"If you are having any trouble picturing it, I am going to help you out," Keller said. "Do you remember when Stacey was on the witness stand and Mr. Fitzpatrick was asking her questions? Remember what that was like? That was in a courtroom with a jury and a judge and a defense attorney. Could you imagine what it was like for Stacey with that detective behind closed doors? She had nobody. Could you imagine? How bad was it?" Keller wondered.

"Think about the level of law enforcement scrutiny Stacey endured during her last days of freedom," Keller said. Police watched her. They listened. Long-range photographs were taken. A camera had been mounted on a pole outside her house. "They put a wire at the grave site," Keller said. "They were following her around—but do you know what they didn't do? They didn't record their interrogation of Stacey. Why not? What don't they want *you* to see?"

Perhaps if a tape recording had been made of the various interrogations of Stacey Castor, we would find that there weren't any discrepancies in her statements at all, and that all of those differences were in the faulty memories of police investigators.

And then there was this question of "did she say 'antifree' or did she say 'antifreeze'?"

"Guess what?" Keller said. Use a tape recorder or a video camera and you have it forever on tape, and there's no question as to what she said or didn't say. "We wouldn't have a question if they recorded it," Keller said, "but they didn't—so we don't know what happened."

Keller told the jury to think back upon Spinelli's testimony and how he described Stacey's interrogation. "He said in his calm Detective Spinelli voice that he asked her this, and he asked her that, and she said, 'And then I poured the antifree.' As if that was how she talked. Is that how she talked? 'Hey, I'm having problems with my radiator. I need some more antifree.' Come on!" The jurors had heard her on the witness stand. She was very articulate—a legal secretary! Did they really believe she didn't know the word "antifreeze"?

It reminded him of a game Keller remembered from when he was a kid. "Milk, milk, milk, milk, what does a cow drink?" Everybody answered the question too quickly and said milk. Of course, cows didn't drink milk, they drank water—but the idea of milk had been planted, so it was the first thing that popped out of everyone's mouth.

"It is a trick, a game," Keller said. "Just like interrogation is a trick and a game."

That was why there was no recording. Spinelli was shouting at Stacey, getting in her face and yelling. If that word popped out of her mouth, it was because she'd been tricked. She was nervous. Everyone got nervous under stressful circumstances. Keller placed his fingertips on his own chest and admitted that right then, as he made his closing argument, he felt nervous. Maybe some of the jurors were feeling nervous, too. It was important work they were all doing. So could they imagine how nervous Stacey must have been when the detective was yelling at her and playing games to get her to misspeak?

And the game was not being played fairly. Stacey knew that all she had to do was say the wrong thing once and she might go to prison for the rest of her life. Misspeak once, and there was no taking it back. Could the jurors imagine how nervous she must have felt?

How did they know that Spinelli was telling the truth? How did they know that Spinelli heard Stacey say what he claimed she said? They had Detective Brogan testify. She had been listening from behind the glass. What did she say? "She didn't say the same thing as Detective Spinelli," Keller noted. "She said that Stacey used the word 'antifree'—and caught herself, perhaps midword, and then continued on." That corroborated Stacey's testimony, not Spinelli's.

Had Detective Spinelli told them that Stacey caught herself? No. He'd left that part out. In fact, he'd made it clear that Stacey did not catch herself. So now they had two detectives who were giving two different accounts of what happened. Perhaps they hadn't gotten together to figure it out. One said one thing. One said another. "Who are we to believe? I don't know. If we had a tape, if it was recorded, there would be no question as to which one of them was correct." Once again, a piece of the puzzle had been denied the jury. Bottom line: police hadn't done their job.

It was as simple as that. Perhaps if there had been tapes made of Stacey's interviews, this trial would not have been necessary.

Okay, okay, maybe Stacey did forge a will to make business matters less complicated after she was widowed for a second time. Maybe she did. But it was still a "far cry" from that to thinking she was a cold-blooded murderer. Ashley was clearly the murderer—an angry, difficult woman, perpetually on the edge of losing control.

The motive? It was right there in the note.

Stacey wasn't quick to respond to David Castor's illness—it was true—but there was a solid reason for that. They'd had a huge fight, so bad that she moved to a friend's house. That was why she didn't realize just how sick David was.

Keller was hot now. During the trial, it had been the prosecutor who wore his emotions on his sleeve, while the defense attorney remained cool. Now it was Keller's voice that rose as he delivered his closing argument.

He explained that his opposing counsel on this case, William Fitzpatrick, was the singlemost impressive lawyer he'd ever encountered. He knew all the tricks. "Let me talk about a couple of things that you saw, a couple of things that I call 'lawyer tricks,'" Keller said. Just because he used the word "tricks" didn't mean they were bad. He was a lawyer and he used them, too. Maybe "tactics" was a better word. "Lawyer tactics." One common one was asking a question, usually to a hostile witness, to which you know there is no good answer.

"Why do you ask that question that there's no good answer to? Because you want to force them to give you an answer that doesn't sound good," he said. Keller had an example. Fitzpatrick had asked Stacey this question: "Mrs. Castor, isn't your daughter a psychotic monster?"

"Is there a good answer to that question that would have satisfied any one of you?" Keller asked the jury. "No, there isn't. That's why the question was asked."

He pointed out that if Stacey had said, "Yes, my daughter is a psychotic monster," they would have recoiled in horror because the woman was attacking her daughter. But if she were to say, "No, my daughter is not a psychotic monster," then guess what? That meant that Stacey was guilty.

Another example of a lawyer tactic used by the prosecution was Fitzpatrick's yelling, which Keller referred to as "aggressive cross-examination."

Keller placed his palm on his chest, a sign of sincerity, and said, "I wish I could be that skilled. I'm not." He couldn't cross-examine someone like that. Why was Fitzpatrick that aggressive? Again, it was a trick. There were only two possible responses Stacey could have to it, and neither one looked good in front of the jury. She could break down, and the prosecution would point at her and say, "The innocent don't break down. Only the guilty break down." Or she could keep her cool, which was the case here, and the prosecution would say what a "cold and heartless killer she was."

These tactics represented fantastic lawyering, Keller said, but not evidence. It meant nothing. Would any of them know how they would behave on that witness stand under that cross-examination?

"I sure as heck don't know how I would," Keller said.

He was going to contrast systematically the credibility of the two suspects. Ashley had told them that she had only one drink at noon, or in that vicinity, on Thursday, and that she woke up in the hospital on Friday. If Ashley was lying about that drink, they knew Ashley was guilty. It was as simple as that. "Period, end of story," Keller said. "There was no other reason to lie about it. There was only one reason—that she tried to kill herself and she was guilty."

And it was hard to believe that Ashley was telling the truth, he said. At eight o'clock on Friday morning, many hours later, Ashley's blood-alcohol count was 0.14. All the experts—everyone—agreed that you couldn't get a blood-alcohol level anywhere near that high with a single drink.

"Not possible," Keller said.

The alcohol wasn't the only problem with Ashley's scenario, either. There were the drugs to consider as well. Lots and lots of drugs. Keller pointed out that if Ashley had taken enough drugs, or if Stacey had given her enough drugs, at noon on Thursday to leave the residue that scientists found on Friday morning, the dosage would have been fatal.

"Ashley would have been dead ten times over, long before anyone found her," Keller said.

So they knew it wasn't true. It couldn't have happened that way. Where did the prosecution go from there? Keller guessed as to what they would hear during Fitzpatrick's closing, that the jury would be told that Ashley consumed all of that alcohol and all of those drugs around four o'clock on Friday morning. Experts agreed that that was when the stuff must have been consumed, so that was what the prosecution was going to have to say. Keller pointed out that there was a bit of wiggle room when it came to the accuracy of toxicology reports. It wasn't like math, where two plus two always equaled four, or with a computer where there's a clear-cut correct and incorrect. Different toxicologists handled things in slightly different ways. So taking that into consideration, Ashley had to have ingested the various intoxicants late Thursday night or early Friday morning—certainly not noonish on Thursday.

"So let us ask ourselves this question," Keller said. "How does Ashley Wallace get a bottle of vodka and at least sixty pills in her at four o'clock in the morning? The answer to that question is literally the answer to this case."

The answer was a simple one: it was not possible for Stacey to have done it.

"Why do I say sixty pills?" Keller asked. He asked the jury to recall the testimony of Dr. Gengo, who had testified that sixty was the "absolute bare minimum" number of pills that Ashley must have taken for toxicology results to have reached the levels they did.

Keller walked up to a white board that had been set up at the front of the courtroom facing the jury. With a black Magic Marker, he wrote a large numeral *60*. That number of pills, he reiterated, was the conservative estimate. The witness had said that it was probably more.

"And I submit to you that it is probably a lot more," Keller added. "Let's take a look at this." Writing down the numerals in a column to the right of the big *60,* Keller itemized the drugs that he thought Ashley had consumed.

An empty bottle of Lexapro—a brand name version of escitalopram, used to treat depression and generalized anxiety disorder—was found near Ashley, and the prescription had been for ninety pills. A bottle of amoxicillin, an antibiotic, was found. The prescription had been for twenty pills and there were nine left. He wrote *11* on the board. Also found was an empty hydrocodone bottle, a strong opiate painkiller, and the source of the codeine and morphine that had been found in Ashley's system. That scrip was for twenty-four pills. There was an empty bottle of Ritalin, Ashley's own pills, recently refilled. Keller wrote a *30* at the bottom of the column. There was an empty bottle of Ambien, a prescription sleep medication. That was another thirty pills missing.

Keller started to add the column up, commenting, "I'm not saying that this is exact, or that this is the actual number of pills. And this wasn't even all of the medications they found." The sum: one hundred eighty-five pills.

"I ask you this—how do you get a bottle of vodka and a hundred and eighty-five pills into someone when they are asleep? Involuntarily. How do you do it? You can't."

Keller explained that complex explanations were suspect in this world they lived in. The simplest explanation was most often—almost always, in fact— the truth. In this case, the simplest answer of all was that Stacey Castor did not murder David. The simplest answer was that Stacey Castor did not try to kill her daughter and frame her for it. The simplest explanation was that the suicide note was real. No matter how hard someone labored over this case, no matter how much time someone put into it, a simpler answer was not to be found.

He had been meticulous and he wished the jury to be meticulous as well. He urged them to take their time during deliberation, and to go over all of the evidence methodically, just as he had.

If they did look at everything, it wouldn't matter how much they puzzled over things; they could not conclude that events occurred as the prosecution said they had. No matter how much the jury didn't want to believe that a twelve-year-old was capable of patricide, of murdering her own father, there was no way to be sure she was innocent.

"All you can do is take a guess," Keller said. "There are only two people on this whole planet that actually know what happened." Everyone else was guessing.

A jury could not guess about whether someone is guilty of murder. There was no guessing when it came to deliberations.

"You can't take someone's life away because of a

guess," he added. "You have to *know* it! You have to know it beyond all reasonable doubt. I thank you for your time, ladies and gentlemen."

Keller sat down, and Judge Fahey called the lunch recess.

29

Fitzpatrick's Closing Argument

William Fitzpatrick told the jury that this was a case where the defendant's words and actions spoke for themselves.

"I want to talk to you about one word that may be the most overused word in the English language and that is the word 'love,'" the DA said. Sometimes, he explained, we say, "I love blank." And you could fill in the blank, a sports team or a particular food. That, Fitzpatrick said, was not the essence of the word "love." "In its truest and purest form, it is the greatest gift that has been bestowed on us—our ability to love."

Though there may be loves equal to it, he said, there was no greater love than a mother's love for her child. He offered the jury a quick anecdote, starting by stating that he had been lucky enough to be a father. When his oldest was an infant, he and his wife traveled in early winter to a store.

"And this might not seem like any big thing to you, but it was a remarkable thing to me, because when my wife got out of the car with my infant son cradled in her arms, she hit a patch of ice and went down. Now two million years of evolution tells us that the instinctive, natural thing to do when someone hits a patch of ice, loses their balance and is perhaps about to seriously injure themselves, is to put your arms out, extend them, to brace yourself. My wife never moved her arms. And she took a pretty big whack to her back. My son just kind of smiled and burped and had a good time with that. There it was, in its simplest form. That is what a mother is supposed to do. It is one of life's constants."

Using that example of motherly love fresh in the jurors' minds, Fitzpatrick asked them to recall some statements Mr. Keller had made during the trial, that this didn't make sense, or that didn't make sense.

"How could you possibly expect the defendant's actions to make sense?" the DA asked. "I'm just happy that we are all here trying the defendant for the *attempted* murder of her daughter. Because sense and love have both taken a holiday in the life of Stacey Castor."

The DA explained that it was the little things that got people convicted in courts of law. Here was an example: The defendant called 911, and she was worried about the room being a pigsty. Here was a woman who had already lost two husbands to poisoning, and whose daughter was lying in front of her near death. Naturally, she was going to be worried that the EMTs would think she was a bad housewife.

"That's normal," he said. "She stays at Dani's home on August twenty-first, first time ever. That's normal. She checks the alarm on Bree's phone on September the thirteenth to make sure that Bree is going to be there to find Ashley. That's normal. She's looking for Matt Gandino's ATM card in the dark. That's normal. With her husband, according to her, she's worried about whether or not he's taken his own life. And she makes one phone call. One phone call to the house. That's normal. She says the word 'antifree' on September the seventh, and it appears four times in 'Exhibit 1.' But that's normal. On the 911 call of September fourteenth, she wants to make darn sure that everyone knows there's a note. She is shaking by herself in the dining room while her daughter is in her bedroom dying. And Bree comes up and tries to console her and she tells her to eff off. And that's normal."

There were other little things, little indicators of the defendant's guilt. She knew that Gatorade was mentioned three-quarters of the way through the note, even though she claimed to have only skimmed the first couple of lines. "And that's normal," he added.

The first time the defendant ever answered her daughter's cell phone and talked to Ashley's boyfriend, Matthew Gandino, was on the afternoon Stacey tried to kill her. She told Matthew not to come over. Normal. The defendant phonied up a will, allowed her friends to come close to facing criminal charges. Normal. She hid the Lexapro bottle behind the toilet paper and her fingerprints were on it. Normal.

Back in the year 2000, she tried to convince the

doctors that her first husband, Mike, had died of a heart attack. In 2005, she tried to convince the police that David had taken his own life. Now the defendant claimed that she wasn't trying to convince anyone that David had committed suicide.

"Sure she was," Fitzpatrick said. "Remember? Remember the seven-hour marathon in the garage? And they're drinking Pepsi, and she's alone with him."

The defendant had made it clear that David was drinking Pepsi and he didn't want to share it with Stacey. He made her get her own Pepsi. He must have put something in that Pepsi to hurt himself and he wanted to protect her.

"She's trying to set it up as a suicide—and it almost worked," the DA said. "She was getting good at it. This was number two. When number three came around, she's a pro! Now, with Ashley, she's going to do this note.

"Now this trail of horror and deceit and evil and murder is about to come to an end. Mike Wallace and David Castor, linked forever, by a common killer. They were two regular guys. Everybody knows a Mike Wallace or a David Castor in their lives. 'Hey, Mike, can you shovel my walk for me? I hurt my back. Hey, Dave, can you stop at the store and pick up an extra carton of milk for my mother?' They were guys that you meet a thousand times a day. And only one person shed a tear— Ashley Wallace. They were killed by their own wife, in an agonizing, irrefutable, plain-as-day way. They died an agonizing death."

The police merely followed the evidence when they investigated Stacey Castor, like the expertly trained professionals that they were. They didn't investigate Ashley Wallace, because there was no reason to.

The defense claimed it was impossible for Stacey Castor to have tried to kill her daughter because of the quantity of drugs Ashley took. Well, think about what the prosecution's expert said: Ashley was unconscious already when the great bulk of the drugs were ingested. There was the proof. There was the proof that Stacey Castor had tried to murder her own daughter in an attempt to frame Ashley for the murders of both of her husbands.

The prosecutor acknowledged that there were some discrepancies in Ashley Wallace's story. But nothing that couldn't be explained away easily by her youthful emotions. Maybe her words weren't always precise—but the emotion she displayed while on the stand, that rang clearly with the truth. Those were honest emotions. You couldn't fake that. Ashley Wallace was a young woman who obviously had been deeply wounded by the events that led to this trial. And as for Stacey Castor, the contrast could not have been sharper. The defendant was eerily cool on the stand. She didn't seem to *have* emotions.

The defense wanted the jury to think of Ashley Wallace as a murderer. How unfair was that? The assault on this young woman was continuing. There wasn't now, and there never had been, a reason to suspect Ashley was a murderer. Even the defendant admitted that. There was only one reason to suspect Ashley, and that was the note, the note that the jurors heard the *defendant* typing, the tippy-tap sound of guilt preserved through the wonders of clandestine electronic surveillance.

There was another reason Stacey made a better suspect than Ashley for the murder of David Castor, a reason that had not been enunciated upon, one the DA hoped the jury would pick up on intuitively. And that was a matter of intimacy. The murder took place in David's bedroom, a place where the defendant was no doubt more comfortable than her daughter. "Do you know how many of Ashley Wallace's fingerprints were in her stepfather's bedroom? None! She didn't go in there. She had no reason to go in there."

Fitzpatrick noted that the person who wrote the so-called suicide note had tried to disguise it. There was no reason for Ashley to disguise her own note.

The defendant wanted the jury to believe that she "forgot" a trip to the post office, when that trip should have been fresh in her mind, but remembered it for an interview years later. How unlikely was that?

The district attorney said it was time to stop the attacks on Ashley. She had suffered enough. It was time to convict her mother and lift the weight of suspicion off Ashley's shoulders once and for all. Think about it, he said, how unlikely was it that a twelve-year-old girl would be able to pull off "the perfect crime"? It was ridiculous. What Ashley needed was sympathy, and an apology from some. She needed compassion! Here was a girl who could honestly say that at twelve she lost her dad, at seventeen she lost her stepdad, and at twenty her mother tried to kill her.

"She deserves a break," the DA said.

Fitzpatrick reminded the jury of something he had said when the trial began. He'd admitted from the start that he was at a loss for words when it came to the defendant. During the course of the trial, he'd tried to think of words, but he'd failed. The defendant's depravity was truly unspeakable, so he wasn't going to try to speak on it. Instead, he implored the jury to do the right thing.

"You can solve that problem for me, because the word for this defendant is 'guilty,'" Fitzpatrick said.

Fitzpatrick talked about a time back when he was in law school. He said he took many courses, many of which he had mercifully forgotten, but there was never a course called "Justice 101."

"Different professors might have had different definitions of it. Some professors might have said this or that was justice, or whatever, but no one ever had a definition of justice. But today, right now, right today, justice is sitting in front of me. You are about to bring justice to this case. Ladies and gentlemen, I can't think of twelve people more qualified to do that."

As he had when cross-examining the defendant, he finished with the "it" motif in a couple of the case's written works—the so-called suicide note, and also in a letter Stacey wrote to a friend. The writer had used the word "it" instead of "I."

"*It* did it," Fitzpatrick said.

Both attorneys played against type during their closing arguments. Charles Keller, who was cool throughout the trial, gave a heated argument, and William Fitzpatrick, who had exploded with rage during some cross-examinations, was reserved as he delivered his case's ultimate summary.

30

Deliberation

Following the closing arguments, Judge Fahey gave the jury their instructions. If there was testimony that they wanted to review, they were not allowed to have a transcript in the jury room. They would have to submit a request to the judge for a read-back, and the testimony would be read to the jury in the courtroom. The panel then returned to their familiar home in room 351 of the courthouse to decide Stacey Castor's fate.

During deliberation, the jury considered Ashley's suicide note, and the question of who had written it as the crux of the matter.

Among the read-backs requested was the testimony of Frank Brackin and Gerald Grant, the computer experts on either side, testimony involving the so-called suicide note. The prosecution expert said the last time either of the two suicide note fragments found on the Castors' home computer was accessed was at 2:27 P.M. on September 12, 2007—about forty hours before Ashley was rushed to the ER. It was, of course, Ashley's alibi, as she was away at school when the file was last edited, miles away from the computer on which it was edited. Chuck Keller had made a big point of the fact that, because it was deleted from the computer hard drive, there was no way of telling when the suicide note was completed and printed. This struck the jurors as a moot point since the earlier editions of the note, the so-called "note fragments," *were* dated. It only stood to reason that the same person who edited the note also wrote and printed it.

The jury also listened again to the testimony of the phone company experts who testified regarding the number of phone calls Stacey made to her house on her cell phone during David's demise.

They asked for a read-back of a portion of Ashley Wallace's testimony—the part during which she discussed her whereabouts during the weekend that her stepfather lay dying. Then they asked for a read-back of Bree's testimony regarding the same time frame.

During the long, long wait for a verdict, Fitzpatrick was asked if he was confident. The DA said he was. "She's as guilty as hell. Juries generally do the right thing."

For Stacey's daughters, the wait was excruciating. It was hard to imagine how Ashley's psyche in particular processed the events. How could she not be conflicted? The defendant was her own mother; yet her own well-being was best served by a jury confirmation of her mom's guilt. Ashley and her mom . . . once best friends—and yet now a guilty verdict would mean a personal vindication for Ashley. How could she not hate her mother so much for all of this?

31

Verdict

On February 5, 2009, after four days (approximately
sixteen hours of deliberation), the ten-women, two-
man jury notified Judge Fahey that they'd come to
a decision. Word of this went forth through the
courthouse and beyond; within minutes, all parties
convened in the courtroom. The jury filed in last.

Judge Fahey said, "*The People of the State of New York*
versus *Stacey R. Castor.* As to count number one,
murder in the second degree, what is the verdict?"

In many courtrooms across America, defendants
are asked to stand for the verdict. This often
caused wobbly knees, and the defense attorney's job
became physical, literally to support his or her
client. In this courtroom, Stacey Castor was allowed
to sit. Chuck Keller sat, too—and there was a decent
amount of space between the lawyer and his client.
He not only wasn't lending any physical support,
he was barely within arm's reach of her. As the
moment drew down on her, Stacey sat forward

toward the defense table, supporting her weight with folded fingers. Keller leaned back in his chair, reclining a tad. His eyes lowered and he folded his hands across his stomach.

The foreperson spoke softly. "Guilty," she said.

Stacey's face, as it had been during her scintillating cross-examination, was inanimate. No twitch, no blink, no anything—completely impassive.

"As to count number two, attempted murder in the second degree, what is your verdict?"

"Guilty."

Again, Stacey didn't react. But there was quite a reaction in the spectator section on the other side of the courtroom. Ashley and Bree embraced. The second charge had been that Stacey tried to kill Ashley. Now Ashley was off the hook. Bree pressed her face against Ashley's cheek and the sisters cried together. The weight of suspicion was lifted from Sissy's shoulders, and Bree could feel it, too.

The jury found Stacey Castor guilty on all charges. Stacey's hands were cuffed behind her back, and two female officers led her from the courtroom.

After it was over, and Ashley stepped outside the courtroom, she was asked how she'd felt when she heard the verdict.

"I can honestly say that this is the best day of my life—because I knew they knew I didn't do it," Ashley said.

A reporter asked Bree how it felt to watch her mother exit in handcuffs.

"It was sad seeing her being led out of the courtroom

that way," Bree said. "But I was happy they decided she was guilty, because we all knew that was true."

Only a few feet away, a reporter asked David Castor Jr. for his thoughts. "Justice was served," the son replied. Any message for his father's murderer? No, he had nothing to say to her.

What would be an appropriate punishment?"

"She does not deserve to see the light of day," he replied. "The family always suspected she did it. There isn't enough punishment. But we'll take what they give her."

The moment dissolved for some spectators into a series of revealing snapshots. Stacey sitting stone-faced as the jury decided her destiny. Her family gasping. Ashley crying. Stacey in handcuffs. Family members. Hugs in pairs, group hugs. Hugs within families. Hugs between families. Hugs all around.

It was a victory for the friends and relatives of Michael Wallace as well, because it was now almost certain that Stacey had killed her first husband. Would Cayuga County bother to prosecute Stacey for Michael's murder, or would they figure she was behind bars, anyway; why spend the taxpayers' money? It was too early to make that call.

Michael Wallace's sister, Rosemary, said, "I'm just glad that it's over, and that Ashley is vindicated. I believe my brother was there by those sisters' sides—all the way."

Rosemary explained that the Wallace and Castor families had formed a bond. It was too bad that it was a bond forged by grief, but it was strong, nonetheless. The Wallaces had been in attendance at this trial, and if there was another one, for Mike's murder, the Castors would be there as well.

Outside the Onondaga courtroom, Bill Fitzpatrick told the press that he had been confident all along that the state would be able to prove its case.

"I am also confident that Stacey is going to receive the maximum sentence . . . twenty-five to life."

"What key mistake did the defendant make?"

"I don't think she made one key mistake. She made a series of mistakes."

"Where does Stacey Castor stand in the pantheon of criminal justice?"

"If there is a ceiling in terms of evil, she is at the ceiling," the DA proclaimed.

The next question almost overlapped his answer: "Who do you think was the trial's key witness?"

"I believe that Ashley Wallace's testimony was the key to the case," Fitzpatrick said. "And the phony suicide note was also crucial." After giving a quick shout-out to the forensic lab for their stellar work and testimony, Fitzpatrick noted that Ashley was a true hero in all of this. Here was a girl who had almost died. She probably came within a couple of doses of Lexapro of dying.

About Stacey Castor, the DA opined, "No one that I have ever prosecuted was so cold-blooded and heartless as this woman was—and so unemotional about it."

* * *

Just as cameras had tagged along with Chuck Keller on his way into the courthouse for closing arguments, now they trailed the losing attorney on his way out. Of course, Stacey Castor would appeal the verdict. That was a given. On what grounds? Take your pick. There were many things wrong with the trial, Keller maintained, and Stacey clearly deserved another one, another more fair trial.

Could he be more specific?

For one thing, the judge allowed in all of the evidence regarding the death of Michael Wallace. That was irrelevant and had no business being allowed. All it did was prejudice the jury against his client.

"Essentially, it was piling on," he said.

How did his client feel?

"Obviously, she is disappointed, and that is probably the least of it."

A video camera tracked him even as he rode down in the elevator, a leather briefcase slung over his right shoulder, tugging at the collar of his trench coat and pulling on gloves in preparation for the Syracuse winter.

"Well, that's that, I guess," Keller said with a note of resignation. "At least for now."

He walked from the courthouse to his office several blocks away. Cameras followed every step. There was something resembling eye-in-the-sky technology—ABC had a rooftop camera tracing Keller's route as he exited the courthouse and walked along the snowy sidewalk toward his office.

Along the way, Keller didn't have a lot to say. Sometimes it was the wise thing to keep one's mouth shut. He had worked for years to develop evidence that would create reasonable doubt in the mind of just one juror. But he couldn't do it.

Not then, but later, after Keller had an opportunity to think about it, he was willing to go on the record regarding his client's guilty verdict. He analyzed the machinations of the jury he'd failed to sway. It came down to one thing, he believed, as it so often did with juries. "They considered Stacey's motives as opposed to Ashley's motives, sure, but what it really came down to was opportunity," Keller said. "The fact is—and it doesn't matter if you're on the prosecution or the defense—Stacey had more opportunity."

Jurors are under no obligation to talk to the media after a trial is through. If jurors want to, they can disappear the instant the verdict is read and remain forever anonymous. In this case, nine jurors volunteered to participate in a posttrial news conference, willing to discuss the inner workings of the panel's deliberation. It was a consensus that the two most important facts in the case were: Was Stacey Castor believable? And who had the most access to the two male victims?

One female juror pointed out that some of the things Stacey said were believable, but the biggest things she said were not believable. The jury apparently believed that Ashley Wallace drank the foul-tasting drink just because her mother told her it was okay. Another female juror said, "I, for one, did not find the defendant believable. I definitely did not."

32

Sentencing Hearing

At nine in the morning on March 5, exactly one month after Stacey Castor's conviction, many of the parties were back in their places. Only the judge and the defendant were missing, and they entered more or less simultaneously.

The bailiff announced Judge Fahey's entrance and instructed the courtroom to rise. When Judge Fahey reached the bench, the bailiff said, "Please be seated," and the hearing was under way.

The session began with some lengthy legal rhetoric. Two days earlier, Chuck Keller had asked Judge Fahey to set aside the conviction on the grounds that the jury did not follow the judge's legal instructions during deliberations. The judge had instructed the jury to be sure of two things before they came back with a guilty verdict: one, that they were convinced "beyond a reasonable doubt" that Stacey Castor had killed her husband David, and two, that they were convinced "to a moral certainty" that Ashley Wallace was not the killer. After several minutes of legal banter, Judge Fahey denied Keller's motion.

The argument was in legalese, difficult to understand. The defendant no doubt didn't follow it well, her brain swimming with dread. In mere minutes, she would be sentenced, and she didn't know how it would go. Judge Fahey would fix her in his sights and blast away with the news. But would he have mercy on her?

When the preliminaries were through, Judge Fahey quickly read the charges against Stacey—murder, attempted murder, filing a false instrument—and noted that a jury in a court of law had convicted her of those charges. As a formality, he turned to the prosecution and asked if the people wished to hear the sentence.

"We do, Your Honor," the district attorney answered.

"And, Chuck, is there any *legal* reason why the sentence shouldn't be imposed?" Judge Fahey asked.

"No, Your Honor," Keller replied.

Turning again to the prosecution table, the judge said, "And you have with you, Bill, two individuals who wish to address me with respect to sentencing in this matter?"

"Yes, Your Honor. And, with your permission, I would also like to address you briefly," the DA said.

"Sure," the judge said agreeably.

William Fitzpatrick offered the court an outline of what was about to occur, and then noted that this would be his last opportunity to thank some people personally.

"It might be a little outside what you are looking for in terms of sentence recommendations, but I ask the court's indulgence," Fitzpatrick said. After his thank-yous, he explained, he would ask David Castor Jr. to "step forward and speak on behalf of his family, and certainly on behalf of his dad. And then I ask you to hear Ashley Wallace, who will speak on behalf of herself and her sister, Bree, as well as her family and loved ones. Finally, Your Honor, Chief Assistant District Attorney Christine Garvey will speak to the court on behalf of the people of the state of New York."

Fitzpatrick began his long list of thank-yous with the men and women of the OCSO. He complimented their fine work in putting the case together. "We might not be here today if it weren't for their efforts," the DA said. He lauded Dominick Spinelli and Valerie Brogan, the lead detectives on "both of these cases," he said, referring to both the murder and attempted murder charges.

There were people the DA wished to thank who, unlike the lead detectives, were not frequently mentioned during the course of the proceedings. This included Steve Smith, of the Cayuga County Sheriff's Office, who offered the prosecution's case the fruits of his "conscientious hard work." And it included Tim McCarthy and Phil Nolan, the DA's investigators whose work had been "nothing short of phenomenal." He thanked the men and women of the Onondaga County Center for Forensic Sciences, then mentioned how pleased he was that the proceedings had been filmed and were being made available to the public in a variety of media. Now the entire community, the very people he represented, had and would continue to have an opportunity to watch the trial.

He thanked the relatives and loved ones of Michael Wallace and David Castor. "I am a better person for having met many of the individuals I've encountered during the course of this investigation and trial. That certainly includes Ashley and Bree, who are two absolutely remarkable and heroic young women."

Fitzpatrick told the people how lucky they were to have someone like Christine Garvey working on their side, a woman who had "dedicated her life to the service of justice."

Lastly the DA thanked the members of the jury, some of whom, he noted, were in the courtroom as spectators. So caught up were they in the machinations of the trial that they needed to witness all of it, even after their role was completed. The jury was comprised of a dozen extraordinary citizens who had given up their time selflessly and had deliberated conscientiously. "They deliberated the way a jury was *supposed* to deliberate," he said. He was proud of them.

After a pause, Fitzpatrick said, "I would ask you now to take the opportunity to listen to David Castor, Jr."

David Castor Jr. stepped to the pulpit and said, "Pain. The amount of pain Stacey R. Castor has put our family through is indescribable and immeasurable! She tortured my father."

The son spoke of a dad who loved living life, who had many passions and hobbies: watercrafting, four-wheeling, boating, motorcycling, camping, racing, and snowmobiling. He was a man who both worked hard and played hard, a man who had "so much life" ahead of him.

It had been painful just to listen to the horrible details of his father's murder, "to hear how the antifreeze slowly, painfully, shut my father down." What could be worse than seeing pictures of his dead father lying naked in his own vomit, than knowing the pain he went through?

Then there was the pain of having to watch Stacey lie, perjure, and slander.

And it wasn't just his dad's pain or his own pain, either. It was everyone's pain he was talking about. His father's murder had caused a "chain reaction of pain to everyone's life that he touched." The pain was immeasurable. He was only expressing some of the pain he and his family were going through, not to mention what Stacey had put the Wallace family through, and all the pain Ashley and Bree had to go through.

"I can't begin to imagine how this has been for them," he said, referring to the sisters. "If what doesn't knock you down only makes you stronger, then nothing will ever knock them down after standing through all of this."

Then, as one might in a eulogy, David Castor Jr. listed the roles his father had played in life. He'd been a friend to many, but so much more. "He was a son, a brother, a companion to my mother for twenty-seven years, and, of course, he had been a father."

Sometimes, the son said, it took all of his effort to keep from exploding with anger right there in the courtroom. Every lie he heard made it harder to maintain control. In particular, it was hard to stay composed when Stacey's mom came on the stand and said his father touched Ashley inappropriately.

"That is a lie!" he said. "Let me set one thing straight. My father was a good man with a moral compass that pointed north—certainly *not* a pedophile."

He then called out Mike Colman by name, the man who helped Stacey carry his father into bed as David looked deathly ill.

"I guess to him he looked normal, too. I don't think he can look in the mirror and be proud of himself," David Castor Jr. said.

Mike Overstreet was next on his list, a man who got up on the witness stand and "lied and perjured repeatedly." Castor called Overstreet a "piece of work" and pointed out that Stacey's boyfriend had also profited from the death of David Castor Sr.

"These are the people who get to enjoy my father's life earnings due to Stacey's contracting this fake will," Junior pointed out. He added that Stacey said she gave David Jr. his father's car and $2,500 because that's what his dad would have wanted. What a crock!

"She seems to have forgotten that I contested this false will. With the Pulaskis signing a sworn statement that they witnessed my father signing the will, my lawyer said it was too hard to prove, so I settled with the car because it meant a lot to my dad and me. I would think—no, I would know—that my father would have wanted his only son and his grandchildren to enjoy his life earnings, not his murderer and her friends," Castor said.

Castor concluded: "Your Honor, Stacey Castor is a

monster and a threat to society." He told the judge that there was a criminal ladder and its ascending rungs represented growing levels of evil. Using that measure, Stacey was at the top. She'd created so much pain and death, multiples of pain and death in the families of those that she had hurt. "I will never, ever get to see my dad again. Our relationship was torn when she took him, and we will never have a chance to fix it," he said. He knew it was impossible, but his wish would be that Stacey be imprisoned forever with no visitation, so she would always be alone—alone with her guilt. "She deserves to be penalized to the highest extent the court can impose. She deserves to spend the rest of her life in prison!"

As David Castor Jr.'s mother, Janice, sat in the courtroom and watched her son give his statement, she recalled the long trial process. Charles Keller had subpoenaed her, which prevented her from being in the courtroom during the testimony of others. Janice Poissant was convinced Keller subpoenaed her just to keep her out. She knew Keller had had no intention of calling her as a witness, and he didn't. So the trial had been a matter of waiting out in the hall, staring at the double doors, often with her son and his wife and Mike Wallace's sister. There were moments of drama in that hall. Ofttimes Stacey Castor's mother and Stacey's fiancé would be out there as well, and the two sides would glare at each other. Janice admitted that, though it wasn't like her at all, she enjoyed "branding" Michael Overstreet with her stare. She could tell she was making him uncomfortable.

Now, as she listened to her son speak of pain, Janice thought about Stacey. There wasn't enough justice for what she'd done. Still, she was going away for a long time, and that was as it should be. Janice had never stopped loving David Sr. Her greatest regret involving her marriage was the psychological effect their divorce had on David Jr. He and his dad were estranged because of it—temporarily, she was sure. And now, because of Stacey, her two Davids would never have an opportunity to reconcile.

Next to speak was Ashley Wallace, who said to the judge, "The biggest question I ask is 'Why? Why did she do these things?' I know that it is probably never going to be answered."

As Ashley spoke, Bree Wallace stood at her side, but behind a little bit, their shoulders almost touching. As had been the case when she testified at the trial, Ashley's voice rose higher and screeched when she understandably lost her composure.

"There are so many things she has ruined," Ashley said. Her mother would never see Bree graduate. Her father would never walk her down the aisle. Her mother would never get to see her grandchildren. All those things Stacey Castor took away.

"She killed two people and then she tried to kill me and blame me for the other deaths," Ashley said. That was the thing that bothered her so much. She had to pretend for a year that everything was okay, that nothing was bothering her, even though she was worried about the trial, and worried whether a jury would believe her. She hated her mother for ruining so many people's lives.

"And I don't even know why she did it," Ashley said. "What gave her the right to play God with people?"

She hated her mother for having her be the one to find her father's body, just like she hated her for having "Bree be the one that found me." Ashley said she hadn't previously known what hate was. Now she understood; yet she hated and loved her mother simultaneously. That bugged her, confused her.

"I just wish she would say she was sorry for everything she did, including all the lies. And though I feel bad for her today as she sits there all by herself, she is the one that did this to herself, and nothing bothers her," Ashley said. Ashley, on the other hand, had a future to look forward to. After her mother was sentenced, Ashley got to go back to a loving home with people who cared about her. Mom wasn't going home, though. She could have been, without a worry, going home with her and Bree, but no.

"I have cried enough tears about this. I do not want to cry anymore. I just want it all to go away, but I know it won't ever go away. I have to live with this for the rest of my life."

Ashley admitted that there were times when she considered genetic inevitability. Was she destined to turn out to be just like her mother? Mom was good sometimes.

"But I know I won't," Ashley concluded. "I know I could never hurt my children like she did."

Ashley hated how Stacey tried to make her look stupid in that note she wrote. Ashley had tried so hard to make something of herself. She had a 3.9 GPA, and Stacey still tried to make her look stupid. But William Fitzpatrick made Stacey look stupid with her lies. Ashley hated how Stacey made friends and family members choose sides.

"Bree and I are children," Ashley said. "People are supposed to stand up for us. But she is an adult, and that is the decision she made."

Sometimes late at night, she would ponder her mother, try to figure out what made her tick, try to think like her mother thought. Sometimes she would become frightened. What if her mother was released and tried to hurt her again? What if Stacey got out and tried to hurt Bree?

Ashley wrapped it up: "She has to listen to me this time. I did not get a chance to say good-bye, and this will be the last time I will get a chance. And, as horrible as it makes me feel, this is good-bye, Mom. As hard as you tried, I survived, and I will survive, because now I am surrounded by people who love me. I am going to do good in this world, despite you making me, in every sense of the word, an orphan. Thank you, Judge Fahey, for letting me express my feelings."

You could hear a pin drop.

Following the statements from the victims' relatives, Christine Garvey spoke on behalf of the people of New York State. She said, "It is very humbling to stand here and listen to the words of David Castor Jr. and Ashley Wallace, and to hear about how the defendant has affected their lives." Garvey explained that the rest of us would never truly understand how the sisters and other members of their family had suffered from the evil of Stacey Castor.

She talked about the victims. David Castor Sr., by all accounts of the people she had spoken with, was a good man with many hobbies who loved life and lived it to the fullest. He was entitled to a long life full of those fun times, but Stacey Castor took it all away. She pulled the plug on that life. In August of 2005, she poisoned him in a sadistic manner—then went about her life like nothing was happening. Still, her thirst for cold-blooded homicide was not quenched. She saw murder as a viable way to solve life's problems, the way others might view telling a white lie. In September of 2007, she poisoned her daughter, and while the toxic cocktail was affecting her daughter's organs and killing her, Stacey Castor partied in her backyard with friends, like nothing was happening.

"Ashley Wallace is very fortunate to be alive. She is one of the strongest people I have encountered in my lifetime. In circumstances that might have emotionally destroyed others, she is excelling in school and taking care of her sister, while dealing with the reality that her own mother tried to take her life," Garvey said. Ashley deserved to have a mother to love and protect her. Instead, she had a mother who decided her own life was more important than her daughter's life.

Stacey Castor had stolen happiness in so many ways from so many different people. She was "cold, calculating, and without any emotion." Human life was sacred—yet Stacey placed *no value* on human life, not even her own flesh and blood. Human beings were, to her, disposable. Luckily for the people of New York State, a very good jury heard this case. Stacey's days of deciding who in her family should live and die were over. "We ask the court for maximum and consecutive sentences to ensure she spends the rest of her life in jail," Garvey said.

The victims' statements read, all eyes turned to Judge Fahey, Stacey Castor's fate in his hands.

The judge told Stacey that in his thirty-four years in the criminal justice system as a lawyer and a judge, he had seen serial killers, contract killers, killers of every variety and shape, but she was in a class by herself. She was a first. He had never before seen a parent who was willing to sacrifice a child in order to shift blame away from herself. Her behavior had been reprehensible. He then rendered the sentence for her murder of her second husband and attempted murder of her oldest daughter.

"I sentence you to twenty-five years to life for the murder of your husband, David Castor, and to *another* twenty-five years to life for the attempt to murder your daughter, Ashley Wallace. In addition, I sentence you to one-third to four years in prison for forging your husband's will."

Stacey would have to serve fifty-one and one-third years behind bars before she was eligible for parole. In light of her age, she would probably die in prison.

David Castor Jr. and Ashley Wallace held hands, a sign of solidarity, as the sentence was read. Behind them sat Bree Wallace and Janice Poissant. David cried, an outpouring of pent-up emotion that had nothing to do with sympathy for his dad's killer. "Justice was served. I was so relieved," he explained.

Was it enough punishment? *There could never be*

enough. Even the maximum. Not enough. Did he have anything to say about *her?*

"I don't have words for Stacey. There are no words for Stacey," he said.

Stacey Castor was transferred from the Onondaga Jail to the Bedford Hills Correctional Facility for Women in Westchester County, the only maximum-security prison for women in New York State. The facility originally opened in 1901 as the Westfield State Farm and had been the home of infamous inmates such as Pamela Smart, who with the help of her underage lover and his friends, murdered her husband in New Hampshire; Carolyn Warmus, who murdered her lover's wife; Amy Fisher, the "Long Island Lolita" who shot her boyfriend's wife in the face; and Jean Harris, who killed her ex-lover, Dr. Herman Tarnower, inventor of the Scarsdale Diet.

33

Aftermath

Sometime not long after Ashley Wallace read her emotional statement regarding her mother at Stacey Castor's sentencing hearing, Ashley sat down to talk to ABC. She was relaxed, her voice low and soft. She'd gotten all of that emotion out of her system and was again in control.

Her statement in court had been hard to deliver, one of the hardest things she'd ever had to do. Now that it was done, she could feel a tremendous weight lifted from her shoulders. She'd gotten the opportunity to say all of the things to her mother that she always wanted to say—things that she wanted to say when she was on the witness stand, but hadn't gotten the chance.

Yes, she hated her mother, and those were painful feelings. It wasn't just hatred that didn't feel good, but insecurity as well. She was an orphan. With the realization that her mother was evil came a reevaluation of everything that had come before. Every happy moment now had to be thought about in a new light. She felt like a ship that had been just fine as long as it had its anchor. But now cut adrift, the waters were choppy, and she had to hold on tight not to be thrown overboard. She tried not to feel hate, but she couldn't do it. She couldn't help it. She hated her. Hated her so much. "She killed two people and tried to kill me!" Ashley said. It was too much. How could that ever be forgiven?

Now, talking quietly despite the questions screaming in her brain, she let the tears flow freely. How could her mother be so evil? She had grown up with the Devil, and she hadn't even realized it until two men were dead, and she was almost in a grave herself. She felt pretty stupid sometimes, but she doubted that anyone else, placed in her shoes, could have handled herself any better. Ashley never had the slightest inkling that her mother was a homicidal maniac, because—to be blunt—it would have been kind of nuts to think that way. You start out life with a certain number of strong assumptions, and one of them was that your mom was on your side. You start out loving your mother from the moment you are born, when you are a baby, and then growing up. You're supposed to always love and trust your mother. Take that away and a person's mind can feel like it's being held together by bubble gum. How could it be? Ashley shrugged. She would never know the answers.

When it was Bree Wallace's turn, she said that she never took her eyes off her mother when the verdict was being read, and she vouched for the fact that Mom hadn't moved a muscle. There wasn't so much as a flicker of an eyelid. Regrets? Yeah. Bree had hoped that her mother would apologize. Even if it came off as way too little, too late, Bree wanted her to do it, anyway. Just say those two little words "I'm sorry." It would have meant a lot, but her mother didn't do it. Didn't even come close. She was too ashamed and too stuck in her lies, selling out the daughter she failed to kill, making Ashley the scapegoat for her misdeeds.

Both Ashley and Bree Wallace knew better than to go anywhere near their grandma. Judi Eaton told the press that she had not changed her mind about anything. The jury was wrong, simple as that. The DA screamed like a maniac and they gave him the verdict. Maybe the fix was in from the beginning. Judi said that she was never going to give up on her daughter, not until the day she died. "I do *not* believe Stacey did this." Judi didn't care if the bridge between her and her granddaughters was burned beyond repair. She repeatedly spoke words about Ashley, from which there was no return. Their relationship was dead, and probably had been long before Judi testified on her daughter's behalf at the Stacey Castor murder trial.

For William Fitzpatrick, the Stacey Castor case was yet another feather in his cap. Only three days after the sentencing, Fitzpatrick agreed to give a presentation at Le Moyne College's Reilly Hall regarding his prosecution. The event was open to the public. After a speech, he fielded questions and refreshments were served.

Some who had followed the case closely noted how the pro-Stacey, anti-Ashley witnesses, Eaton and the Colmans, had acted as a team in defending Stacey. Did Fitzpatrick ever suspect a conspiracy? Was he ever close to charging anyone with being an accessory, before or after the fact?

"No," the DA said. "It's funny, you hear the expression sometimes, usually on television, 'I'm going to charge you with accessory after the fact.' There's no such thing. You can be an accessory before or during, but not after the fact. There were some people in this case who were total assholes, but I never thought about charging them with anything."

How was the trial affected by the presence of network TV?

Fitzpatrick explained again that he personally was unaffected, and he believed the jury was also. "The jury knew it was a high-profile case, but I don't believe they were affected by the cameras," he said.

What lessons did he learn during the prosecution of Stacey Castor?

This was a case where, for the investigative bodies, some very important lessons were learned. The case had led to important changes in the way deaths in New York State were investigated. This was a case that might never have broken if it hadn't been for the exhumation of Michael Wallace.

Stacey and her mother wanted everyone to believe that it never occurred to anyone that Michael Wallace needed to be autopsied after he died of a "heart attack." The doctor said it was his heart, they trusted the doctor, and everyone agreed. Janice Poissant, however, had learned this wasn't true.

"Mike's sister, Rosemary, did want an autopsy,"

Janice said. "Today, what we really want is to pass a Wallace-Castor Autopsy Law, which would make it easier for members of the family to request an autopsy even if a spouse says no."

The law would make an autopsy mandatory if there were any suspicions about the cause of death. If such a law had been in effect when Michael died, David would still be alive.

The movement to pass the new law had support from the DA, who concurred that all too often in cases in which an autopsy might shed light, no autopsy was performed at the wishes of a family member. Authorities could order an autopsy anytime they wanted as well, of course, but all too often, unless the case was clearly suspicious, the body would be cremated at the behest of the grieving widow or widower before authorities began to suspect foul play.

William Fitzpatrick noted that the question of which deaths required autopsies was a standard that varied widely from county to county within New York State, particularly wide in counties where the coroner was an elected official. The coroner in such cases would hesitate before making politically incorrect decisions—like performing an autopsy on a dead husband against the wife's wishes. The system needed to be revamped.

"In the twenty-first century, the coroner system is, in my judgment, outdated," Fitzpatrick opined. He favored medical examiners' offices with complete laboratories, which followed specific criteria for reportable deaths. The criteria would include violent deaths, suicides, accidental deaths, and suspicious, unusual, or drug-related deaths. Any sudden death of a healthy person qualified for a mandatory autopsy.

Someone asked about the yelling Fitzpatrick did in court. Did he ever worry that his loud cross-examination might one day turn a juror off?

"If I thought that, I wouldn't do it," the DA responded.

How did he decide when to yell? How calculated was the yelling?

Fitzpatrick noted that he was a fanatic preparer. But he did not write out or preplan what questions he was going to ask. He knew the subjects he wanted to cover, but nothing more specific than that. This way, he explained, he could listen—really, listen—to what the witness had to say, and to ask questions specifically about their testimony.

"I think too many lawyers prepare their cross-examination on what they think someone is going to say—or based on what they've said at some other time," the DA said. "To do it my way, you have to think quick on your feet." A lawyer didn't have a lot of time between questions if he or she didn't want the jury to go to sleep. "You have to make your moves on the spot."

Fitzpatrick thought of a perfect example from the Stacey Castor trial. It occurred when he was listening to the defendant testify.

"You've heard the old admonition 'Don't ask the question why.' I totally disagree with that." The DA cited Vincent Bugliosi, the former Los Angeles County district attorney who nailed Charles Manson. Bugliosi was a big proponent of asking why.

"So, when I started my cross-examination of Stacey Castor, one of the first subjects I hit on was 'You

knew Ashley Wallace better than anyone, correct?'
She had to acknowledge that. 'No one knew her in-
nermost thoughts better than you, correct?' She said
yes. 'Why did she kill her father? Give me the top
four reasons.' She sat there, flummoxed. I thought
that was devastating, because that was straight out of
the box, and that was what the jury was seeing. So I
said, 'You've been sitting in jail for sixteen months
for a crime that you didn't commit. You know your
daughter committed this crime. And when I ask you
why she did it, you sit there and go, 'Huh?'"

Fitzpatrick got back to the question of yelling.

"I didn't write in my notes, 'Yell here.' I didn't plan
that—but the more laissez-faire she got on the witness
stand, the more blasé she was, the more—in all
honesty—the more outraged I was at her description."

Fitzpatrick recalled how, to Stacey's regret, the defendant had used the word "normal" in her testimony. Talking about Mike Wallace, she had said he
was normal. It wasn't the only time she'd used the
word to describe one of her victims. In a wiretap of
a phone conversation Stacey had not long before
Ashley was rushed to the hospital, she said Ashley
was "drooling normally."

It was when Fitzpatrick asked about this quote, his
outrage enveloped him, and the decibel level of his
cross-examination rocketed upward.

"I remember saying, 'Was she drooling normally,
Mrs. Castor?' I might as well have been asking,
'What planet do you come from?'"

Because his outrage was genuine, he didn't worry
about jurors being turned off. He was outraged,
and there was every reason to believe the jurors
were outraged as well by the substance and manner

of the defendant's responses. He considered every jury to be an extension of himself in the courtroom. They were a team. It never occurred to him that one of the jurors would hear him yelling and think, "Come on, stop picking on her."

Fitzpatrick had the opportunity to talk with several of the jurors after the trial, and confirmed his belief that they were as outraged as he by Stacey Castor's behavior on the stand—by the defendant's behavior in general.

The DA had thrown everything he had at her. He accused her, insulted her, pounded away at the shakiness of her scenario of the facts, and she just sat there, not moving, not changing expression. There was an overwhelming urge on his part to do something, anything, to make her *flinch*.

Just give me something, he thought during his cross-examination, *some indication that you are a human being with something resembling human feelings*. But there was nothing.

After a while, though, the DA realized that her stony behavior was to his benefit. If she had been up there crying about her dead husbands and alienated daughters, griping bitterly about being falsely accused, there was a chance that some of the jurors might have felt sympathy toward her. Someone might have thought, *Hey, maybe the daughter did do it*. But the way she really was up there, so stone-faced— no way.

Stacey Castor's behavior in front of the jury, the DA noted, couldn't have been in sharper contrast to that of Ashley Wallace, who seemed on the verge of falling apart as she testified.

"After she testified, Ashley came up to me and said, 'I'm sorry I cried.' I said, 'Don't worry, you did good.'"

Not long after Stacey Castor's trial, plans were initiated to exhume David Castor's body, not to be examined for further evidence of foul play, but rather for relocation. With Stacey's conviction, David's family was irked that David was buried in an adjacent plot to Stacey's first husband, her other alleged murder victim. The family wanted to move David as fast as possible to Pine Plains Cemetery, but it was going to cost money, and they would have to go to civil court over the matter.

Nothing against Mike Wallace, but as it existed, David's grave was like a trophy honoring Stacey's black widowhood.

Janice Poissant didn't believe David could not rest in peace where he was currently buried. "We feel it's her 'evil shrine,' and we want to move him so he can be near his dad, who was buried one month to the date before him," said Janice. "Where he is now is out in the middle of nowhere, and the family doesn't feel comfortable going there."

On April 23, 2009, a hearing was held before Judge Fahey to decide on a request by the Cayuga County district attorney to unseal and turn over minutes from the Onondaga County grand jury's hearings regarding the Stacey Castor case.

For the hearing, Judge Fahey allowed Stacey to move temporarily from her home in the Bedford Hills Correctional Facility back to the courtroom jail in Syracuse. In court, Stacey wore her green prison jumpsuit and sat beside the indefatigable Chuck Keller, who argued why Cayuga County should not receive minutes from the Onondaga County grand jury hearing.

"All grand jury testimony is meant to be secret and should remain that way," Keller said. He noted that the Cayuga County grand jury had full subpoena power and could subpoena any witness they wanted to come in and talk to them—so there was no "essential reason" for another county's grand jury minutes to be turned over.

Arguing the issue for the people was Onondaga County chief ADA James Maxwell, who crisply communicated the positives of releasing the transcripts, saying they would be useful as an "investigative guide" for Cayuga County prosecutors.

Judge Fahey said that he would take ten days to consider the matter before he made a ruling. On Monday morning, May 4, 2009, he ruled that he would not release to Cayuga County authorities grand jury minutes regarding the case against Stacey Castor for the murder of David Castor. The decision did not surprise Keller, who said he was unaware of the type or strength of the case Cayuga County was making against his client.

"I sent a letter to the Cayuga County District Attorney's Office to initiate some communications about what their intentions are, just to let them know what our positions are, and I have not heard anything from him," Keller said.

* * *

Cayuga County sheriff David Gould said that Judge Fahey's refusal to unseal the grand jury minutes would do nothing to impede his attempts to get an indictment on Stacey Castor for the murder of Michael Wallace.

Gould said that the judge's decision was not terribly detrimental to his investigation because, although there were similarities between the murders of Michael Wallace and David Castor, the crimes were not identical.

"We had to interview our medical people at the scene when Mr. Wallace died—certainly, they weren't at the scene when Mr. Castor died, so there's a whole different crew that we have to interview," Gould said.

Asked why he was determined to prosecute Stacey for her first husband's murder, Gould said he owed it to the people of Cayuga County: "If we just let this go and say she paid her dues, we would still have an open murder case in Cayuga County. It is not off the books, and it would never be off the books, because there is no statute of limitations. For us to close it, we need to make an arrest, and we need to get a conviction."

Gould was not swayed by arguments that prosecuting Stacey for Mike's murder was a waste of taxpayers' money because she was already sentenced to life in prison. There was a larger point: Michael Wallace's family deserved closure. "If that was one of our family members who had been murdered, and we knew that Stacey did it, and I was the son of that person and the DA didn't prosecute the case, I would be out of my mind," Gould said. Before there could be a trial, however, the investigation had to be complete to everyone's satisfaction. "We have to make sure that everything that needs to be done is done, and that she is the right person."

Cayuga County DA Jon Budelmann concurred but warned about overconfidence. It would be no slam dunk, he said. The case was so old that potentially valuable evidence was gone.

And, because it was so notorious, part of the backdrop for a famous murder trial in Syracuse, it might be difficult to find twelve jurors who hadn't heard about the case and made up his or her mind about who was responsible for what.

Budelmann refused to say that convicting Stacey Castor in Cayuga County would be easier because she'd already been found guilty in Onondaga.

"Well, it's not harder," he conceded. "Had she been acquitted over there, the file would've been sealed and we would've had to unseal it to move forward on ours."

None of this was going to happen overnight. The official status of the Wallace case was that it was an open homicide, and Stacey Castor was just one of several key suspects in that crime.

Obviously, this understated Stacey's role as primary suspect, but the sheriff was an expert at erring on the side of safety when it came to public statements.

They did not, he emphasized, have enough evidence at that moment to convict Stacey in a court of law. He anticipated, however, there would come a time when there would be enough evidence. At that time, the case would be presented for a Cayuga County grand jury for indictment.

They were not suddenly reopening the Michael

Wallace case because Stacey Castor had been convicted of killing David Castor. The case had never closed, and had been officially open since Michael Wallace's body was exhumed two years before. The district attorney's office had been in contact with the Wallace family throughout that time.

In May 2009, the Stacey Castor case became national news, the sole subject of a two-hour television special episode of the ABC show *20/20*. The show began as if it were about a mystery. Anchor John Stossel, sitting in for Elizabeth Vargas, said, "Our correspondent David Muir spent the summer with the killer. But which one was the killer?" Photos of Stacey Castor and Ashley Wallace flashed on the screen. That might have been the tease to induce the audience to stay tuned, but it wasn't representative of the body of the show. No one was intended to seriously consider Ashley guilty. The first clue was the show's title: "The Black Widow."

So it was a bit of a false tease when host John Stossel at the beginning of the show said, "A mystery between a mother and a daughter, once best friends, who accused each other of slowly poisoning the men in their lives . . . which one did it?"

Those who had followed the trial closely noticed that a lot of the evidence was omitted. Perhaps this was because of time constraints, and perhaps because a disclosure of how strong the prosecution's case was might hurt the program's suspense, dilute the power of their whodunnit angle. For example, they hardly mentioned the *drafts* of the note, the ones that had been dated and timed by the computer they were written on, or the fact that that date and time gave Ashley a strong alibi.

Before his big postconviction interview with Stacey Castor, ABC's David Muir had hopes. He'd later admit that there was a part of him that was thinking this was it—this was the moment when Stacey was finally going to shed her cocoon of deception. This was when she would finally admit that she did it, finally apologize to her daughter for what she did.

Instead: "She was defiant to the end," Muir recalled.

In that interview, Stacey came off as soft-spoken and heartbroken. She told Muir that David Castor had been her rock, her anchor—her knight in shining armor. For others to think she would hurt that man was ridiculous. He conjured up words like "strength" and "security" and "support." Even behind bars, she felt this every day, maybe more than ever because of the things she'd been through. Sure, she could step back from the situation far enough to see events as others saw them. She could see how people would think she was guilty. How did she explain those facts?

"You're asking the wrong person," she said. "I can't explain these facts." To whom should the question be addressed? Stacey was mum on the subject. "I will never say I did something that I didn't do," Stacey added. "I will maintain my innocence until the day I die. I did not kill Michael Wallace or David

Castor. I did not try to kill my daughter—and I will never say I did."

She refused to accuse her daughter directly of murder, but she did say she "absolutely" agreed that police and the district attorney's office hadn't strongly enough considered Ashley as a suspect.

And if they had?

"Then I would not be the one sitting here," she said.

Did her conviction come as a surprise? Yes. In fact, that was putting it mildly. She was in shock—couldn't *believe* that she had been found guilty. Chuck Keller had tried to prepare her for the worst. They had talked about the possibility that she would be found guilty, right from the beginning of the trial. But hearing it was still shocking—unbelievable, really. The jury had listened to the prosecution and looked in the wrong direction. Regardless of what they thought or felt, Stacey knew Ashley was the one who brought this on. "I know the truth," Stacey said. "She knows the truth. Bree, I do feel for Bree, and the fact that she didn't ask for any part of this, and she is another one of those innocent victims." Stacey noted that her case was not over. It was headed toward appellate court, where Charles Keller would argue that she had not received a fair trial. "I still have my mom and my stepdad and some other relatives who still believe in me, but I lost my daughters. I lost my husbands. I lost my freedom." Stacey was asked what was the main point, the one thing that was most unfair about her trial. She answered broadly, saying that her entire defense was the problem. "We weren't allowed to put on a defense—period," she said.

The interviewer would not let up. If there was something Stacey knew that the rest of the world didn't know, now was the time to reveal it. Muir reminded her that she was free to say whatever she liked. What was the thing that went unsaid, that if said would have resulted in her acquittal?

Again, Stacey answered in the broadest—almost vague—terms. "Anything that made me look bad or pointed a finger at me was allowed. Everything else was shut down and not allowed to be presented," Stacey said.

The reporter tried a different tack. He asked her, if she could have asked one question during the trial, the answer to which might have resulted in her acquittal, what question would that be?

Stacey couldn't say, noting that she wasn't in the jury room and she had no idea what the deliberation was like. Stacey never did suggest a piece of evidence or a witness's testimony that if allowed into her trial might have reversed her fate. Instead, she emphasized that the charges against her were ridiculous. The charges, Stacey maintained, should never have been taken seriously, to begin with. It was ludicrous enough to think she would hurt the men she loved. But it was light-years beyond incomprehensible to think that she would have done anything to harm either of her daughters.

Ashley's version of events did not make any sense. How does one get a young woman to drink something so offensive to the taste? "Ashley was twenty years old and I supposedly gave her this vile, disgusting drink, and told her to drink it," Stacey said, a flabbergasted note in her voice. "If my mother gave me a drink like that and told me to drink it, I would have dumped it out and said, 'Sorry, Ma. I'm not drinking that.'" Ashley said she drank because she trusted her mother. Huh? That didn't register, as far as Stacey was concerned. "What does trusting me have anything to do with drinking something that tasted so horrible?" Stacey asked.

The interviewer made note of something Stacey had said after the death of David Castor, but before the exhumation of Michael Wallace. She'd said that David must have gotten the idea to kill himself with antifreeze because of a television program they'd watched together, a show in which a woman killed not one but two husbands by poisoning them with antifreeze. He asked Stacey if she ever considered the fact that the program they were working on right then, the *20/20* episode about the case, was also going to be a TV show about a woman who killed both husbands by poisoning them with antifreeze. Did she consider that a strange coincidence?

Stacey disagreed with the premise: "No, this program is going to be about a woman who was accused of killing both husbands," she said.

Since their mother's arrest, Ashley and Bree Wallace were living with Ashley's boyfriend, Matthew, and his mother and father. Bree, who was nineteen years old in 2009, was considering college. Ashley, who was close to getting straight A's in college, was looking forward to graduating with honors in 2010. They had a new family now and called Mr. and Mrs. Gandino "Mom and Dad." Neither had plans ever to communicate again in any way with her mother. She was gone forever and never coming back, and good riddance. As for the pain, it never went away, and it never diminished. The nightmare was ongoing. Now Ashley had shared her bad dream with the rest of the world, but that didn't mean it would stop. She could never, ever wake up.

The sisters felt a strong alliance. It was Ashley and Bree against the world. It had always been the two of them against the world. Ashley didn't know how she would have gotten along if it hadn't been for the two of them. Interestingly, one of the great mysteries of her life had been solved by the murder trial and the subsequent conviction of her mother. As a child, Ashley had wondered why God had been so mean to them. He'd taken her father, and then her step-father. What had she and Bree done to deserve that kind of fate? But now she didn't wonder those things anymore. She now knew it wasn't God who was doing it.

"It was *her*," Ashley said.

Stacey Castor had always been fodder for prolific amateur editorials on the Internet. With the TV show, a fresh wave of "Stacey comments" flushed over the Web. One blogger felt it was weird that even after the public learned of women like Stacey, there were still those who refused to believe that violence in the home was anything but a one-way street, and that all of the victims of domestic abuse were women. There were those who said that Stacey was no more than a product of her environment—after all, Stacey's mom seemed chilly, too—and that she deserved mercy. The great majority, however, felt she was simply a horrid and evil person, and that was that. Some argued for capital punishment; others said that they didn't want the chair, that life in prison without chance of parole *was* a death sentence, a punishment more severe than a comparatively quick stint on death row. That was rebutted with the story of Charles Manson, who claimed he could get anything in prison that he could get on the outside. Another blogger questioned the second-degree murder charge, feeling that proving premeditation should have been a snap. Even if she had to go to the garage to get the antifreeze, that meant she had schemed, and that meant first-degree murder.

After the broadcast of the *20/20* special, William Fitzpatrick was asked for his criticism of the TV show. Was there anything ABC missed?

"It's not so much that they missed anything, it's that they lent the case more suspense than there actually was," the DA said. "Who did it? Was it the mother or was it the daughter?" Fitzpatrick said that it might be a fact that Stacey Castor had friends and relatives who thought her daughter did it, but any unbiased person analyzing the facts in this case would quickly decide that Stacey was the culprit.

Regarding the postconviction interview in which Stacey calmly continued to deny her guilt, Fitzpatrick was asked his thoughts on Stacey's demeanor. It wasn't what Stacey exhibited in the interview that bothered him most, the DA replied. It was the thing that was absent. "Where is her moral outrage?" Fitzpatrick asked. He mocked the expression on her face. "Me? Me? . . . She's a cold customer. She knows she killed her two husbands. She is just getting better at denying it, that's all."

When it came to Stacey Castor and her mystifying attitude, Fitzpatrick was the utmost authority. After all, he had been listening to her phone calls for a long period of time, including her jail phone calls for over a year. Stacey had been absolutely convinced that she was going to be acquitted. "So this is all made up that they were preparing from jump street for the conviction," Fitzpatrick said. She and her boyfriend had planned to go away on trips after the trial. "If you believe, as I do, that she did what she did, then her reaction and demeanor are incomprehensible," the DA said.

She was, after all, an anomaly—unique in the annals of crime.

Infanticide, no matter the age of the child, is almost always an act of passion, desperation, and deep depression. It is a hot-blooded act, usually a suicide gone awry, a suicide turned outward.

But Stacey was different. She was cool. She knew how to maintain an even strain, even as the noose of the law slowly tightened around her neck. Desperate times called for desperate measures. That was her thoroughly chilly line of reasoning.

The DA thought about the marathon argument that Stacey and David had in their garage two and a half days before David was found dead. Stacey claimed that during this altercation, she became worried that David was thinking of hurting himself. Oh, someone was thinking about hurting David, all right, but it wasn't him. That was when the plan went into motion, he believed. Perhaps she eyed the antifreeze during that long night in the garage.

But why was it so simple for her? Other women would consider any line of action before murder, but Stacey's course was clear. She looked and sounded like Mrs. Jane Six-pack, and, in reality, she was a homicidal maniac.

How could she see death as the best answer to her problems, whatever they were?

She had *purposefully* shattered her own nest. She was Bad Mom—*Mommy Deadliest*. The worst mom ever. This mother, after murdering her two husbands, tried to kill her own child in cold blood. And why?

To save her own skin.

Epilogue

In 2007, DA William Fitzpatrick was appointed New York State representative to the National District Attorneys Association. He is extremely active in his community and has been involved with Vera House (the same local shelter for abused women where Janice Poissant once stayed), the Ronald McDonald House, the Make-A-Wish Foundation, the Rape Crisis Center, and several other community groups.

Fitzpatrick has lectured extensively on various aspects of the criminal justice system at numerous colleges and public forums across the nation, including New York State governor Mario Cuomo's and governor George Pataki's Law Enforcement Forums. He was a member of the New York State Forensic Science Commission and served on Judge Judith Kaye's Drugs and the Courts Commission. He also played an instrumental role in establishing the Onondaga County Center for Forensic Sciences, which is used statewide and has DNA testing capabilities.

* * *

In March 2009, Dr. Robert Stoppacher, the doctor who performed the autopsies on David Castor and Michael Wallace, was promoted from deputy chief medical examiner, a position he had held since 2004, to the chief medical examiner position. Dr. Stoppacher replaced Dr. Mary Jumbelic, who retired earlier that year.

Dani Colman, who was willing to talk to reporters before and during Stacey Castor's trial, clammed up afterward. During the fall of 2009, she wrote, *I really have nothing to say. She was my best friend and so many people have been hurt by this.*

Mike Wallace's stepdaughter Renee says life is good now. She is no longer the rebellious wild child she was when she came to live for a couple of months with Mike and Stacey and the girls when she was fourteen. She is now Renee Tawczynski. "Just got married, bought a house," she said.

Renee's mom, Nancy, Mike Wallace's first wife, is also thriving. When the author last spoke with her by phone, she was multitasking, simultaneously answering questions and fixing dinner for her "other half," Maurice.

In January 2009, Onondaga County Surrogate's Court judge Peter Wells, the man who had issued the order barring Stacey Castor from disposing of any of David Castor's property until the matter of the forged will was solved, retired from his post. In a ceremony, Judge Wells himself swore in his successor, Ava Shapero Raphael, whose father once presided over the Onondaga County Legislature.

Stacey Castor's boyfriend at the time of her arrest, Michael Overstreet, was contacted about participating in this book. He called the author's office repeatedly between two and three in the morning, and left ten e-mails during that same hour. His message was that the interview had to occur then, or forget it. Other messages: **Last chance to talk about the love of my life,** and **If u don't answer ur phone then dont contact me again.**

Dr. Christine Stork, of the Upstate New York Poison Center, who testified at the trial, said her center saw between sixty and eighty cases of ethylene glycol poisoning per year, most of which were treatable. Although a small amount of antifreeze could cause death if a patient went untreated for long enough, a large amount of antifreeze could be consumed and the patient still be treatable if the patient got emergency care within the first couple of hours. She had known of patients who drank upward of half a gallon of antifreeze and lived. After the Castor case received so much publicity in the Syracuse area, there were more rather than fewer cases of ethylene glycol poisoning. The publicity popularized the poison, talk of its pleasant taste apparently outweighing repeated warnings that death by antifreeze was a slow and painful way to go.

* * *

On November 2, 2009, Detectives Valerie Brogan and Dominick Spinelli, as well as Sergeants Michael Norton and Robert Willoughby, were given certificates of merit for their part in the investigation that led to Stacey Castor's conviction. The annual sheriff's office awards ceremony was held at the Gillette Road Middle School on South Bay Road in Cicero.

Christine Garvey has spent hours pondering this case, and somehow it still doesn't register. What was the word David Castor Jr. had used? Surreal, that was it.

"This case seems more like a TV movie. How could something like this happen in real life?" Garvey wonders.

Would the day ever come when Stacey Castor would admit to the things she'd done? Sheriff Walsh, for one, doesn't think so. "I don't think she'll ever take responsibility for what she did," Walsh said. There was a stubbornness to her. Perhaps she had trained herself to believe she was innocent.

As of January 2010, Cayuga County is "still building" its case against Stacey Castor for Michael Wallace's murder.

David Castor's first wife, Janice Poissant, is a night manager at an East Syracuse hotel. She remains the loving mother of David Jr. and grandmother of her three "absolutely great" grandkids. She is suing the Colmans, Michael Overstreet, the Pulaskis, and, of course, Stacey Castor for their alleged respective roles in denying her son his rightful inheritance.

She worries that because of her marital difficulties with David Castor, readers of this book will fail to understand how close and loving their relationship actually was.

"I never thought anything like [his murder] would happen," Janice said. "He was all I knew, all I had, all I ever loved. I loved him more than anyone could ever imagine loving anyone."

Janice didn't like to admit it, but she felt guilty. She tried to talk herself out of it, but the best she could do was create a mental maelstrom. She felt that if she hadn't left David, then David would not have gotten married again and he would be alive today. She started the ball rolling that led to his demise. David Jr. would still have a father. Mom Castor would still have her son. *If only, if only, if only*—a woman couldn't live her life like that. Look at it another way, and, as Janice put it, "if I had stayed with him, I probably wouldn't be here today. That's because when I left him, I was dead." But then she'd think again. "I am the reason he is dead." The guilt would return. Why did she have to flourish inside as well as out? Why did she develop these needs for freedom and independence? Why had she demanded something more, and lost a husband?

It was hard looking at the pictures in the newspapers about the murder. That house on Wetzel Road used to be Janice's house. The death room used to be their room. The "Evil It Alien" had taken Janice's place in that house and she'd destroyed everything.

Her son, David Jr., still has not received any part of his father's estate. That fake will had befuddled the court system. Nothing could be done until Stacey was convicted, and even after that, progress was snaillike.

Janice fumed. Michael Overstreet, the fiancé of David's murderer, had more of David Sr.'s possessions than David Jr. had.

The house on Wetzel Road has new owners. They are growing impatient with writers, TV producers, and drive-by sightseers, and wish to be left alone.

Stacey Castor remains in the Bedford Hills Correctional Facility, just north of New York City in Westchester County. She will first be eligible for parole on June 15, 2055. On that date, she will be one month shy of her eighty-eighth birthday.

Antifreeze continued to be a popular weapon for women killers. In October 2009 a fifty-one-year-old Canandaigua, N.Y., woman allegedly exacted revenge on an abusive boyfriend by pouring a shot glass of antifreeze into a margarita mix. After his death and her arrest, she told state police she intended only to sicken him. She was eventually indicted on a manslaughter charge.

* * *

With Stacy Castor in prison for a long while, her friends and family began to rethink other sudden deaths in Stacey's past. There was her father, who was recovering in St. Joseph's Hospital from a lung ailment when he quickly took a turn for the worse and died. One of his last visitors had been Stacey, who brought with her an open can of soda. Gerald Daniels was cremated without an autopsy and Stacey became the executrix of his will.

Then there was Stacey's niece, who as an infant died suddenly, supposedly of SIDS, but hadn't Stacey been babysitting earlier that day?

Both cases may forever remain a mystery, but Gerald Daniels's demise was suspicious enough to get the attention of the Onondaga County District Attorney. In late January 2010, Bill Fitzpatrick confirmed that his office was investigating the circumstances surrounding the death of Stacey's dad. He admitted, however, that any investigation would be difficult due to the cremation. "We're not optimistic we're going to get proof beyond a reasonable doubt," he said.